Suicide in Sri Lanka

Why people kill themselves remains an enduring and unanswered question. With a focus on Sri Lanka, a country that for several decades has reported 'epidemic' levels of suicidal behaviour, this book develops a unique perspective linking the causes and meanings of suicidal practices to social processes across moments, lifetimes and history.

Extending anthropological approaches to practice, learning and agency, anthropologist Tom Widger draws from long-term fieldwork in a Sinhala Buddhist community to develop an ethnographic theory of suicide that foregrounds local knowledge and sets out a charter for prevention. The book highlights the motives of children and adults becoming suicidal and how certain gender, age, class relationships and violence are prone to give rise to suicidal responses. By linking these experiences to emotional states, it develops an ethnopsychiatric model of suicide rooted in social practice. Widger then goes on to examine how suicides are resolved at village and national levels, tracing the roots of interventions to the politics of colonial and post-colonial social welfare and health regimes. Exploring local accounts of suicide as both 'evidence' for the suicide epidemic and as an 'ethos' of suicidality shaping subjective worlds, *Suicide in Sri Lanka* shows how anthropological analysis can offer theoretical as well as policy insights.

With the inclusion of straightforward summaries and implications for prevention at the end of each chapter, this book has relevance for specialists and non-specialists alike. It represents an important new contribution to South Asian Studies, Social Anthropology and Medical Anthropology, as well as to cross-cultural Suicidology.

Tom Widger has conducted ethnographic fieldwork on suicide in Sri Lanka for more than ten years. He received a PhD in anthropology from the London School of Economics, UK in 2009. He has since held positions at Brunel University, UK, the University of Sussex, UK, the University of Colombo, Sri Lanka, and Durham University, UK.

Routledge contemporary South Asia series

1 **Pakistan**
Social and cultural transformations in a Muslim nation
Mohammad A. Qadeer

2 **Labor, Democratization and Development in India and Pakistan**
Christopher Candland

3 **China–India Relations**
Contemporary dynamics
Amardeep Athwal

4 **Madrasas in South Asia**
Teaching terror?
Jamal Malik

5 **Labor, Globalization and the State**
Workers, women and migrants confront neoliberalism
Edited by Debdas Banerjee and Michael Goldfield

6 **Indian Literature and Popular Cinema**
Recasting classics
Edited by Heidi R.M. Pauwels

7 **Islamist Militancy in Bangladesh**
A complex web
Ali Riaz

8 **Regionalism in South Asia**
Negotiating cooperation, institutional structures
Kishore C. Dash

9 **Federalism, Nationalism and Development**
India and the Punjab economy
Pritam Singh

10 **Human Development and Social Power**
Perspectives from South Asia
Ananya Mukherjee Reed

11 **The South Asian Diaspora**
Transnational networks and changing identities
Edited by Rajesh Rai and Peter Reeves

12 **Pakistan–Japan Relations**
Continuity and change in economic relations and security interests
Ahmad Rashid Malik

13 **Himalayan Frontiers of India**
Historical, geo-political and strategic perspectives
K. Warikoo

14 **India's Open-Economy Policy**
Globalism, rivalry, continuity
Jalal Alamgir

15 **The Separatist Conflict in Sri Lanka**
Terrorism, ethnicity, political economy
Asoka Bandarage

16 **India's Energy Security**
Edited by Ligia Noronha and Anant Sudarshan

17 **Globalization and the Middle Classes in India**
The social and cultural impact of neoliberal reforms
Ruchira Ganguly-Scrase and Timothy J. Scrase

18 **Water Policy Processes in India**
Discourses of power and resistance
Vandana Asthana

19 **Minority Governments in India**
The puzzle of elusive majorities
Csaba Nikolenyi

20 **The Maoist Insurgency in Nepal**
Revolution in the twenty-first century
Edited by Mahendra Lawoti and Anup K. Pahari

21 **Global Capital and Peripheral Labour**
The history and political economy of plantation workers in India
K. Ravi Raman

22 **Maoism in India**
Reincarnation of ultra-left wing extremism in the twenty-first century
Bidyut Chakrabarty and Rajat Kujur

23 **Economic and Human Development in Contemporary India**
Cronyism and fragility
Debdas Banerjee

24 **Culture and the Environment in the Himalaya**
Arjun Guneratne

25 **The Rise of Ethnic Politics in Nepal**
Democracy in the margins
Susan I. Hangen

26 **The Multiplex in India**
A cultural economy of urban leisure
Adrian Athique and Douglas Hill

27 **Tsunami Recovery in Sri Lanka**
Ethnic and regional dimensions
Dennis B. McGilvray and Michele R. Gamburd

28 **Development, Democracy and the State**
Critiquing the Kerala model of development
K. Ravi Raman

29 **Mohajir Militancy in Pakistan**
Violence and transformation in the Karachi conflict
Nichola Khan

30 **Nationbuilding, Gender and War Crimes in South Asia**
Bina D'Costa

31 **The State in India after Liberalization**
Interdisciplinary perspectives
Edited by Akhil Gupta and K. Sivaramakrishnan

32 **National Identities in Pakistan**
The 1971 war in contemporary Pakistani fiction
Cara Cilano

33 **Political Islam and Governance in Bangladesh**
Edited by Ali Riaz and C. Christine Fair

34 **Bengali Cinema**
'An Other Nation'
Sharmistha Gooptu

35 **NGOs in India**
The challenges of women's empowerment and accountability
Patrick Kilby

36 **The Labour Movement in the Global South**
Trade unions in Sri Lanka
S. Janaka Biyanwila

37 **Building Bangalore**
Architecture and urban transformation in India's Silicon Valley
John C. Stallmeyer

38 **Conflict and Peacebuilding in Sri Lanka**
Caught in the peace trap?
Edited by Jonathan Goodhand, Jonathan Spencer and Benedict Korf

39 **Microcredit and Women's Empowerment**
A case study of Bangladesh
Amunui Faraizi, Jim McAllister and Taskinur Rahman

40 **South Asia in the New World Order**
The role of regional cooperation
Shahid Javed Burki

41 **Explaining Pakistan's Foreign Policy**
Escaping India
Aparna Pande

42 **Development-induced Displacement, Rehabilitation and Resettlement in India**
Current issues and challenges
Edited by Sakarama Somayaji and Smrithi Talwar

43 **The Politics of Belonging in India**
Becoming adivasi
Edited by Daniel J. Rycroft and Sangeeta Dasgupta

44 **Re-Orientalism and South Asian Identity Politics**
The oriental other within
Edited by Lisa Lau and Ana Cristina Mendes

45 **Islamic Revival in Nepal**
Religion and a new nation
Megan Adamson Sijapati

46 **Education and Inequality in India**
A classroom view
Manabi Majumdar and Jos Mooij

47 **The Culturalization of Caste in India**
Identity and inequality in a multicultural age
Balmurli Natrajan

48 **Corporate Social Responsibility in India**
Bidyut Chakrabarty

49 **Pakistan's Stability Paradox**
Domestic, regional and international dimensions
Edited by Ashutosh Misra and Michael E. Clarke

50 Transforming Urban Water Supplies in India
The role of reform and partnerships in globalization
Govind Gopakumar

51 South Asian Security
Twenty-first century discourses
Sagarika Dutt and Alok Bansal

52 Non-discrimination and Equality in India
Contesting boundaries of social justice
Vidhu Verma

53 Being Middle-class in India
A way of life
Henrike Donner

54 Kashmir's Right to Secede
A critical examination of contemporary theories of secession
Matthew J. Webb

55 Bollywood Travels
Culture, diaspora and border crossings in popular Hindi cinema
Rajinder Dudrah

56 Nation, Territory, and Globalization in Pakistan
Traversing the margins
Chad Haines

57 The Politics of Ethnicity in Pakistan
The Baloch, Sindhi and Mohajir Ethnic Movements
Farhan Hanif Siddiqi

58 Nationalism and Ethnic Conflict
Identities and mobilization after 1990
Edited by Mahendra Lawoti and Susan Hangen

59 Islam and Higher Education
Concepts, challenges and opportunities
Marodsilton Muborakshoeva

60 Religious Freedom in India
Sovereignty and (anti) conversion
Goldie Osuri

61 Everyday Ethnicity in Sri Lanka
Up-country Tamil identity politics
Daniel Bass

62 Ritual and Recovery in Post-Conflict Sri Lanka
Eloquent bodies
Jane Derges

63 Bollywood and Globalisation
The global power of popular Hindi cinema
Edited by David J. Schaefer and Kavita Karan

64 Regional Economic Integration in South Asia
Trapped in conflict?
Amita Batra

65 Architecture and Nationalism in Sri Lanka
The trouser under the cloth
Anoma Pieris

66 Civil Society and Democratization in India
Institutions, ideologies and interests
Sarbeswar Sahoo

67 Contemporary Pakistani Fiction in English
Idea, nation, state
Cara N. Cilano

68 **Transitional Justice in South Asia**
A study of Afghanistan and Nepal
Tazreena Sajjad

69 **Displacement and Resettlement in India**
The human cost of development
Hari Mohan Mathur

70 **Water, Democracy and Neoliberalism in India**
The power to reform
Vicky Walters

71 **Capitalist Development in India's Informal Economy**
Elisabetta Basile

72 **Nation, Constitutionalism and Buddhism in Sri Lanka**
Roshan de Silva Wijeyeratne

73 **Counterinsurgency, Democracy, and the Politics of Identity in India**
From warfare to welfare?
Mona Bhan

74 **Enterprise Culture in Neoliberal India**
Studies in youth, class, work and media
Edited by Nandini Gooptu

75 **The Politics of Economic Restructuring in India**
Economic governance and state spatial rescaling
Loraine Kennedy

76 **The Other in South Asian Religion, Literature and Film**
Perspectives on Otherism and Otherness
Edited by Diana Dimitrova

77 **Being Bengali**
At home and in the world
Edited by Mridula Nath Chakraborty

78 **The Political Economy of Ethnic Conflict in Sri Lanka**
Nikolaos Biziouras

79 **Indian Arranged Marriages**
A social psychological perspective
Tulika Jaiswal

80 **Writing the City in British Asian Diasporas**
Edited by Seán McLoughlin, William Gould, Ananya Jahanara Kabir and Emma Tomalin

81 **Post-9/11 Espionage Fiction in the US and Pakistan**
Spies and 'terrorists'
Cara Cilano

82 **Left Radicalism in India**
Bidyut Chakrabarty

83 **"Nation-State" and Minority Rights in India**
Comparative perspectives on Muslim and Sikh identities
Tanweer Fazal

84 **Pakistan's Nuclear Policy**
A minimum credible deterrence
Zafar Khan

85 **Imagining Muslims in South Asia and the Diaspora**
Secularism, religion, representations
Claire Chambers and Caroline Herbert

86 **Indian Foreign Policy in Transition**
Relations with South Asia
Arijit Mazumdar

87 **Corporate Social Responsibility and Development in Pakistan**
Nadeem Malik

88 **Indian Capitalism in Development**
Barbara Harriss-White and Judith Heyer

89 **Bangladesh Cinema and National Identity**
In search of the modern?
Zakir Hossain Raju

90 **Suicide in Sri Lanka**
The anthropology of an epidemic
Tom Widger

91 **Epigraphy and Islamic Culture**
Arabic and Persian inscriptions of Bengal and their historical and cultural implications
Mohammad Yusuf Siddiq

92 **Reshaping City Governance**
London, Mumbai, Kolkata, Hyderabad
Nirmala Rao

93 **The Indian Partition in Literature and Films**
History, politics, and aesthetics
Rini Bhattacharya Mehta and Debali Mookerjea-Leonard

Suicide in Sri Lanka
The anthropology of an epidemic

Tom Widger

LONDON AND NEW YORK

First published 2015
by Routledge
2 Park Square, Milton Park, Abingdon, Oxon OX14 4RN

and by Routledge
711 Third Avenue, New York, NY 10017

First issued in paperback 2017

Routledge is an imprint of the Taylor & Francis Group, an informa business

© 2015 Tom Widger

The right of Tom Widger to be identified as author of this work has been asserted by him in accordance with sections 77 and 78 of the Copyright, Designs and Patents Act 1988.

All rights reserved. No part of this book may be reprinted or reproduced or utilised in any form or by any electronic, mechanical, or other means, now known or hereafter invented, including photocopying and recording, or in any information storage or retrieval system, without permission in writing from the publishers.

Trademark notice: Product or corporate names may be trademarks or registered trademarks, and are used only for identification and explanation without intent to infringe.

British Library Cataloguing in Publication Data
A catalogue record for this book is available from the British Library

Library of Congress Cataloging in Publication Data
Widger, Tom.
Suicide in Sri Lanka : the anthropology of an epidemic / Tom Widger.
  pages cm. – (Routledge contemporary South Asia series ; 90)
Includes bibliographical references and index.
1. Suicide–Sri Lanka. I. Title.
HV6548.S72W54 2015
362.28095493–dc23   2014021043

ISBN 13: 978-1-138-49161-8 (pbk)
ISBN 13: 978-1-138-82074-6 (hbk)

Typeset in Times New Roman
by Wearset Ltd, Boldon, Tyne and Wear

Contents

	List of figures	xii
	List of tables	xiii
	Preface	xiv
	Acknowledgements	xx
	Transliteration	xxii
	Abbreviations	xxiii
1	The anthropology of suicide	1
2	Of villages, courts and clinics	23
3	Suicide *there*, suicide *here*	51
4	Relational flows	69
5	Suffering, frustration, anger	95
6	One life, one love	116
7	The Black Demon	131
8	The search for compassion	153
9	The suicide process	173
	Glossary	179
	Bibliography	181
	Index	191

Figures

P.1	Map of Sri Lanka and the Puttalam District	xvi
1.1	The Sri Lankan suicide rate, 1948–2008	5
2.1	Map of the fieldsite	24
2.2	Male self-harm and suicide cases in the Madampe Division	29
2.3	Female self-harm and suicide cases in the Madampe Division	29
2.4	Religion of suicides compared to religious communities in Madampe	30
4.1	Relational flows of male suicides	74
4.2	Relational flows of female suicides	75
4.3	Relational flows of unmarried male self-harm	75
4.4	Relational flows of unmarried female self-harm	76
4.5	Relational flows of married male self-harm	77
4.6	Relational flows of married female self-harm	78

Tables

2.1	Ethnic communities in the Madampe Division, 2001	25
2.2	Religious communities in the Madampe Division, 2001	25
2.3	Employment by sector in Puttalam and five neighbouring districts	26
2.4	Agricultural land use in the Madampe Division, 2004	26
2.5	Self-harm and suicide cases recorded at GPHU and MPS	28
2.6	Methods of self-harm and suicide by gender	31
2.7	Ethnic communities in Udagama and Alutwatta, 2001	33
2.8	Occupational classes in Udagama and Alutwatta	34
2.9	Religious communities in Udagama and Alutwatta, 2001	35
2.10	Discrepancies in lists of causes of suicide recorded by MPS and the Sri Lanka Police	42
2.11	Transformations from mundane to formal categorisations of self-harm and recommendations for treatment at CMHC	46
2.12	Generative arenas of suicidal practice in Madampe	48
5.1	An ethnopsychiatric framework of suicide *here*	112

Preface

Every three seconds someone in the world intentionally harms themselves, and every forty seconds one dies as a result. Each year some 800,000 suicides take place worldwide (World Health Organization 2012). Most deaths occur in the developing world – and 60 per cent in Asia – where health and social resources for the treatment and prevention of self-harm are often limited (Beautrais 2006). Just 10 per cent of the world's suicide research and intervention resources are spent in middle- and low-income countries, which produce 90 per cent of the world's deaths by self-harm (Yip 2008: vii). It is not only economic disparities between high- and middle- or low-income countries that drive global inequalities in suicide rates and interventions. The field of 'suicidology' – the interdisciplinary study of suicidal practice that encompasses the social and medical sciences – is, in the main, heavily indebted to Western understandings of suicidal practice. These do not easily translate to other contexts around the world, where the cultural representation of suicide may be constructed in very different ways. Combined, a lack of resource investment and a failure to account for global variations in suicidal practice means that little progress is likely to be made towards the development of context-specific suicide interventions.

The overall aim of this book is to develop an anthropological approach to the study of suicide: a subfield of anthropological inquiry that remains relatively unexplored but has enormous significance as global suicide rates continue to rise. The book presents the results of ethnographic fieldwork conducted in the South Asian island-nation of Sri Lanka over the past decade: a country where rates of self-harm and self-inflicted death have existed at 'epidemic' proportions since the 1980s. The book argues that to understand suicide cross-culturally we need to rethink the dominant paradigms of Western suicidology and, through an ethnographic approach, pay close attention to how ordinary people experience and explain suicide in their lives. By conducting an anthropological analysis of suicide in Sri Lanka, I aim to show how we are better able to understand the ways in which practices of self-harm and self-inflicted death are both produced by and produce wider social, cultural and emotional processes. My argument is that suicide is never a single event in time and space, but is rather deeply embedded in, and constitutive of, on-going relationships across time and space – at the level of suicide events, lifespans and history. As people 'live through suicide', the practice of suicide becomes the effect of a cause and the cause of its own effects, manifesting socialities in a processual sense. In this book I will argue that through the 'suicide process' social and moral personhood is 'created' as it is 'negated,' leading to new ways of living through agentive ways of dying.

While speaking to broad themes, the focus of the book is on suicide in a peri-urban district of Sri Lanka called Madampe, in the Northwest Province of the island (see Figure P.1). I have known Madampe intimately since 2001, when I was posted there while working for a British development NGO, Voluntary Services Overseas (VSO). It was during that time that I first became interested in suicide and decided to return at a later date to study it. With interests in anthropology, I enrolled on postgraduate courses at the London School of Economics and wrote about suicide in Sri Lanka for my Master's dissertation, and then formulated a research proposal for a Ph.D. based around the subject. My doctoral fieldwork was carried out principally over twenty-one months, between October 2004 and June 2006, and was complemented by follow-up visits in 2007 and 2012/2013. During that time I have had the privilege of becoming part of my informants' lives, many of whom are much better described as friends, sharing in each other's fortunes and misfortunes, celebrating good times and commiserating bad times. My parents, siblings and cousins visited from the UK during my main fieldwork period, extending the network of relationalities further still. More recently, I introduced my partner and baby daughter, changing my status in the village from 'youth' to 'householder'. These friendships proved invaluable throughout the fieldwork period, during which my focus on suicide necessitated engagement with extremely troubling questions, but which I was able to navigate due to the love and care shown towards me by others who became close confidants.

The anthropological study of suicide, based on deep qualitative methods including 'participant-observation', raises significant practical and ethical challenges. An important constraint on my research was the extent to which I could – and indeed should – encourage previously suicidal people to talk about their experiences. Although in most cases suicidal informants were not suffering from psychiatric illness, they were usually socially and emotionally vulnerable and often victims of abuse. To limit the risk of my work having adverse effects on informants, first interviews were only followed up when expressly invited to do so by the interviewee. When informants were less than sixteen years of age parental consent was sought. Even then, I quickly noticed that having a notebook present was often off-putting for informants both young and old, so I would put it away. For this reason, the interviews I conducted with self-harmers were rarely recorded verbatim, and instead written down from memory later in the day. As such, many of the cases I relate are in my own voice rather than the voices of my informants. In more mundane or neutral spaces, I used notebooks to record the results of interviews, most of which were conducted in Sinhala and translated by my assistants as conversations progressed.

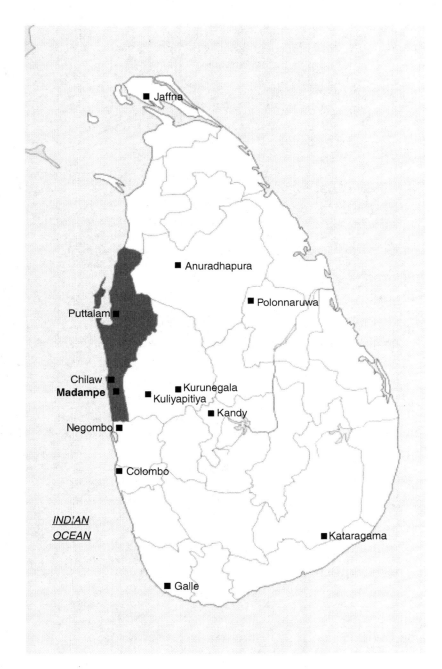

Figure P.1 Map of Sri Lanka and the Puttalam District (source: http://commons.wikimedia.org/wiki/File:Sri_Lanka_districts_Puttalam.svg).

Fieldwork comprised research across village and institutional settings, including the offices of police investigators and coroners, and frontline medical staff and mental health clinicians. This enabled me to develop close understandings of suicidal practices from a range of different perspectives and at different stages of the suicide process: from before an act took place, through treatment and management interventions, and into the aftermath for those who survived and of those left behind. At village level I conducted three surveys using an interview schedule: a household census to establish patterns of kinship in the present and past, a 'love and marriage attitudes' survey, and a 'village development satisfaction' survey. The purpose of these surveys was not simply to collect quantifiable pieces of data to complement my qualitative work but also to get to know residents and importantly to give them a chance to get to know me, and what I was there to do. The completion of the surveys usually took a long time as respondents were encouraged to raise issues that were of interest or concern to them, and, as we chatted freely about this and that, I significantly expanded my understanding of context issues.

Although over the two years of my primary fieldwork trip I spoke to literally hundreds people around Madampe, ethnographers are often dependent on a handful of key informants who are especially willing to share their time and knowledge, and my research was no exception. First, my two research assistants, Nalin and Shon, Sinhala Buddhist men aged in their early twenties and residents of Udagama and Alutwatta respectively, the two villages I studied in-depth, were a source of daily consultation. Likewise, Nalin's older sister and mother often sat with us on the front porch of their home in Udagama, and we discussed at length matters both connected and unconnected to my primary research concerns. Similarly, Nalin's and Shon's groups of male friends and male and female cousins were also regular informants, and over the years we spent many hours together playing *carom* on front porches, during which we would debate the causes and representations of suicidal practices at great depth. From these sources, I developed a detailed knowledge of youth social worlds and self-harm, including the issue of primary importance for many of them: love and romance.

Next was the family at Alutwatta I was lodging with: a retired bank manager, his wife and their three children with whom I had also lived during my visit in 2001. Upon my return, I was accepted back into the household and called 'Tom *puththa* [son]' and 'Tom *ayya* [brother]'. This also meant an expectation to behave like a family member and I quickly found myself subject to the same social and moral regulations as their own children, which was itself a unique research experience. Adjacent to my lodging place was a tiny shack that was home to a woman and her three grandchildren, including an eighteen-year-old daughter who came and went from the Gulf to work in garment factories. Their own mother also worked abroad and the father was living separately; a few months after my arrival he died from alcohol poisoning. The children would often spend time at my lodging place as well. These two families provided a more intimate understanding of the high- and low-status households I was studying in Udagama and Alutwatta.

At divisional level, I spent time with a group of older men from around Madampe who formed a drinking circle, a crucial space of male sociality. My regular meetings with them provided unique insights into men's social and emotional worlds, which was essential for understanding male suicide. Meanwhile, my organisational research allowed me to observe staff at the local hospital, the Galmuruwa Peripheral Health Unit (GPHU), Madampe Police Station (MPS), Kuliyapitiya Coroner Court (KCC) and Chilaw Mental Health Clinic (CMHC). One clinician at CMHC in particular became a close and trusted informant and I often stayed at his home. These individuals helped me to understand the ways in which suicide was treated and managed in Madampe, including the creeping process of medicalisation and 'psychopharmaceuticalisation' that has been underway in the country since the 2004 tsunami. Combined, this group of around thirty key informants spanning from 'village to clinic' provided a network of trusted individuals from various social backgrounds with whom I could discuss my research and from whom I often received clarifications or counter-arguments.

During the second year of my research, I asked 1,000 children in two Madampe schools to complete a psychosocial survey (Achenbach and Rescorla 2001). The aim of this research was to gain additional information regarding the social and emotional lives of Madampe youth, including the frequency at which they might think about committing suicide or actually perform self-harm. The survey was translated into Sinhala and participants completed it under exam conditions. More than 80 per cent of the forms were returned to a standard suitable for analysis. Importantly, it seemed that many children appreciated the chance to take part in the survey: 'Thank you for taking an interest in us, Mr Tom!' wrote one. While I do not report the quantitative results of the survey in this book, I do make use of the many qualitative statements children made about their lives, including those relating to suicidal practice.

Finally, I spent around one month at the Sri Lanka National Archive in Colombo, collecting secondary materials including British and Ceylonese Administration Reports dating from the mid-1800s to the mid-1900s and selected copies of national (English-language) newspapers from the mid-1800s to the late 1900s. This work allowed me to delve into Madampe's colonial and post-colonial past and to collect fascinating accounts of economic and social life in the area. At the same time I looked more broadly at the national scene, and came to build a picture of how successive governments have thought about and managed the suicide problem, as well as its presumed causes and correlating concerns.

By conducting intensive, long-term fieldwork research alongside complementary survey and archival work, I have been able to elucidate what I call the 'processual sociality' of suicide in Madampe. This is an 'ethnographic theory' of suicidal practice that has been developed from informants' understandings of what kind of behaviour suicide is, and what its causes and consequences might be. It is a theory that stands apart from, but not necessarily in opposition to, normative sociological and psychological theories of suicide that have been formulated on experiences of suicide in different parts of the world and thus have little a priori validity in the Sri Lankan context. My 'local theory' of suicide is one that could only have been discovered via ethnography, which allows the researcher to collect extremely detailed data over several years and so become conscious of how apparently singular events like suicide exist as part of historical processes at both individual and social levels. As suicide rates continue to rise across the world and cross-cultural suicide research becomes increasingly important an ethnographic method must become central to our efforts at explaining and ultimately preventing this expression of human suffering. This can only be achieved in and through the ideas and practices of the people affected, and by understanding how suicide exists within their own social and relational worlds.

Acknowledgements

My greatest thanks go to the people in Madampe who have shared with me their stories of self-harm, suicide and much more besides. They have entrusted insights into a problem of such personal but also global significance – often at a time of extreme pain and uncertainty in their own lives – that I can only hope to have reflected accurately and fairly what they meant to convey. If by doing so improved understanding of suicide can be reached, and better forms of intervention and support designed, then perhaps my intrusions will have been worthwhile.

My fieldwork benefited from the patience, support and enthusiasm of so many people it would be impossible to name them all. In Madampe, my thanks go to: S.G.K. Piyadasa, Karunawatti, Dilrukshi, Usman ('*Loku*'), Rajiv, H.M. Nalin, H.M. Indika, D. Shon. Somawatti, Sriyantha Liyanage, Satsura, Kapila, Chandani, Bandara, Nalika, Upali, Wasana, Chandana, Hasitha, Malith, Thilak, Sharika, Bandara and Warana. I thank staff at Galmuruwa Peripheral Health Unit, Chilaw Mental Health Clinic, Madampe Police Station, Kuliyapitiya Magistrates' Court and Madampe Divisional Secretariat for allowing me access to records and to observe working practices. I also thank staff and students at Madampe Central College and Herath Gunarathna Vidalaya. Finally, I thank the residents of Udagama and Alutwatta who over many years have put up with my presence in their lives, first as a volunteer worker, second as an ethnographer, and third, I hope, as a friend.

In Colombo, I must thank staff at Sri Lanka Sumithrayo, and Melanie Paranavitana in particular, whose valuable work over several decades offers still the only specialised community-based route for supporting suicidal people. Thanks also to staff at the Sri Lanka National Archives for providing access to valuable historical documents, and Centre for Women's Research, Centre for Poverty Analysis, International Centre for Ethnic Studies, Marga Institute, National Institute of Mental Health and Social Scientists' Association for access to their libraries. Also: Prabath Kularathna, Ridma, Jayananda, Shyamalie, Nilmini, Sasanthi, and Lalith and Janaki, Ranjan. Finally, I thank Sally and Arjuna Hulugalle for their introduction to the work of Nest and fascinating discussions on Sri Lankan society and politics.

The research and writing of this book was generously supported by a number of grants, including from the Royal Anthropological Institute (Emslie-Horniman Fieldwork Grant and Firth Trust Fund), the Wenner-Gren Foundation (Dissertation Fieldwork Grant, Gr. 7259), the London School of Economics (Alfred Gell Studentship), the University of London (Travel Grant), the University of Essex (LS Grant) and an ESRC Post-Doctoral Fellowship (PTA-026–27–2739). My Ph.D. fieldwork was conducted as a Visiting Student in the Department of Sociology at the University of Colombo. The manuscript for this book was finished while I was employed as a Research Fellow in the Department of Anthropology at the University of Sussex under an ESRC-DfID research grant (RES-167-25–0713), a Visiting Research Fellow in the Department of Sociology at the University of Colombo, and a Visiting Research Fellow in the Department of Anthropology at Brunel University.

I would like to thank James Staples, Jeanne Marecek, Jock Stirrat, Jocelyn Chua and Dennis McGilvray for their insightful comments on earlier chapter drafts, and the two anonymous reviewers from Routledge. Krishantha Fredricks very kindly provided assistance with Sinhala–English translations and transliteration. Over the years my thinking on suicide in Sri Lanka has benefited significantly from the discussions, debates, arguments and casual asides provided by, in no particular order: Tharindi Udalagama, Maurice Said, Bob Simpson, Chandanie Senadheera, Kalinga Tudor Silva, Elizabeth Frantz, Michael Eddleston, Melissa Pearson, David Gunnell, Duleeka Knipe, Ravindra Fernando, Raveen Hanwella, Nalaka Fernando, Neil Fernando, Daniel Muenster, Filippo Osella, Jonathan Spencer, David Lester, Malathi de Alwis, Ananda Galappatti and Junko Kitanaka. My Ph.D. supervisors, Jonathan Parry and Chris Fuller, provided an unparalleled training in anthropology and I hope this book does some small justice to what they taught me. I thank Jillian Morrison and Dorothea Schaefter at Routledge for believing in the project when they only had a few draft chapters to consider, and for their patience as I completed the rest.

Various sections of the book were presented to audiences around the world, and I would like to thank organisers and participants for the opportunities to share my work: Brunel University, University of Warsaw, University of Colombo, King's College London, the Max Plank Institute for Social Anthropology, the Annual Conference on South Asia at the University of Wisconsin, and annual meetings of the Association of Social Anthropologists (ASA), the International Association of Anthropological and Ethnological Sciences (IUAES), and the American Anthropological Association (AAA).

Chapter 4 contains material originally published in: Widger, T., 2012a, 'Suicide and the Morality of Kinship in Sri Lanka', *Contributions to Indian Sociology*, 46(1/2), 83–116. DOI: 10.1177/006996671104600205.

Chapter 5 contains material originally published in: Widger, T., 2012b, 'Suffering, Frustration, and Anger: Class, Gender and History in Sri Lankan Suicide Stories', *Culture, Medicine, and Psychiatry*, 36(2), 225–244. DOI: 10.1007/s11013-012-9250-6.

Completing a Ph.D., pursuing a post-doctoral career and writing a book are all activities that place often entirely unfair burdens on those whom we love the most. I thank my parents, Alan and Yvonne Widger, whose inspiration and support over the years has never wavered. Finally I thank Jordan Mullard, and our beautiful daughter Alba May, whose love, encouragement, understanding, patience and humour have made it all possible.

Colombo, March 2014

Transliteration

Krishantha Fredricks of the Department of Sinhala at the University of Colombo kindly prepared transliterations. We have used a simple version of the International Phonetic Alphabet (IPA) to denote Sinhala pronunciations of vowels and some consonants. To aid legibility, standard Latin script is used to spell personal names and place names.

Table A

a	Short vowel, as in s<u>u</u>n
a:	Long vowel, as in <u>a</u>ardvark
ə	Mid-central vowel, as in sof<u>a</u>
æ	Near-open front unrounded vowel, as in c<u>a</u>t
ɖ	Voiced retroflex stop, as in
e	Short vowel, as in t<u>e</u>n
e:	Long vowel, as in t<u>a</u>ke
i:	Long vowel, as in J<u>ee</u>ves
ŋ	Velar nasal, as in su<u>ng</u>
ɳ	Retroflex nasal, as in <u>n</u>eck
ʃ	Voiceless palato-alveolar fricative, as in <u>sh</u>ip
o:	Long vowel, as in c<u>oa</u>t
ʈ	Voiceless retroflex plosive, as in

Abbreviations

CMHC	Chilaw Mental Health Clinic
GMH	Global Mental Health
GPHU	Galmuruwa Peripheral Health Unit
KCC	Kuliyapitiya Coroner Court
LDO	Land Development Ordinance of 1935
LTTE	Liberation Tigers of Tamil Eelam
MPS	Madampe Police Station
NGO	Non-governmental organisation
NYSC	National Youth Service Council
PHU	Peripheral Health Unit
SLFYC	Sri Lanka Federation of Youth Clubs
UNP	United National Party
WHO	World Health Organization

1 The anthropology of suicide

Mr Tom where are you? Come quickly. Ravi ayya has died.
Udagama youth, male, aged twenty-four

A few weeks after arriving in the peri-urban Madampe Division of the North-west Province of Sri Lanka, Ravi, aged twenty-three,[1] drowned in a monsoon-swollen river. It was late November 2004 and I had travelled to the South Asian island to carry out a two-year research project on self-harm and suicide in the country, where for several decades suicide rates had ranked among the highest in the world. For the past few days I had been attending a conference in the capital Colombo, and was travelling the seventy kilometres north to Madampe on board an intercity bus when I received an SMS. It was from Preshan, a mutual friend, who informed me of Ravi's death and urged that I return as quickly as possible to attend the funeral house (*maḷə gedərə*), where Ravi's body was lying in wake.

Upon returning to Madampe, I learned that the police had recorded Ravi's death as being accidental, even though villagers were suggesting it was a suicide. By the day of Ravi's funeral, two competing stories of how he had died were circulating the area. While close family and friends were maintaining that the death was an accident, most others in attendance were saying that it was self-inflicted. Among those who believed the death had been intentional were three of Ravi's friends who had actually witnessed the death. Ravi, who had been drinking *toddy* (fermented coconut sap) and smoking *ganja* (marijuana), was reported to have taken a drag from his roll-up, declared 'that was my last', and jumped into the water. He resurfaced a short way downstream, caught up against a branch, by which time he was dead.

While for me personally coming to terms with Ravi's sudden and tragic death had been about trying to establish whether it was an accident or a suicide, for people in Madampe a more pressing concern existed. Regardless of what kind of death it was, the more important question seemed to be who could be blamed for it, only after which people began to speculate about an appropriate classification. For my informants there was no discussion about the state of Ravi's mental health, although there was considerable discussion about the social circumstances of his death. During the days and weeks that followed, two other accounts emerged in the wake of the accident and suicide stories. Both of those stories attempted to explain why Ravi, a 'good boy' (*hoñdə lamay*) who had done well at school and had always been polite to his elders, had met his demise under the influence of alcohol and drugs in the waters of a monsoon-swollen river. Whether an accident or a suicide, it was clearly a dangerous place to be, and people thought that Ravi should have known better. Who, Udagama villagers asked, had allowed this to happen?

The first story told, and mostly by those of Ravi's age, simply explained how he had been in love with a woman who had broken his heart. Out of desperation, Ravi turned to *toddy* and *ganja* and cared less for his life; wilfully or not, he put himself into dangerous situations that eventually cost him his life. Many people told me that this was typical of young people in love, and that love was a dangerous thing that youth were all too ready to declare, often leading to frustrations, disappointments and deaths. Over the months that followed Ravi's death, the woman in question was teased by her schoolmates and older boys in the village: 'She's very dangerous!' Ravi's friends would tell me, half in jest. Even before Ravi's death, her beauty had been famous in the village, but now that she had 'caused' Ravi to kill himself, she was infamous. 'Like a siren!' one friend joked.

The second story told, in this case mostly by older men and women, was of how Ravi had been 'abandoned' by his mother. They explained how she had migrated to the Middle East to work as a housemaid, upon which Ravi's father took a mistress and left home. Said to be experiencing desperation in the face of his loss of 'mother's love', Ravi took up drink, drugs and other foolhardy pursuits. The stories I heard, which all placed the blame squarely on the mother, went something like this:

> Ravi came from a broken home. His mother has worked as a housemaid in Saudi Arabia for the past five years, and some people say that she has a second husband there. In fact, some people say she once brought him back to visit Sri Lanka. As a consequence Ravi's father was heartbroken and left Udagama to marry a woman who lives in Anuradhapura. Together with his younger sister, Ravi went to live with his *ma:ma:* [mother's brother]. With his mother absent, Ravi lacked the love and care that would guide him along the correct path in life. He became addicted to drink and drugs and did other dangerous things that eventually cost him his life. If his mother had not been so greedy, if she had love in her heart and not only wanted money, Ravi would still be alive today.

Both sets of stories, I was to discover, fitted within well-worn theories expressed by women and men of all ages and backgrounds concerning the roots of problems and misfortunes in their lives. Their theories often explained personal and relational crises such as suicide in terms of 'family problems' (*pavul praʃnə*), and the failure of close kin, friends, neighbours and society at large, to help people enjoy a 'good family life' (*hoňda pavul ji:vite*). The ways in which 'a good family life' were imagined, and the definitions and theories of suicidal practice arising from them, were always contingent on gender, generation and social class. At the same time, they reflected more popular theories about how people in general might live and die. Thus, men and women of a certain age or social status might assume themselves likely to resort to suicidal practices of certain kinds using certain methods when faced with certain problems, and equally be assumed by others of doing the same. The fact that Ravi had died in the context of love problems and/or of migration led almost everyone in Udagama to agree that Ravi had committed suicide. They further agreed that Ravi's suicide was not only an accepted but *expected* outcome of such troubles. In Madampe, causal theories of suicide provided both a motivation for, and an explanation of, Ravi's death, which only served to reproduce those theories further and direct similar kinds of suicidal practice in the future.

This book tells a story about how people in Madampe 'live through suicide', and in so doing how they generate social life: of how suicidal practices shape social practices and representations of society at large. By 'live through suicide', I mean two things. The first is how people in Madampe have lived *through* a period of extremely high rates of self-harm and self-inflicted death over the past few decades: a phenomenon which my informants knew all about. Their explanations of the national suicide rate spoke to general concerns about Sri Lanka's experiences of development and globalisation in the modern period, and revolved around core narratives concerning the troubles of farmers and youth and the role of religion in their lives. The second is how people *live* through suicide. Suicidal practices are never simply the effects of a cause but a cause of their own effects; in Madampe, they may be understood as a manifestation of social and moral orders as well as being constitutive of those orders, and in particular imaginings of how family lives 'ought' to be, and what this means in social, moral and political terms. By integrating both perspectives, I show how suicidal practices give rise to suicide representations, through which people in Madampe come to make sense of their lives and the nation at large.

The Sri Lankan suicide 'epidemic' and self-harm 'endemic'

Suicide is a serious global health and social problem, with significant societal, economic and developmental effects. According to the World Health Organization (2012), every year almost one million people across the globe die from suicide. Over the past half-century, reported suicide rates around the world have risen 60 per cent and, based on current trends, the number of suicides will grow to 1.53 million yearly by 2020. It is estimated, furthermore, that between ten and twenty times the number of people who commit suicide, *attempt* suicide – elevating 'deliberate self-harm' to the level of a major health and social crisis outpacing that of suicide itself. The toll of suicide and self-harm on individuals, families, communities and nations is thus enormous, representing considerable levels of physical and social suffering.

Ravi's death was just one of hundreds of acts of fatal and non-fatal self-harm that occurred in and around the Madampe Division during the twenty-one-month period of my fieldwork. On average, suicides occurred on a monthly basis, acts of self-harm on a weekly basis, and suicide threats – existing as part of everyday discourse – on a daily basis. They were in turn just a small percentage of the many thousands that occurred across Sri Lanka over the same period, and hundreds of thousands since the middle of the twentieth century – as many as 90,000 between 1983 and 1993 alone (Pradhan 2001: 383) – that have created what has been called Sri Lanka's 'suicide epidemic' (Eddleston *et al.* 1998: 134; IRIN News 2009). During the same period that global suicide rates rose 60 per cent, the Sri Lankan suicide rate rose a staggering 870 per cent (Silva and Pushpakumara 1996: 73). Kearney and Miller (1985) showed how this rise had affected all demographic and social groups in Sri Lanka in equal measure, leading them to argue that the 'spiral' of suicides in Sri Lanka was being fuelled by 'fundamental forces' of economic, social and political change affecting all sections of society.

After 1996, however, something strange appeared to happen. First, the suicide rate began to fall, and is currently at its lowest level in more than thirty years. Second, the rate of *attempted suicides* began to rise, and according to some estimates by more than 300 per cent (IRIN News 2009) – i.e. at a magnitude greater than the fall of *completed* suicides. The fall may be understood as the consequence of government interventions restricting the import and sale of the most toxic pesticides (the most popular method of self-harm in Sri Lanka), improved access to and treatment in first aid centres, an apparently spontaneous shift away from pesticides to medicinal drugs which have a lower fatality rate (de Silva *et al.* 2012; Gunnell *et al.* 2007), and, I have argued, shifting representations in the social significance of self-inflicted death compared with non-lethal self-harm (Widger 2013). The 'up-and-down' behaviour of the suicide rate – the causes of which are located in 'fundamental forces' of social change as well as changing methods of self-harm – problematises mainstream theories of suicidal practice (ibid).

Traditionally, the academic study of suicide has been the concern of sociologists and psychologists, who have addressed self-destructive behaviours as a normative phenomenon: that is, as a problem universally definable and measurable. This may be understood as reflecting the status of suicide in European thought, traditions of which have come to shape understandings of suicide in particular ways (Hacking 1995; Giddens 1965; Minois 1999; Staples and Widger 2012). Since the European Middle Ages, there has been a long debate – first among religious scholars, moralists, philosophers and administrators, and from the nineteenth century within and between the emerging disciplines of sociology, psychology and psychiatry – concerning the proper representation of suicide. The term itself was only coined in the seventeenth century, taken from the Latin *sui* (of oneself) and *caedes* (murder) (Minois 1999: 182). It passed into English

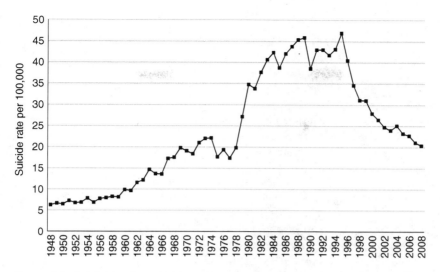

Figure 1.1 The Sri Lankan suicide rate, 1948–2008 (source: after Gunnell *et al.* 2007: 1236; raw data kindly provided by David Gunnell. Additional data obtained from Sri Lanka Sumithrayo at www.srilankasumithrayo.org/statistics-a-data (accessed 16 July 2012)).

usage first, then French, and by the eighteenth century Spanish, Italian and Portuguese (ibid.: 183). Prior to that, the terms 'self-murder' and 'self-homicide' were used instead. Acts of self-murder or suicide were variously regarded as affronts to God, natural law or society, and thus deemed a criminal act. By the nineteenth century, an argument had erupted between two new professions, moral statistics (a precursor to modern sociology) and psychiatry, with the one locating suicide in social deviancy and the other in mental pathology (Hacking 1995).

A central and on-going controversy ever since has thus been *where* to locate the causes of suicide: in macro-level social forces or internal emotional states. Social scientists have tended to argue for the former, and psychologists and psychiatrists for the latter. For the French sociologist Emile Durkheim (1951), who was writing at the end of the nineteenth century, suicide in Europe was best understood as the malady of a broken, egoistical and anomic society. Durkheim (1951: 210) argued that the suicide rate could be read as an artefact created by the 'suicidogenic current': the conditions in society that compel individuals to end their own lives. Durkheim posited that the suicidogenic current fluctuated according to degrees of social integration and moral regulation within society. With one or both too strong or too weak, the suicide rate rose or fell depending upon conditions and experiences of what he termed egoism, anomy, altruism and fatalism. Egoistic suicide was produced by a lack of social integration, which exposed individuals to suicide because they lost adequate levels of social support for dealing with their problems. Processes of social change that led people to lose their moorings in the social world, and thus their sense of belonging to a social group and the moral regulation that came with it, produced anomic suicide. Altruistic and fatalistic forms of suicide, for their part, were produced by strong social integration and moral regulation respectively, and for this reason were assumed to be only found in traditional, small-scale societies. Altruistic suicide was compelled not by some individual problem but rather by a sense of commitment to the group, while fatalistic suicide followed in contexts where individuals were so constrained by their social position that they could envisage no other life when that position disappeared.

In psychology and psychiatry, however, it has been the pathology of the individual that has garnered attention, with suicidal behaviour considered perhaps the most tragic manifestation of troubled minds. While social scientific studies of suicide almost inevitably locate their roots in Durkheim, even if they soon depart from him, in psychology no such obvious founding figure exists. The psychoanalytic tradition and even Freud himself had little to say on the matter (Alvarez 2002). Freud's early formulation was concerned with the status of suicide as a kind of violence and thus an 'internalised' form of homicide. A later formulation may be found in Freud's discussion of the 'life drive' (Eros) and the 'death drive' (Thanatos), in which suicide becomes a manifestation of the 'death wish'. It was the early formulation that became most influential during the mid-twentieth century and appeared in such influential works as Karl Menninger's (1938) *Man against Himself* and Shneidman and Farberow's (1961) *The Cry for Help*.

Today the debate has evolved and tends to concentrate on what Freud would have described as the processes through which people overcome the 'life drive' to embrace the 'death drive'. Since the time Freud and his immediate followers were writing, the diagnostic of 'depression' has come to dominate the field, and suicide and self-harm are today routinely associated with what might be termed 'mental illness'. Most health research supports the thesis that the vast majority of suicidal acts are caused by depression (Williams 2001), and indeed in popular Western culture it would be difficult to separate one from the other. 'Even though I know that each suicidal death is a multifaceted event,' wrote Edwin Shneidman (1998: 5), one of America's leading suicidologists, 'I retain the belief that, in the proper distillation of the event, its essential nature is *psychological*.' Echoing this, Mark Williams (2001: 139), one of Britain's most renowned suicide specialists, argued against the 'cry for help' theory to suggest that '[s]uicidal behaviour is best seen as a cry of pain'.

The 'inevitable' relationship between suicide and depression has been modelled in different ways, although often with the aim of understanding how people can overcome fears of pain and death to commit suicidal acts.[2] For example, Shneidman (1998) argues that suicide may be understood as the result of extreme psychological disturbance, what he called 'psychache', manifesting as negative self-image. This negativity makes it possible for people to overcome an 'instinctual' fear of pain and death and commit suicide. Similarly, Thomas Joiner (2005) contends that the risk of suicidality develops in individuals through their exposure to bodily pain and suffering which helps them to 'overcome one of nature's strongest forces ... self-preservation' (ibid.: 48). Joiner argues that '[t]he diminution of fear [of one's own death] through repeated self-injury is ... necessary for serious suicidal behavior to occur' (ibid.: 58). Thus, in much contemporary psychology, suicide has become a case of 'mind over matter'.

The Sri Lankan suicide rate has been similarly explained in terms of macro-level forces and worsening psychological states. First, several decades' worth of sociological analysis (Dissanayake and de Silva 1974; Gombrich and Obeyesekere 1988; Kearney and Miller 1985, 1987, 1988; Ranasinghe and Jayawardene 1966; Silva 2000, 2006; Silva and Pushpakumara 1996; Straus and Straus 1953; Wood 1961) have located the causes of suicide in processes of modernisation, urbanisation, population movement and violence. Factors identified include: the breakdown of 'traditional' caste, kinship and village structures; conflicts between parents and children over marriage preferences ('arranged' vs. 'love'); growing mismatches between educational levels and employment opportunities leading to the creation of a large class of 'educated unemployed'; high levels of internal migration as part of government resettlement programmes, and the effects of violent political insurgencies in the south and north of Sri Lanka leading to mass killings and disappearances and three decades of civil war. Second, a smaller but recently expanding number of psychological explanations have begun to appear (Abeyasinghe and Gunnell 2008; de Silva 2003; Marasinghe *et al.* 2012; Jayasinghe and Foster 2011; Samaraweera *et al.* 2008, 2010). These writers have tended to argue that similar experiences of rapid change, disjuncture and violence have led to increasing levels of depression and attendant issues of alcoholism and domestic violence in the population, resulting in self-harm and suicide.

The suicidal practices I encountered in Madampe were not so easily explained by either paradigm. On the one hand, 'fundamental forces' of change, disjuncture and violence, while obviously crucial, were experienced, represented and practised by different people in different ways. Processes of modernisation, urbanisation, migration and violence were not simply regarded as pressures put to bear on a society transitioning from a state of (traditional) order to (modern) disorder, but had ramifications for people's lives depending on their own experiences of those changes.

Jeanne Marecek's (1998, 2006) research in Sri Lanka stands as the most important ethnographic contribution to understanding this phenomenon thus far. Rejecting mono-causal theories, Marecek concentrates on the representations that self-harming and suicidal people themselves give to their acts. Marecek's work has shown how patterns and representations of suicidal behaviour are highly gendered, and of being significantly related to relationships of inequality and violence in the household. An important aspect of her research has been to show how self-harm exists as a kind of 'protest' or 'complaint' in people's lives. Drawing from Steve Taylor's (1982) work on the performative aspects of suicide, Marecek and Senadheera (2012) distinguish between dialogue suicides and monologue suicides. Dialogue suicides are those cases wherein the self-harming individual is clearly seeking to make some kind of point, while monologue suicides are those cases where individuals are perhaps only wishing to die. Although not suggesting an absolute distinction, Marecek's work points to one of the ways through which people in Madampe make sense of suicidal acts occurring around them, including the relationship between suicide and gender violence.

A further problematisation of sociological and psychological readings of suicide in Sri Lanka comes from historical sources. There is evidence to suggest that practices of self-harm were widespread in the island even before the 1960s and certainly before the escalation of civil violence from the 1980s. European travellers and colonialists had long commented on the prevalence of self-poisoning in Ceylon (as Sri Lanka was then called), which they identified as a customary recourse to interpersonal 'protest' (Amerasinghe 1999; D'Oyly 1929; Knox 1981). The practice was widespread enough to warrant the establishment of formal legal codes on the matter, and coroners had the power to impose sanctions and fines upon individuals and even whole villages for their wonton lack of care for the suicidal person. In the 1960s the sociologist A.L. Wood (1961) commented that the code, by then disappeared, was 'hyper-modern' in its dealings with suicidal people as victims rather than as criminals. Thus even if fundamental forces of social change, psychological disturbance and spread of pesticides combined to produce Sri Lanka's contemporary suicide *epidemic*, Ceylon was home to a much older self-harm *endemic* clearly pre-dating modernisation, globalisation and civil war. What all this amounts to is, I suggest, a recurring social practice of suicidality that while crucially contingent upon local contexts in time and space, has nevertheless been a persistent feature of social life for many centuries (Widger 2013).

The need for an anthropology of suicide

The historical depth and social specificity of the Sri Lankan suicide epidemic and self-harm endemic complicates the validity of the theoretical and analytical tools of suicidology. If, as I have suggested, mainstream sociological and psychological theories of suicide struggle to account for the behaviour of the Sri Lankan suicide rate as well as the nature of individual cases, would an anthropological approach fare any better? Anthropology is often defined as the study of the 'large issues' of human existence in the 'small places' in which people actually live (Bloch 2005; Eriksen 2001). Ethnography, the methodological tool of anthropologists that incorporates participant-observation in the daily lives of research subjects, may be understood as the means through which anthropologists come to comprehend, in intricate detail, 'small places' and their importance for 'large issues'. As 'anthropologists' we are interested in human beings in a universal sense, while as 'ethnographers' we are interested in what being human means in a highly particularistic sense. Maurice Bloch (2012) has argued that this dual interest has given rise to a tension within anthropology between, on the one hand, a pull towards general theories of large issues (the 'questions of anthropology' (Astuti *et al.* 2007)) and, on the other hand, a descent into relative specificities of small places (the 'complexities of ethnography').

On one level, suicide may be understood very simply as an action of and outcome for people who intentionally inflict harmful or fatal wounds upon the body. Around the world, this might be accomplished by poisoning, cutting, drowning, hanging, shooting, jumping or whatever, and in all cases raises some fundamental questions about the meaning of life and death and the nature of self-inflicted death. This is the level of large issues: of what is arguably a universal human phenomenon and one that is quite possibly found in other species as well, indicating a shared evolutionary origin (Anderson and Chamove 1985; Brown *et al.* 1999; Cross and Harlow 1965; Jones and Daniels 1996; Lester and Goldney 1997). But this apparent simplicity becomes complicated very quickly when those actions and outcomes are investigated in small places: what 'self-inflicted' wounds upon the body and their methods mean, what it takes for people to engage in those practices, how 'intentionality' is constructed and understood, what the causes and consequences of self-harm and suicide might actually be, and how suicide deaths are distinguished from other kinds of deaths. Borrowing from the philosopher John Searle (1995), it could be said that suicide as a large issue is 'epistemically objective', while suicide in small places is 'ontologically subjective'.

However defined, suicide would appear to be a subject ripe for anthropological investigation. Nevertheless, when compared with the voluminous materials produced by sociologists and psychologists, anthropological studies of suicide have remained surprisingly limited.[3] When they have appeared, they have tended to challenge the normative approaches of sociology and psychology, and argue instead for a closer attention to the cultural practice and representation of suicide in small places. While Durkheim was preparing *Le Suicide*, anthropologists were noting that suicide outside of Northern Europe and (white) North America did not fit the sociological or psychological models popular at the time. Steinmetz (1894: 59), writing in the pages of *American Anthropologist*, argued that suicide was far more prevalent in 'primitive' societies than sociologists such as Guido Morselli (Durkheim's inspiration) had allowed, who considered suicide a correlate of human social and psychological evolution and complexity. Steinmetz also lamented the lack of attention anthropologists were paying to suicide. 'It is a matter of regret,' Steinmetz suggested, 'that in so rich and suggestive a publication as the "Notes and Queries on Anthropology,"[4] ... there are so few questions in reference to suicide' (ibid.: 60).

Half a century later the founder of modern British social anthropology, Bronislaw Malinowski, published what was once considered 'the best known suicide in the ethnographic literature' (Bohannan 1960: 4). Today it has perhaps become one of the most overlooked elements of Malinowski's work. Malinowski (1949 [1926]) modelled suicide in the South Pacific Trobriand Islands as a socially legitimate form of redress used by people in the face of specific problems. Malinowski reported the suicide of a sixteen-year-old Trobriand man called Kima'i, who threw himself out of a coconut tree. Kima'i had been in a love affair with a parallel cousin, his mother's sister's daughter. Within the Trobriand kinship system, this affair constituted an act of incest. Although the affair had been publicly known, the couple had been discreet and in such a situation kinsmen were unlikely to make a fuss. However, in an attempt to end the affair and win the girl for himself, a rival male publicly accused Kima'i of incest. Following his accusation, which brought greater attention to the relationship and meant that it could no longer be overlooked, Malinowski (ibid.: 78–79) explained:

> [T]here was only one remedy; only one means of escape remained to the unfortunate youth. Next morning he put on his festive attire and ornamentation, climbed a coco-nut palm and addressed the community, speaking from among the palm leaves and bidding them farewell. He explained the reasons for his desperate deed and also launched forth a veiled accusation against the man who had driven him to his death, upon which it became the duty of his clansmen to avenge him. Then he wailed aloud, as is the custom, jumped from the palm some sixty feet high and was killed on the spot. There followed a fight within the village in which the rival was wounded; and the quarrel was repeated during the funeral.

The suicide thus expiated Kima'i of the shame of incest and directed public attention to the man who drove Kima'i to his death, causing him to be physically attacked:

> The person publicly accused admits his or her guilt, takes all the consequences, carries out the punishment upon his own person, but at the same time declares that he has been badly treated, appeals to the sentiment of those who have driven him to the extreme if they are his friends or relations, or if they are his enemies appeals to the solidarity of his kinsmen, asking them to carry on the vendetta.

Malinowski's argument may be read in two ways. The first is as a commentary on suicide in small places – what we might call suicide as an ontologically subjective phenomenon – in this case in the Trobriand Islands of the South Pacific. Malinowski argued that among the Trobrianders suicide did not arise owing to varying levels of social integration or moral regulation as Durkheim might have argued, but rather existed as a functional social institution in its own right, meeting the needs of individuals who found themselves in certain problematic circumstances. Both suicide and attempted suicide could be used as a response to personal slight, with the intent to die or to survive dependent on the gravity of the initial insult, and with each leading to different consequences for those implicated as the cause of that insult. The second reading problematises suicide as a large issue – which is to say, suicide as an epistemically objective fact. The implication of Malinowski's argument is that the *definition* of suicide (its epistemic objectivity) can only be derived from the ontological subjectivity of small places: ontological subjectivity *gives rise* to epistemological objectivity; particularism *gives rise* to normativism; *practice* gives rise to *representation*.

Malinowski's 'practice theory' of suicide is distinct from the 'cultural theory' approach to suicide that has arguably since become dominant. This theory is found in the work of anthropologists writing within the American cultural tradition of anthropology (e.g. Brown 1986; Counts 1980; Hezel 1984), and, in a simplified way, a growing body of work produced by suicidologists borrowing from it (for discussions see Colucci and Lester 2012). Explanations developed in this tradition may be understood as deriving a theory of culture from the anthropologist Franz Boas, in which culture is understood as 'an integrated system of meanings which enables people to deal with the world by classifying it according to their own, culturally inherited, unique way of seeing things' (Bloch 2012: 154). On one level, cultural theorists of suicide hold that ontological subjectivity gives rise to epistemological objectivity: that the large issue of suicide can only be grappled through its discovery in small places. However, on another level they hold that 'culture' is a pre-existing lens that *mediates*, via language, the construction of suicide in a subjective sense. In this view, *representation* comes before and gives rise to *practice*, so that practice becomes nothing more than the result of culture.

Suicidologists who are interested in understanding suicide cross-culturally have picked up on this idea. The trend is towards a theory of suicide and culture that tends to designate the latter as little more than one other 'factor' that might cause people to kill themselves, or shape the ways in which they may do so. This is evidenced most clearly in the way writers in the suicidological tradition list 'cultural factors' of suicide alongside 'social factors', 'psychological factors', 'genetic factors' and so on. Thus the suicidologist Boldt (1988, emphasis added) writes: 'No one who kills himself does so *without reference* to the prevailing normative standards, values and attitudes of the culture to which he belongs.' In this view, culture is an epiphenomenon that one can do away with and *still* commit, and *still* make sense of, suicide. My reason for highlighting this particular view of suicide and culture is to demonstrate the inadequacy of a culturalist approach. Culture exists as a kind of template that directs practice, and the part played by the agent in learning, adapting, performing and reacting to suicide is minimalised. This view of suicide obscures the dynamic social processes through which its practices generate the conditions of its own representation, and thus the importance of understanding the relationship between suicidal practices and suicidal representations as a first step towards understanding suicidal people, and ultimately suicide prevention.

This discussion brings us to the wider field of medical and particularly psychiatric anthropology, and its dialogue with mainstream and cross-cultural psychiatry. The field is large and this is no place to provide a comprehensive introduction (see Kitanaka (2011: ch. 1) for an excellent summary). However, one issue of on-going debate is the relationship between what might be termed the 'biology' and 'culture' of distressed psychosocial states on the one hand, and self-destruction on the other. Like anthropologists generally, medical and psychiatric anthropologists have had little to say about suicide. On the other hand, they have had a lot to say about depression which, as we saw, many suicidologists believe to be a primary cause of suicide.

The debate on depression is very similar to the debate on suicide. Thus on one side we find the medical anthropologists and cultural psychiatrists who in the Boasian cultural tradition argue that depression is a culturally and socially situated phenomenon (Jadhav 1996; Jadhav et al. 2001). Extreme forms of this argument posit that depression, and the biomedical industry behind it, has been *imposed* upon both Western and non-Western societies as an operation of power and social control (Goffman 1961; Scheff 1966; Zola 1972). An alternative view is that depression has spread around the world through a more subtle process in which psychiatric truths become *normalised* via the self-discipline of subjects buying into the psychiatric life view accompanying neoliberal capitalism (Nye 1984; Petryna et al. 2006; Rose 1999; Turner 1996). As with suicide, then, both approaches place culture before practice and limit the role of human agency in the ways in which people may understand, adopt, perform and respond to mental and emotional states that may be defined as 'ill'. In particular, there tends to be a general agreement that the spread of biomedical understandings of emotional and social problems is necessarily a 'bad thing', at the very least because those understandings exclude social causalities and foreground individual pathologies at the expense of 'indigenous' cultural practices and representations.

Thus on the other side we find the psychologists and psychiatrists who argue that depression is a disease found in all humans, sometimes with biological aetiology, but which is properly understood as a problem of individual minds. The most recent manifestation of this debate exists in relation to the 'Global Mental Health' (GMH) movement, which presses for development aid financing to be directed towards mental health programmes in middle- and low-income countries (Collins et al. 2011; Patel and Bloch 2009; Prince et al. 2007). For advocates of GMH the export of Western models of mental illness and treatment should be considered a fundamental human right. The important point here is that language and culture are not only dismissed by GMH as epiphenomena which again one can do away with and still make sense of depression, but that by focusing on language and culture *barriers* are put in place to extending the benefits of 'modern' psychiatry to the rest of the world. This is a challenging ethical criticism that demonstrates how cultural theorists risk 'exoticising' human suffering and in so doing creating a 'double exclusion' from mental health care: the first, economic, and the second, cultural.

Gananath Obeyesekere (1985) argued that cultures provide their own ways of managing psychological disturbance, and thus formulated a pre-emptive defence of this criticism. Taking the example of Theravada Buddhism in Sri Lanka, Obeyesekere points to how religious practices within that tradition provide symbolic means of understanding and dealing with psychic stress, transforming negative feelings of 'depression' into positive experiences of worship. Indeed, Obeyesekere argues, there is no such thing as depression in Buddhist culture because for Buddhists the supposed symptoms of depression (e.g. hopelessness, helplessness, worthlessness) are inevitable facts of life with which all good Buddhists must come to terms. It would thus be meaningless to suggest that the symptoms of depression have universal validity, as to do so would be to argue that all Buddhists, by virtue of their religious beliefs, are depressed. Obeyesekere does not invite us to speculate that by the same token all depressed people are also therefore Buddhist, and if so a cure for the Western malaise of depression could quite simply be mass conversion to Buddhism. However, what we may take from his argument is the importance of ontological subjectivity in the generation of affective states and behaviours, and the inherent difficulty applying without criticism the terms and tools of modern psychiatry.

Elements of a practice theory of suicide

Anthropological and suicidological approaches to suicide specifically, and mental health and illness more generally, may thus be understood as local battles in the long-running 'culture wars' that have plagued social and natural sciences for decades. In this book, I wish to reinvigorate Malinowski's approach and to understand suicidal practice as something that gives rise to cultural representations of suicide through processual socialities. In so doing I wish to show how some of the problems facing anthropologists, sociologists, psychologists and psychiatrists in the ways they deal with suicide may be overcome. By adopting this approach I do not want to suggest that when people in Sri Lanka engage in suicidal practice they do so without reference to pre-existing theories or representations that might be called 'culture': far from it, in fact. My aim rather is to argue that those pre-existing representations are not simply a kind of 'reference book' to which people refer in order to commit suicide in a way that suits the tradition into which they were born, and could still commit suicide without reference to it (and if doing so would therefore commit suicide in some kind of 'acultural' way). Equally, I find the ethical challenge posed by GMH an interesting one, especially as national health systems around the world are increasingly struggling with questions of culture and diversity, and are forced to find new ways of conceptualising, managing and treating mental health complaints across heterogeneous communities. 'Culture' is not necessarily 'good', just as 'medicalisation' is not necessarily 'bad'.

First, 'cultures' are never homogeneous or uniform, and even in the small Madampe area there are multiple representations – and corresponding arguments and counter-representations – concerning the 'whys', 'ways', 'whens' and 'wheres' of suicidal practice. Second, these representations are always learnt, adjusted and practised across the life-course, from childhood through teenage years and into adulthood and old age, and this means that while a great deal of imitation takes place there is also a great deal of innovation to be found (Widger n.d.). The performance of suicidal practice is something that may be understood as taking place in spatial and temporal 'arenas' at event, lifespan and societal levels that are both constrained by history and set free by unfolding contexts of practice. Suicidal practices and representations are 'generated' from those arenas as products of both history and contemporary socialities. To put it another way, the pages of the reference book are being written even while they are being read: practice and representation are integrally linked in processual terms.

By developing a practice theory of suicide, I locate myself within the larger field of practice theory, especially Bourdieu's (1977, 1984, 1990) concept of 'habitus', Lave and Wenger's (1991) work on 'situated learning', and Bandura's (2001) work on the agentive processes of learning. As a set of theories, they provide models for understanding the social processes through which individual practices and representations are shaped by what Lawrence Goldman (1998: xviii) has called 'mimesis and mythos': imitation and creativity. Pierre Bourdieu's (1990) famous concept of habitus – defined as '[s]ystems of durable, transposable dispositions ... principles which generate and organize practices and representations' (ibid.: 53) – sets out a theory of socialisation that links individual positions and position taking in society with representations in and of the world. For Bourdieu, formative experiences and practices shape habitus and these further shape experiences and practices, so that practices and representations become mutually generative. Thus, subject positionalities in the world are both constrained by structural positions ascribed by gender, age, race, class and so on, but are also embodied and performed through practices that have the potential to transform representations and realign structured positions.

Jean Lave and Etienne Wenger (1991) have illuminated the processes through which people come to learn practices and acquire representations or ideas about the world. Lave and Wenger studied apprentices and the ways in which they move from a 'peripheral' position in a trade to becoming full members of a 'community of practice'. Lave and Wenger's (ibid.) studies showed how apprentices learn the knowledge and skills required to join a community of practice through what is usually non-verbal instruction and copying. This exposure facilitates the slow development of relevant expertise in apprentices as they 'hang around' with master craftsmen and 'absorb' their knowledge. Lave and Wenger's insights have been important for two reasons. The first concerns how they demonstrated the relative *unimportance* of language in the transmission of knowledge, which may be typical of how everyday knowledge is passed on (Bloch 2012: 193). The second is in how they pointed to the importance of situated learning as a means of overcoming marginality to become accepted community participants. It is literally through doing that people learn and habitus develops to make fully-rounded adults, and again this may be typical of how cultural knowledge – including suicide knowledge – is acquired.

Focusing on the everyday contexts of socialisation and knowledge acquisition leads to questions concerning the role of the agent in the process and the extent to which individuals take charge of their own learning: the extent to which those in peripheral positions may situate themselves to maximise learning potential. The field of educational psychology that engages with the subject of self-regulated learning is large (see Martin (2004) for an introduction), but a key figure remains Albert Bandura. Bandura (e.g. 2001) has argued that the learning process is agentive in the sense that learners take control of what they come to know, but also, as a result, come to understand themselves as people *with* agency. For Bandura, agentic learning as self-regulation 'is ... both determined and determining' (Martin 2004: 139). As for Bourdieu, then, learning is a cumulative process in that it shapes both the ability to learn as much as it does what is learnt, and these processes spiral together.

This triad of practice theories has particular relevance for the study of suicide. First, the theories suggest how a *disposition* for suicide must be acquired through socialisation processes in history that define particular kinds of practice as suicidal and particular kinds of experiences as worthy of a suicidal response. As an element of habitus, the disposition for suicide must be shaped by structural position, and reflect, for example, gender, age and class constraints, while being embodied and performed through practices that have the capacity to transform them.

Second, they suggest how the *acquisition* of suicidal dispositions in terms of both structured and structuring practices and representations must proceed through processes of situated learning that move individuals from peripheral to central positions. There are, according to one's gender, age and class positions, 'right ways' and 'wrong ways', and 'right reasons' and 'wrong reasons', to kill oneself, in the sense of social values and meanings that can be attached to suicide, and how the effects of suicide are played out in social contexts during and after the event. Thus the 'ability' of individuals to 'correctly' perform suicidal practices has significant bearing on how others will react to such acts, the ways in which others may be expected to react, and how the suicidal person may envisage the consequences of the act for themselves and others beyond the corporeal facts of injury, pain and possible death.

Third, if agency may be understood as manifested through learning practices, then learning to become a suicidal person implies learning how suicidal agency – and agency more generally – comes into being. The ability to end one's own life, as an acquired and mastered response, is perhaps an ultimate expression of agency allowed or disavowed, and what Camus (1955: 3) called the 'one truly serious philosophical problem'. Suicide may be understood as a singular event that only exists within much longer processes stretching before and after the act, with ramifications both distant and near, and often, if not always, posing considerable problems for people to deal with. The voluntary removal of self from life, family and community – what might be called a 'denial of sociality' – injects that singular event with a long-lasting recurring and rebounding resonance of its own, shaping the flow of events both before and after it.

A re-examination of Ravi's death helps us to figure the implications of a practice theory of suicide that will be developed in this book, and finally summarized in its totality in the Conclusion. First, as we saw, assumptions concerning Ravi's disposition to suicide were found to be expressed in different ways. Yet the decision to define his death as suicidal, and to identify particular kinds of experiences as leading to his suicide, was based on his gender, age and social class, as well as the backgrounds of those commenting upon his death. Therefore, for those of Ravi's age, the suicide was the consequence of a love problem and, for those of his parents' age, the consequence of his mother's occupation and family life more generally. While of course we do not know why Ravi killed himself – if indeed he did at all – the numerous similar cases of non-fatal self-harm described in this book suggest that when young men describe their own motivations, they do so often with recourse to similar kinds of concerns. For young men in Madampe it is 'obvious' that love problems people like them to attempt suicide.

Second, as an element of habitus, Ravi's disposition for suicide was shaped by his structural position in family and community. Thus Ravi's suicide may be understood as an embodied response that has the capacity to transform the structures of its own creation: for this reason, we may argue that suicide has structuring effects. Community responses to Ravi's death ignited wider debates in Udagama concerning the fate of young people in the modern age of romantic love marriage and international labour migration. Arguments hardened existing opinions concerning the fate of the nation in the face of economic and cultural modernisation and globalisation, whether they were pessimistic or optimistic about the implications for young people's lives. Perhaps rarely a single suicide could have such an effect on public consciousness that structures radically transform. In most cases, as in Ravi's, change may be understood to accrue slowly, through 'a thousand deaths'. Here we find time to be important. The structured and structuring of suicide occurs from micro to macro levels, at the levels of the singular event, lifespan and society.

Third, the transformations created by suicidal practices may derive from a clear intent of the person who self-harms, even if its reception is highly debated. Here agency may be facilitated or denied, often at the same time or over time, depending on the social status of the suicidal person and the context of his or her actions. This is perhaps the most uncertain element of the practice theory of suicide, as the agentive consequences of suicide are rarely truly known and are always contested – not only by people in Madampe but also centuries of academic suicide scholarship. Nevertheless, how and in what ways agency might be allowed or disavowed at different junctures – up to and after the event, across the lifespan, and in society at large – forms a crucial part of the ways in which people in Madampe made sense of suicide. Simply, they asked: Who caused it? What effects did it have? Opposed to sociological and psychological theories of suicide, my intention is to show how representations of suicide generate from contexts of practice that exist at different temporal and spatial plains.

A definition of 'suicide'

To conclude the theoretical section of this introduction I turn finally to the question of what we might mean by 'suicide'. Thus far, I have used the term and its relatives ('self-harm', 'suicide threat', 'suicide attempt', 'self-inflicted death') without any attempt at defining them. However, as I have been concerned to argue in this chapter, to seek to apply a definition of suicide at the outset would be tantamount to placing representation before practice and limiting the practice theory of suicide I intend to develop. I contend that suicidal practices give rise to suicidal terminologies. This process is most evident in Chapter 3, where I discuss how people in Madampe understand the difference between suicide as a national problem and suicide in the everyday intimate spaces of their lives. To foreshadow that discussion here I quickly summarise what suicidologists have generally meant by suicide and explain the rationale for the approach I will adopt.

With roots in positivist traditions of sociology, psychology and medicine, suicidology has sought to define the scope of its inquiry in 'scientific' terms. This has often focused on – and stumbled upon – the problem of intent. For Durkheim (1951), for example, a rigid definition of suicide was crucial for the development of his sociological method, as the correlation between social conditions and suicide rates could only be proven by the surety of the concepts under comparison. As such, Durkheim boldly stated that suicide would be defined as 'all cases of death resulting directly or indirectly from a positive or negative act of the victim himself, which he knows will produce this result' (ibid.: 44). Despite Durkheim's confidence, however, such a definition is hard to demonstrate in real life. In Sri Lanka, many cases of suicide may be better understood as 'accidental' deaths, even though the hallmarks of both intentional and accidental death – e.g. the consumption of poison – are identical. How are we to distinguish one from other?

For this reason, others prefer to talk of 'self-harm'. Here the focus is placed not on the *outcome* of the act but the *process*, and the problem of intent may be addressed or avoided on a case-by-case basis. In some studies self-harm is to be distinguished from suicide precisely because self-harm is assumed to be an *intentionally* non-fatal act. Drawing from wider debates in the field, Laye-Gindhu and Schonert-Reichl (2005) define self-harm as a 'deliberate and voluntary physical self-injury that is not life-threatening and is without any conscious suicidal intent'. Conversely, other studies seek to exclude intent from the definition of self-harm. Cooper *et al.* (2005: 13) suggest that '[s]elf-harm is defined as an act of intentional self-poisoning or injury irrespective of the apparent purpose of the act'. In a similar move, Skegg (2005: 141) suggests that the 'term self-harm is commonly used to describe a wide range of behaviours and intentions including attempted hanging, impulsive self-poisoning, and superficial [self]-cutting'.

As will be discussed in Chapter 3, people in Madampe are similarly troubled by the problem of intent. To remain faithful to that ethnographic reality, this book seeks to make no assumptions concerning the 'proper' definition of suicide and its relatives. First, I use the terms more or less in relation to the outcome that is immediately apparent. When a person has apparently died by their own action, I shall generally call this suicide, and when a person has deliberately hurt himself or herself but survived, I shall generally call this self-harm. In so doing, I am not seeking to make any comment regarding the intent or otherwise of the person, except in those cases where I make it explicit from readings of the wider contextual and processual environment that such is my aim. Second, I use the term 'practice' rather than 'behaviour' – thus I shall speak of 'suicidal practice', 'self-harming practices' and so on. Here the term 'practice' clearly conveys the practice theory of suicide I wish to develop and serves as a reminder that representations of suicide are always in the process of becoming in practice, rather than practice simply being the consequence of representation. Thus, the term 'suicidal practice' does not indicate a complete or total action or behaviour but one that is always being made through the processual socialities of its existence.

Plan of the book

The practice of suicide as a processual sociality shapes the resulting structure of this book. That is to say, the chapters follow the steps through which suicidal practices are learnt and performed by different kinds of people in differing social contexts, and of how suicidal practices generate forms of social life.

Chapter 2 sets the local scene and contexts of suicide. Through a description of the fieldwork setting, which I define as different 'arenas' of suicidal practice and meaning making (villages, police stations and coroners' courts, and community hospitals and a mental health clinic), I introduce the social and historical foundations upon which different causal theories of suicidality are developed in Madampe. A key concern across all three arenas is the extent to which suicide may be understood as a failure of people to lead 'good family lives' (*hoṅda pavul ji:vite*), and of how ordinary villagers, criminal investigators and coroners, and health professionals deal with this problem. I argue that at once 'evidence' of suicide and an 'ethos' of suicidality, the causal theories of suicide generated by the social practices of villages, courts and clinics engender patterns and understandings of suicide found in Madampe.

Chapter 3 sets the local conditions of suicide. The chapter charts my pathway into understanding causal theories of suicide in Madampe through a description of how informants explained suicide *there*, at the national level in Sri Lanka, and suicide *here*, at the local level in Madampe. Suicide *there* is the suicide of the national epidemic, about which my informants were fully aware, who located its causes in problems attendant to farmers, economic liberalisation, youth frustrations and Buddhism. Suicide *here*, which was routinely described in terms of 'poison drinking', was for my informants much more difficult to understand. The problem lies in the always-uncertain status of intent in any suicidal act, and the relationship of poison-drinking practices to wider social practices of 'lies and make-believe' which thread through social life in multiple ways. It is this 'problem of 'intent', which may be understood as contributing to local ontologies of suicide practices.

Chapter 4 shows how people in Madampe make sense of suicide *here* through recourse to imaginings of the 'good family life', and how this creates particular kinds of 'suicide flows' following the course of everyday relationalities. The focus is on practices of violence 'in and of' the home – a recurring theme of the book – and the processes of 'blaming' and 'shaming' through which gender and generational identities are constructed, adopted and performed. Using anthropological kinship charts to capture 'snapshots' of suicidal relationalities in time, the chapter then explores specific themes through the close examination of individual case studies. Building on the concept of 'good family life', the chapter explains why only particular kinds of kin relationship give rise to suicidal practices when they encounter problems as a function of their special moral endowments. Through suicidal practices, ideas and imaginings of kinship come into being, setting a vision of 'good family lives' in a functioning, moral society.

Chapter 5 develops an emotional framework of suicide by drawing from the popular concepts people use to account for their actions: 'suffering', 'frustration' and 'anger'. The chapter engages with debates in psychological anthropology and cross-cultural psychiatry to argue that practices of emotionality generate particular kinds of suicide defined as 'psychological pathology' under certain conditions. What stands out, however, is the fact that such ascription always implies a denial of the suicidal person's claims, as an operation of power. Thus people in Madampe see middle-class men's suicides as an epitome of calm and quiet suicides that embody a certain respectability, while working-class women's suicides epitomise an impulsive and passionate suicide that embodies shame. At the end of the chapter, I turn again to the dual paradigm of 'evidence and ethos' to outline an ethnopsychiatric framework of suicide in Madampe for future study.

Chapter 6 moves from a description of the general to the specific, and explores suicidal practices that arise in the context of 'romantic love'. Writing against the trend in South Asian anthropology that views romantic suicides as the result of wistful young people coping with the travails of a society adjusting from a tradition of 'arranged marriage' to 'love marriage', I argue that the expansion of the middle classes in Sri Lanka has produced greater levels of interest in 'arranged marriage' than was ever the case in the past. It is in this context of increased pressure on young people on the one hand, and parental surveillance on the other, that suicidal practices emerge as forms of self-discipline used to navigate the difficult terrain of love. Thus, young men come to perform suicidal practices as an attempt to 'push' young women into stating declarations of love, and young women perform suicidal practices to avoid the accusations and violence of parents who suspect them of risking shame by accepting young men's advances. Rather than simply expressing narratives of romance, suicidal practices are also practices of coercion.

Chapter 7 explores adults' suicides, and in particular the relationship between alcohol, migration and masculinity. Here we find a paradox between the conventional wisdom which states that masculinities challenged by female labour migration are leading to increased incidence of drinking, violence and suicide, and the meanings and significances that men invest in alcohol, migration and the 'pursuit of fun' as a *barrier* to suicide. Focused on men's cherished experience of 'movement', the first half of the chapter describes how masculinities are enjoyed in Madampe through practices of 'going somewhere' (*bæ:rakyanəva*) of which drinking and migration are paradigmatic. The second half explores the consequences of movement and in particular men's fears, expressed through allusions to 'Kalu Yaka', the Black Demon, concerning wives' infidelities during their absence.

Chapter 8 shifts the focus to questions of suicide interventions, and explores the social significance of prevention efforts with regard to power dynamics in households, communities and Sri Lanka at large. Focused on the popular Buddhist concept of *metta* (loving kindness/compassion), I argue that suicide and its prevention may be understood in relation to a 'search for compassion'. The chapter reviews the ways in which suicide interventions take place across villages, courts and clinics, and how common strategies of suicide prevention include the imposition of silence at the expense of compassion, each with its own implications for the expression of loving kindness for suicidal people. While, as ever, it is difficult to separate practice from power, I argue that *metta* may offer an ontologically relevant model for understanding suicide prevention in contemporary Sri Lanka, and a means to transform the relational grounds of suicide practice into grounds for suicide prevention.

Finally, Chapter 9 concludes the book by further exploring the implications of a practice theory of suicide in relation to what I call the 'suicide process': the transforming manifold relationships that make up suicide and which give suicide its apparently unique character. I explore this across three socio-spatial scales – the level of individual suicide events, lifespans and the societal level – and demonstrate how through their dynamics suicide practices give rise to suicide representations. I show how history can be found running through individual cases and individual cases can be found running through history in a process of unfolding generation where the 'discrete' and the 'general' feed into one another. The model moves us beyond arguments concerning the biological innateness or social construction of suicide and towards a more dynamic practice-centred approach. I seek not to define suicide as a problem for social science or psychological science or medical science, but rather to establish the value of anthropology as a way of understanding suicide through a humanistic ethic. That ethic allows the right to choose the manner of one's own death while encompassing the crucial fact that suicide may be 'caused' by a withdrawal of rights.

Finally, a word on how this book might be read by non-anthropologists. As they stand, each chapter provides fine-grained details and pointers for suicide interventionists working in Sri Lanka, and South Asia more widely. To understand fully the arguments I make and their relevance for prevention, professionals with an interest in Asian societies would benefit from reading the book in its entirety. However, the book also contains a range of more general insights into the relationship between an anthropological and ethnographic approach to suicide and suicide prevention across different social and cultural contexts. In order to capture and communicate those global insights more effectively, at the end of each chapter (including this one) I have included a box summarising the chapter's main points the implications for understanding and developing suicide prevention programmes in cross-cultural contexts.

Insights for prevention

Summary of the chapter

- Global inequalities in suicide prevention resources are *cultural* as well as financial. Suicidology privileges Euro-American models of suicidality and often overlooks the fact that suicide is a *situated* phenomenon in local contexts.
- But also there is *no such thing* as a 'culture of suicide'. It is better to think of popular cultural representations of suicide as being *generated* by suicidal practices that are continually made and remade in *contexts of practice*.
- Anthropology highlights the importance of adopting a *'local point of view'* when investigating suicidal practices around the world. *Ethnographic methods* can help illuminate the processes through which *practices of suicide give rise to representations of suicide*.
- Practices and representations of suicide are *agentive* in the sense that people adopt, adapt and perform suicidalities according to *their own understandings* of why, ultimately, they may wish to live or die. Learning is cyclical.

Practical applications

- When *developing an approach to prevention* a detailed explanation of how suicidal practices generate representations of suicide is essential to understanding *what we are seeking to prevent*.
- Use anthropological and ethnographic methods to *question assumptions* about suicide and to develop a *context-relevant* model of suicidal practice and representation from a *diverse range of perspectives*.
- Never *assume* that suicide is caused by depression or other deep-seated mental illness; *consider the social practices* through which suicide and social and psychological problems are expressed.
- Ask whether and how suicide *might not be a negative symptom* of illness, despair, or an attempt to 'escape', but is instead *a meaningful and creative social practice* that is generative of social life.

Notes

1 All names and place names smaller than divisional secretariat level are anonymised in this book. Identifying features are masked as far as possible to protect identities.
2 The underlying assumption here is that an insatiable 'will to survive' is the natural state of human beings and voluntary death is an unnatural state. The cultural specificity of this assumption is plain to see, considering the breadth of socially sanctioned reasons for self-inflicted death of various kinds around the world, including, but hardly limited to, suicide.
3 As this book went to press Jocelyn Chua's (2014) *In Pursuit of the Good Life* was published, too late for discussion in my own work, but which explores many similar themes. The book is based on fieldwork in Kerala, southern India, which socially and culturally is similar to Sri Lanka in many ways and thus provides a valuable perspective on the ethnography and theories discussed in this book.
4 *Notes and Queries on Anthropology* was a compendium of anthropological field methods compiled and published by the Royal Anthropological Institute. They were meant to act as a unifying guide for anthropologists working in different societies, and

thus aid the comparative project of anthropology. The *Notes and Queries* were published from the late 1800s to the mid-1900s and, although they came to be seen as rather archaic, they did at least attempt to endow anthropologists with a common charter – something that many are today seeking once again.

2 Of villages, courts and clinics

What are the local spaces of ontological subjectivity that through their practices and processes generate epistemologically objective 'self-'destructive behaviours? Put another way, *where* are people living through suicide and how do those places generate particular representations of suicidality? In what ways are dispositions of suicide created and broadcast so that people may acquire, through practice, suicide as a learned response?

Several 'small places' of suicide are investigated in this book. They include: (1) two villages in western Sri Lanka, Udagama and Alutwatta, and the wider Madampe Division of which they are a part; (2) the crime and legal services responsible for investigating and classifying deaths, including the police station in Madampe and the Coroners' Court attached to the District Court in the market town of Kuliyapitiya, twenty-two kilometres to the east; and (3) the health services responsible for treating self-harmers in Madampe, including the Peripheral Health Unit (first aid medical centre) at Galmuruwa and the Mental Health Clinic attached to the District Base Hospital in the fishing town of Chilaw, fifteen kilometres to the north. Together these places comprise three 'arenas' that have been generated by and generate interrelated representational frameworks of suicidal practice that both explain and produce acts of self-harm and self-inflicted death.

Thus, the chapter explores the local ontological grounds upon which differing representations of suicide come into being through a range of social practices. These include the practices of ordinary villagers and townsfolk, criminal investigators and coroners, and health and mental health professionals. Throughout the book, I will present village- , court- and clinic-generated representations of suicidality at different points to show how cases of self-harm or self-inflicted death may be understood as deriving from multiple causes and as being surrounded by multiple interpretations. In this chapter, my aim is to introduce the actual places and spaces from which those representations emerge, and to make the case for considering them as sources of *evidence* for the causes of suicide in Madampe, as well as signifiers of *ethos* reflecting the particular biographies and worldviews of village residents and court and clinical staff. In so doing, the chapter establishes the basic parameters for developing a practice theory of suicide in Madampe.

General introduction to the fieldsite

My fieldwork took place in a peri-urban locality in western Sri Lanka called the Madampe Division, a southern portion of the wider Puttalam District in the Northwest Province of Sri Lanka (see Figure 2.1). The bulk of fieldwork was conducted between October 2004 and June 2006, and I made brief follow-up visits in 2007 and 2012/2013. The Madampe Division itself has never recorded especially high suicide rates, straddling as it does rural and urban communities (Widger 2013). However, my intention was not to locate myself in a part of Sri Lanka which reported the highest rates of self-harm and suicide, but in a place that would give me the chance to develop a comparative study along class and religious lines, wrapped around a focus on gender and age. Madampe fitted that requirement.

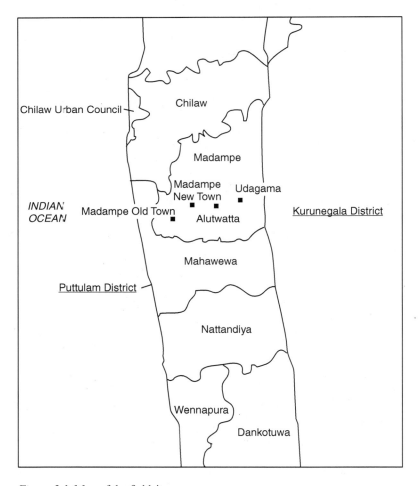

Figure 2.1 Map of the fieldsite.

The Madampe Division

According to the 2001 Census, the Madampe Division had a population of 43,411, of whom 91.4 per cent were ethnically and linguistically Sinhala. The Division is also home to a relatively large Tamil-speaking Muslim community and a much smaller Tamil community (Table 2.1). As is common for the west coast, the majority of Madampe's Sinhala population is Buddhist or Roman Catholic, at 74.1 per cent and 17.2 per cent of the total population respectively. Members of new Evangelical churches account for about 1.6 per cent (Department of Census and Statistics 2001) (Table 2.2). As will be seen below, the highest rates of suicide and self-harm were found in Sinhala Buddhist and Catholics communities, and, reflecting their overall presence in the area more generally, it is those communities and the Buddhists especially that I concentrate on in this book.

Madampe is economically diverse, split between primary, secondary and tertiary sectors, including agriculture, light manufacturing, and government and private sector services (Madampe Divisional Secretariat, unpublished data gathered by the author) (Table 2.3). The coconut, the cultivation of which began on an industrial scale during the early nineteenth century, dominates agricultural production in Madampe. In the division in 2004, 79 per cent of agricultural land use was given over to that crop, with only 4 per cent for other fruits and vegetables (Table 2.4). A

Table 2.1 Ethnic communities in the Madampe Division, 2001

Ethnicity	Population	Per cent
Sinhalese	39,662	91.4
Sri Lankan Tamil	1,106	2.6
Indian Tamil	226	0.52
Muslim	2,359	5.4
Burgher	19	0.04
Other	39	0.09
Totals	43,411	100.0

Source: Department of Census and Statistics (2003: 7).

Table 2.2 Religious communities in the Madampe Division, 2004

Religion	Population	Per cent
Buddhism	32,159	74.1
Hinduism	697	1.6
Islam	2,383	5.5
Roman Catholic	7,452	17.2
Protestant Christian	708	1.6
Other	12	0.03
Total	43,411	100.0

Source: Department of Census and Statistics (2003: 7).

Table 2.3 Employment by sector in Puttalam and five neighbouring districts

District	Primary	Secondary	Tertiary
Puttalam	29.8	32.6	37.7
Colombo	32.2	26.6	41.2
Gampaha	1.9	29.9	68.3
Kurunegala	32.4	31.4	36.2
Anuradhapura	58.6	14.2	27.2
Kegalle	27.4	30.3	42.3

Source: Department of Census and Statistics (2003: 24).

Table 2.4 Agricultural land use in the Madampe Division, 2001

Land use	Acres	Per cent
Coconut estates	92.30	79.50
Banana estates	2.10	1.80
Pineapple estates	1.10	1.00
Cashew nut estates	0.10	0.08
Other fruit estates	1.00	0.82
Vegetable market gardens	0.05	0.04
Paddy (river fed)	8.20	7.00
Paddy (tank fed)	8.30	7.20
Paddy (rain fed)	3.00	2.60
Total	116.15	100.00

Source: Madampe Divisional Secretariat (2004, unpublished).

further 17 per cent was given over to paddy cultivation (ibid.). Meanwhile, between 5 and 15 per cent of the population works abroad with principal destinations being the Middle East, Italy and countries in South East Asia (ibid.). However, these are official figures recording legal migration only, and real levels of overseas migration, especially to Italy, are likely to be very much higher.

When I first visited Madampe in 2001, the legacy of Madampe's location in the coconut economy was still plain to see. Described by one local historian as a 'salubrious suburb' (Edirisinghe 1999), the town and its environs were far more developed than places of a similar size even just to the north of Chilaw, some fifteen kilometres away. Over the decade to come, I witnessed a further transformation in the economic fortunes of the town. Despite its relative prosperity, in 2001 only a very few shops had the bright glass frontages that then characterised modern developments in Colombo and the towns in closer proximity to it, and none of the other symbols of global consumer culture such as mobile phone stores or internet cafés. However, by the time I had returned in 2004, several of the old-style open-fronted *kaḍe* (boutiques) selling simple ranges of food and household items had gone substantially upmarket, with imported European ranges and air conditioning. A number of mobile phone shops had also opened, and the communication centres that once sold local and international calls to the now dwindling number of the telephonically unconnected had begun new lines in web access. When I visited again in 2012, the centre of New Town was dominated by large shops and supermarkets all selling expensive local and foreign ranges, signalling Madampe's transformation into a decidedly middle-class area. These rapid changes have been fuelled mostly from remittances sent by overseas labour migrants to families and relatives in the area.

Patterns of suicide in Sri Lanka

At national level patterns of self-harm and suicide vary by gender, age, ethnicity and geographical location. Studies show how in Sri Lanka men commit suicide at a greater rate – around three times – to that of women (Eddleston *et al.* 2005: 583; Kearney and Miller 1985: 83; Marecek 1998: 72; Silva and Pushpakumara 1996: 73). Although men and women practised self-harm at approximately equal rates, most studies reported either gender parity or a male:female ratio of no greater than 2 : 1 (Eddleston ibid.; Marecek ibid.: 73). With regard to age, suicide in Sri Lanka has generally been a youthful phenomenon, with self-inflicted death the leading cause of mortality in the sixteen to twenty-four age group (Kearney and Miller ibid.; Marecek ibid.; Silva and Pushpakumara ibid.). The suicide rate falls for both women and men after age thirty, before rising again from around age fifty onwards among males (Kearney and Miller ibid.).

Jeanne Marecek (1998: 73) has observed that discussions concerning the ethnic distribution of suicide in Sri Lanka have been a source of much contention, and used to bolster or deny claims of discrimination by one group or another. However, it is generally accepted that Sinhala and Tamil populations report the highest rates, and Muslims and Burghers the lowest rates. Meanwhile, the available evidence would suggest that suicide rates are highest in the Buddhist community first and the Hindu community second, and lowest in Christian and Muslim communities (Thalagala 2009). Only partly reflecting the ethic distribution, then, the variations seen among religious communities suggests that this factor makes considerable impacts on suicide rates.

The comparison of district-level data has long suggested an urban/rural and northeastern/southwestern divide in Sri Lankan suicide rates (Kearney and Miller 1985; Straus and Straus 1953; Wood 1961). Between 1950 and 1978 the highest rates were recorded in the rural Tamil districts of Vavuniya and Jaffna, and the Sinhala Buddhist district of Polonnaruwa, and the lowest in urban Kegalle, Matara and Colombo districts (Kearney and Miller ibid.: 93). In particular, suicide has been considered a major crisis among Sinhala migrant farmers, and especially those settling in the areas being developed for paddy cultivation in the north-central and eastern provinces by the Mahaweli Development Authority (Kearney and Miller 1985, 1987, 1988; Silva and Pushpakumara 1996). Nevertheless, suicide remains a leading cause of death, and self-harm remains a leading cause of injury, in both peri-urban and urban communities in the south and west of Sri Lanka.

Finally, analysis of suicide and self-harm methods shows how self-poisoning has accounted for the majority of cases in Sri Lanka. From the 1960s these were primarily pesticides and since the 1980s the seeds of the *kane:ru* (yellow oleander) plant (de Silva et al. 2012; Eddleston et al. 1998, 1999; Gunnell et al. 2007). Over the past ten years there seems to have been a spontaneous shift away from pesticides and *kane:ru* to medicinal drugs – principally paracetamol – as the leading method of deliberate self-harm in Sri Lanka. Meanwhile, a minority of self-harm and suicide cases have employed hanging, drowning, burning, jumping and trains as the method. The proportion of suicides committed by drowning, burning, jumping and trains has stayed the same over the years, while the proportion of hangings has increased.

Patterns of suicide in Madampe

Representing its peri-urban locality, Madampe reports suicide rates that are about average for the country. Files on suicide held by the Madampe Police Station (MPS) and on self-harm admissions by the Galmuruwa Peripheral Health Unit (GPHU) provide a simple picture of suicide epidemiology in the area. The data suggest that between 2001 and 2006, the period covered by both sets of files, a total of sixty-one suicides and 325 cases of self-harm were recorded (Table 2.5).[1] This suggests an average local suicide rate of 23.4 per 100,000 compared with an average national suicide rate of 23.7 per 100,000 over the same period. Reflecting national patterns too, two-thirds of all suicides were male, while half of all self-harm cases were male and half were female. Overall, the rate of self-harm was more than five times the rate of suicide, although among males the self-harm rate was three times higher than the suicide rate, while among females it was thirteen times higher.

Figure 2.2 shows self-harm admissions to GPHU and suicides logged by MPS for males. The data show a peak of self-harming activity in males between the ages of fifteen to twenty-four, which then steadily declines. However, levels of completed suicide increase during youth and early adulthood to peak between the ages of thirty-five to fifty-four, after which there is a rapid decline. Females (Figure 2.3) display a very different pattern. Levels of both self-harm and suicide peak between the ages of fifteen to twenty-four, after which they rapidly decline; levels of self-harm are especially low after age forty-four. The data thus suggest

Table 2.5 Self-harm and suicide cases recorded at GPHU and MPS, period reviewed, and number of cases reviewed

Source	Period reviewed	No. cases reviewed
GPHU (self-harm cases)	July 2001–June 2006	270
MPS (suicide cases)	Jan. 2001–June 2006	61
Total		331

Sources: GPHU and MPS (unpublished data).

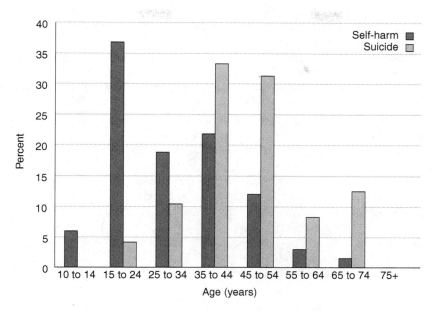

Figure 2.2 Male self-harm and suicide cases in the Madampe Division (sources: GPHU and MPS, unpublished data).

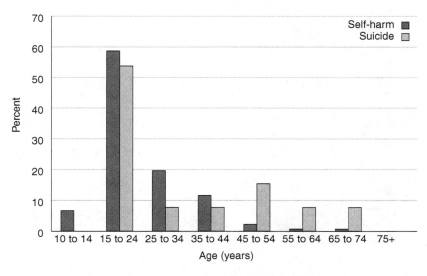

Figure 2.3 Female self-harm and suicide cases in the Madampe Division (sources: GPHU and MPS, unpublished data).

30 *Of villages, courts and clinics*

that while young people and women were most likely to practise acts of self-harm and survive, older people and men especially were most likely to practise acts of suicide attempts and die.

In Madampe, rates of self-harm and suicide were proportionately highest in the Buddhist and Catholic communities, but lowest in the Hindu, Protestant and Evangelical Christian and Muslim communities (Figure 2.4). These figures suggest that although occurring at a rate lower than the national average, in terms of gender, age and religion, patterns of suicide and self-harm resembled those at the national level.

Finally, with regard to methods of self-harm and suicide (Table 2.6), in men poisoning accounted for almost 90 per cent of self-harm cases, with hanging accounting for most of the remainder. Suicides, by contrast, were split approximately evenly between poisoning and hanging. In females, poisoning accounted for 97 per cent of self-harm cases, and just over half of all suicide cases. Like men, most of the remainder of women's suicides were committed by hanging. As such, in both men and women self-harm by poison was considerably less likely to result in death than by hanging, which in turn accounted for half of all suicides. This suggests an extreme example of the national pattern, where the shift to less lethal forms of poisoning means a smaller number of deaths being caused by poisoning and a growing proportion of deaths by hanging.

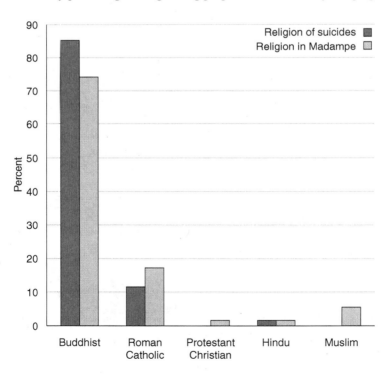

Figure 2.4 Religion of suicides compared to religious communities in Madampe.

Table 2.6 Methods of self-harm and suicide by gender

	Self-harm		Suicide	
	Males	Females	Males	Females
All poisonings	87.2	97.1	47.9	53.8
Plants (e.g. kane:ru)	(39.8)	(11.7)	–	–
Agrochemicals	(8.3)	(11.7)	–	–
Household chemicals	(39.1)	(73.7)	–	–
Hanging	–	–	45.8	46.2
Others	12.8	2.9	6.3	–
Totals	100.0	100.0	100.0	100.0

Sources: GPHU and MPS (unpublished data).

Villages: Udagama and Alutwatta

In this section, I move from a presentation of suicide and self-harm patterns to a consideration of the social contexts within which those patterns are located. The economic and political hub of the Division is Madampe New Town, also known colloquially as 'Silva Town', after the philanthropist who donated the land upon which it was founded in the early twentieth century. At that time, Madampe was at the centre of a booming coconut export industry, which brought new wealth to a local class of landowners and entrepreneurs (Bandarage 1983: 83; de Silva 2005: 366), and encouraged the growth of a local middle class whose children benefited from access to education and white-collar government jobs (*Administration Report* 1877: S1, 27). This in turn had the effect of attracting large-scale labour migration to the area, so that the population of the wider Puttalam District rose from 68,000 in 1871 to 228,900 by 1951 (Department of Census and Statistics n.d.). Combined with increased expansion of the coconut estates, existing villages found themselves hemmed in and overpopulated, leading to pressures on food supply and the risk of social unrest (de Silva 2005; *Administration Report* 1917: S1, F9). In response, the colonial government issued the Land Development Ordinance (LDO) of 1935, which set in motion a process of colonisation and rejuvenation of wasteland and coconut land for residence and small-scale manufacture, placing responsibility for coconut production in the hands of landless and land-poor peasants.

With its extensive coconut plantations and industries, the land in and around Madampe was particularly suited for colonisation by labour migrants. Beyond Silva Town, the Division today comprises two kinds of community that self-identify according to their relationship with the land colonisation process. These include the 'ancient' villages (*pura:ṇa gam*) claiming to pre-date the LDO and populated by people 'native' to Madampe, and colonies (or *estates*[2] as they are locally known) settled under the LDO and populated by 'newcomers' to the area. In 2001, the Madampe Divisional Secretariat recognised fifty-two settlements in the Division, of which thirty-seven were *pura:ṇa gam* and fifteen were *estates*

(Madampe Divisional Secretariat 2004, unpublished data). While many villages in the Madampe Division have no discernible physical borders and run into each other, all nevertheless have strong separate identities derived from their status as *pura:ṇə* or *estate* settlements respectively. For example, *pura:ṇə gam* often boast a foundation myth tied to a royal dynasty and are usually associated with a local *devol* (deity), while *estates* claim no foundation myth and no deity resides in them.

Residents of both communities are also highly conscious of their respective status in Madampe as 'natives' and 'newcomers'. This plays out in terms of how they describe their own communities and in how they speak about each other's. So, for example, residents of *pura:ṇə gam* refer to *estates* as 'poor villages' (*duppat gam*) troubled by family breakdown and civil disobedience caused by the relocation process. Meanwhile, residents of *estates* refer to residents of *pura:ṇə gam* as *gode: minissu* ('backward rural people'), in reflection of the fact that *pura:ṇə gam* tend to be located in remote places and lack the planned layouts of *estates*. Residents of both *pura:ṇə gam* and *estates* often accuse the other's village of being a *kasippu gama*, a place where illicit liquor, *kasippu*, is produced and consumed by drunkards, and so plagued by crime and civil disobedience that is assumed to come with it. Although on one level these expressions may be understood as being little more than forms of prejudice, on another level they indicate important differences in how representations of place, space and person are constructed in Madampe.

The terms '*pura:ṇə*' and '*estate*' refer to much more than the foundational status of a community but say something significant about the kinds of people who live there. Inasmuch as people in Madampe draw their identities from conceptions of grounded locality of persons, local theories of *pura:ṇə gam* and *estates* as 'native place' resemble Sri Lankan Tamil and Muslim concepts of '*ur*'. The concept *ur*, discussed in detail by E. Valentine Daniel (1984) and Sharika Thiranagama (2011), signals 'house' and 'home' as well as 'place' and 'belonging'. As Thiranagama suggests: 'People tell you that they are formed by the particular *ur* in which they reside and have been nourished. This is ... through relationship to both the imagined properties of such soil *and* those others who are assumed to share this with you' (ibid.: 152, emphasis in original). In Madampe, to be seen as belonging to a *pura:ṇə gamə* or an *estate* is to be a particular kind of person and member of a distinct social group. That person and group is made up of different traits that derive from the historical and contemporary formations of *pura:ṇə gam* and *estates* in Madampe, in turn related to processes of caste and class formation and resulting patterns of landownership, household and kinship structure, and religious orientation.

Udagama and Alutwatta

My research in Madampe focused on one *pura:ṇə gam* and one *estate*: Udagama and Alutwatta. Located a few kilometres apart, Udagama, the *pura:ṇə* village, lies on the side of a small, lush, tree-covered hill; by contrast, Alutwatta, the *estate*, is situated in the middle of a flat, dry coconut estate. In 2004, Udagama had a population of 606 and Alutwatta 792, forming seventy-four households (*ge:*) at Udagama and 121 *ge:* at Alutwatta (Madampe Divisional Secretariat, unpublished data). Both communities are in the large majority Sinhala, at 99.8 per cent and 98.7 per cent respectively (Table 2.7). Their respective histories as *pura:ṇə* and *estate* villages shine through on to their contemporary caste, class and religious structures, which I will now briefly summarise.

First, Udagama is home predominantly to the high-caste *goyigamə* (cultivators) community, and within that a high-status patriline which has for several generations controlled the local coconut economy and occupied positions of political power in colonial and post-colonial governments. The Udagama *goyigamə* community is flanked by a low-caste *rada:* (washer) community, who live in a hamlet to the southwest. Although the *rada:* no longer perform ritual duties for the *goyigamə*, the spatial separation is strictly maintained and no socially legitimate marriages take place between *goyigamə* and *rada:* villages. Alutwatta, by contrast, contains a mix of high-, middle- and low-caste groups who live among each other and who do intermarry, sometimes as the result of formal arrangements.

Second, Udagama is considered to be a 'middle-class' village while Alutwatta is a 'working-class' village. This reflects the caste status of Udagama and Alutwatta as well as the fact that Udagama was populated by the owners of the means of coconut production, and Alutwatta by labourers on the coconut estates and in derivative industries. At Udagama today the largest occupational groupings are in white-collar public and private sector jobs and skilled artisanal and labouring roles, while at Alutwatta most employed people work as labourers in one of the several factories located around its borders (Table 2.8). This has allowed the development of higher quality housing at Udagama than at Alutwatta, and higher levels of enrolment in further education among Udagama youth than among Alutwatta youth. Importantly, however, female labour migration from both communities is relatively high, at 6.7 per cent from Udagama and 16.4 per cent from Alutwatta, but ostensibly much lower among men, at 0.8 per cent and 1.6 per cent respectively. The very high rate of female labour migration from Alutwatta does mean that the village is beginning to 'catch up' with Udagama in terms of housing stock and educational levels: a pattern that is

Table 2.7 Ethnic communities in Udagama and Alutwatta, 2001

Ethnicity	Udagama	Alutwatta
Sinhala	99.8	98.7
Sri Lankan Tamil	0.2	1.3
Others	–	–
Totals	100.0	
(*N=606*)	100.0	
(*N=792*)		

Source: Madampe Divisional Secretariat (2004, unpublished data).

Table 2.8 Occupational classes in Udagama and Alutwatta, male and female residents aged 14 years and over

	Udagama		Alutwatta	
	Males	Females	Males	Females
Professional/white-collar	17.1	5.0	6.5	4.7
Skilled/blue-collar	30.9	14.3	47.2	7.8
Unskilled labourer	27.6	4.2	34.3	6.0
Overseas migrant	0.8	6.7	1.6	16.4
Further/higher education	8.1	6.7	5.2	8.6
Unemployed	15.4	6.7	5.2	4.3
Housewife	–	56.3	–	52.2
Totals	100.0 (N=123)	100.0 (N=119)	100.0 (N=248)	100.0 (N=232)

Source: author's household surveys.

found across *estates* and something that is a point of contention for many *pura:ṇə* people.

Third, and as a further reflection of their histories vis-à-vis the coconut economy and caste structure, Alutwatta is more diverse in religious terms than Udagama. At Udagama Buddhists account for 91.6 per cent of the population, while at Alutwatta they account for just 74.7 per cent. Correspondingly, Alutwatta has a large Roman Catholic minority (20.7 per cent) and a growing Christian evangelical community (3.9 per cent) (Table 2.9). The concentration of Roman Catholics in Alutwatta is a reflection of its middle- to low-caste communities, who were more likely to convert to Catholicism when the coastal regions of Sri Lanka were under Portuguese rule. The growth of evangelism, meanwhile, appears to be the result of labour migration, with Buddhist and Catholic women converting while overseas, and to a lesser extent local proselytisation on the part of global evangelical churches springing up across the area.

A 'good family life'

These caste, class and religious differences give rise to conditions that generate different kinds of suicide representations in each village. Of paramount importance is the extent to which social status concerns in each community manifest different ideas concerning family structures and gender roles. In a context of rapid modernisation and globalisation, it is often considered that these structures and roles are at risk of change or breakdown. The most significant threat to village and family life which people in Madampe spoke about was that emanating from international labour migration and the ways in which migration has come to reshape imaginings of the ideal domestic division of labour and roles of women and men in the economy.

In Madampe, as for Sri Lanka more broadly, particular focus is placed on women's increased participation in wage labour, either in garment factories in Sri Lanka or through migration overseas. Women's economic participation and 'empowerment' has been received as both a threat to male dominance over the household unit and to the future of the 'Sinhala Buddhist nation', particularly as women move away from 'traditional' child-rearing roles (Gamburd 2000, 2008a;

Table 2.9 Religious communities in Udagama and Alutwatta, 2001

Religion	Udagama	Alutwatta
Buddhist	91.6	74.7
Roman Catholic	8.3	20.7
Protestant	–	3.9
Hindu	0.2	0.5
Other	–	0.1
Total	100.0	100.0
	(*N=606*)	(*N=792*)

Source: Madampe Divisional Secretariat (2004, unpublished data).

Hewamanne 2008; Lynch 1999, 2002, 2007). The local and national thus converge in imaginings of 'good family lives' (*hoňda pavula ji:vite*) that are constructed as a response to the (perceived) loss of traditional ways of being a family. In so being, people in Madampe invent wholly 'modern' ideals of 'tradition', even as the material gains provided by the growth of female labour opportunities lay the financial basis for the pursuit of 'good family lives' in most cases.

The opportunities and problems presented by Madampe's continued absorption into global economic markets, first through coconut export and second through labour export, form the ontological grounds of suicide representations. At Udagama, a self-consciously *pura:ṇə* village that had benefited from the coconut economy and which created what is today an 'old money' class of high-caste status, family structures and gender roles are seen to be at extreme risk of breakdown should conditions prevail. At Alutwatta, a community reaping the benefits of overseas migration and which is becoming home to a 'new money' class of mixed-caste status, things are seen to be more complicated. However, in both cases the referent for comparison upon which the direction of things, for better or worse, might be judged is an idea of the 'good family life': a concept that is struggled with at the material level through the realities of actual families and family lives.

When people in Udagama and Alutwatta speak of the 'good family' they usually have in mind the family belonging to 'the Kandyan village' four, five or six decades ago. For many of my informants 'the Kandyan village' existed as a location of 'traditional' and therefore 'good' family life and moral virtue. This was usually said to be because the Kandyan region avoided European colonisation until the nineteenth century and was therefore able to maintain 'traditional Sinhala culture' (*sanskrutiyə*) into the modern period – an assumption found in much of the mid-twentieth-century social scientific literature on Sri Lanka.

However, what we know of the Kandyan village and Kandyan family at that time bears little resemblance to the imaginings of people in Madampe. My informants assured me that stable conjugal pairs put together by family matchmakers defined traditional Kandyan families. Nevertheless, the available ethnography suggests a rather different picture. Based on his study of Pul Eliya, a village in the Kandyan district, Leach (1961: 89–91) suggests that 'marriage' in the form of a modern legal contract was the preserve only of well-off landed families keen to protect their holdings, who arranged matches with suitably well-endowed others to ensure the transmission of property to the next generation. For the majority of people, marriages, in the form of common law pairings symbolised through the public sharing of food, were temporary affairs, usually ending in separation after a short period (a similar observation was made by Nur Yalman (1967)). As Leach (ibid.: 90) describes:

> One consequence of this ... is that it is rare to come across any adult, either male or female, who does not admit to having been 'married' more than once. Individuals who have been 'married' five or six times are not thought in any way exceptional, though many long-lasting stable marriages do

occur.... One young lady ... about 22 years of age ... had already been 'married' seven times. Three of the 'marriages' had been with the same husband. She already had two children by two of her five husbands, but showed few signs of any early intention to settle down. This was no doubt an extreme case, but it cannot be considered unique.

One day I discussed Leach's findings with the family I was living with, and they greeted the information with incredulity. As middle-class *pura:ṇə* Sinhala Buddhists their imaginings of the good family life were as rooted in conceptions of the traditional Kandyan village as any others in Madampe I knew. After several minutes of good-natured argument they suggested that if Leach's account *were* true, it was because 'that was *there*' (see Chapter 3), in a remote village of uneducated peasants. Moreover, they pointed out, Pul Eliya villagers had little land or material wealth to protect, and so it was hardly surprising that they did not care much for stable marriage. In Madampe, they argued, middle-class *pura:ṇə* families were both morally respectable and materially conscious, and properly arranged marriages formed an important part of maintaining 'family status' (*pavul tatve*). This would have been the case in the past as well as today. Thus the 'promiscuity' Leach (ibid.) assigned to 'traditional' marriage practices in Pul Eliya which gave rise to extended kinship formations was distanced from Madampe, where ideally at least marriage practices ought to be defined by high moral bourgeois virtues in the form of monogamy, fidelity, stability, and an impossibility of separation or divorce.

Nevertheless, in Madampe, imaginings of the 'good family life' are built up from a belief in what traditional family life was like 'in the past' and what it should again be today. This belief is reinforced by the fact that today very few families in actuality resemble the 'traditional' ideal-type, not least because of the pressures put to bear on households in economic terms. Thus while in practice the ideal-type is rarely or never actually achieved, it is out of the struggles that arise over *how* to define the family and *what* kinds of social and moral rights and responsibilities it ought to imply that theories of suicidality are generated. My informants in Udgama and Alutwatta would usually point to the supposed loss of good family lives and the breakdown of moral virtues in society as being the crucial condition of suicide. However, the relationship between family problems and suicidal practices is better understood as *processual*: as arising from and giving substance to the conflicts and contradictions that emerge when imaginings of the good family life are sought in practice. Village-generated suicide representations thus derive from, and attempt to make sense of, the shifting ideological and material grounds of family life in Madampe, and this will be an issue returned to in subsequent chapters.

Courts: Madampe and Kuliyapitiya

This section moves from the village to the coroners' court: a journey that is also undertaken by Udagama and Alutwatta people who die by suicide, and the witnesses who are called to testify. The move is more than bureaucratic: the deceased and those who are asked to speak on their behalf also commence a shift from the village arena where causalities are generated in one way to the legal institutions of the Sri Lankan state where causalities are generated in another way. The processes through which village-generated theories are translated into court-generated theories occur during moments of formal interview, when first police and then coroners seek to ascertain the 'cause of death', a categorisation that depends upon a host of signifiers relayed by witnesses but also those perceived or assumed by the investigating officer or coroner him or herself. J. Maxwell Atkinson (1978) studied the processes through which coroners in the United States come to define deaths as suicides. Atkinson argued that coroners, tasked with the eminently difficult job of 'making order out of chaos' (ibid.: 172), routinely boiled down the complexities of individual cases by applying 'commonsense' notions of what constituted a 'typical suicide' and why people might die by suicide: notions that are of course highly unstable and dependent upon the whim of individual coroners.

On one level, police and coroners in Madampe shared the theories generated by the *estate* and *pura:ṇə* classes: they are, for example, as equally concerned with 'family problems' as a proximate cause of suicidality. On another level, police and coroners have undergone specific training and this introduces them to theories of suicide generated by the Sri Lankan state (Widger 2012b). These theories do not displace 'family problems' from view, but rather twist the logic and theory of human behaviour underpinning it. In particular, we find a conception of human being derived from the British period, enshrined in the structural dispositions of the national police force that once expressed the colonialists' chauvinisms about the Ceylonese and today expresses middle-class Sri Lankan chauvinisms about their working and labouring class contemporaries (Widger 2012b).

The history of court-generated theories of suicide can thus be traced back to the late British colonial period, when rates of suicide were low but rates of homicide were high (Rogers 1987; Wood 1961). The theories generated by British administrators to account for homicide, key characteristics of which included their 'impulsiveness' in the context of bursts of 'sudden anger', were later applied to suicide. For example, in 1895 the Government Agent for the Puttalam District wrote that the majority of homicides were:

> The result of hasty, ungovernable passion, roused, in the course of disputes, often on a trifling matter and at times inflamed by arrack. The excited person seems completely to lose his head. A blow is struck or a stab is given openly in the presence of witnesses, and apparently without fear of the consequences.
>
> (*Administration Report* 1895: P3, B2)

Similarly, concerning suicide, D'Oyly (1929: 37, 80) remarked that it was 'easily provoked … [by] … slander, non-payment of debt, damage to crops, and thwarted love affairs'. Reflecting the tendency for suicide threats to arise in response to personal slight (Straus and Straus 1953; Wood 1961), British observers often read them as 'trivial'. In 1902, H.R. Freeman (*Administration Report* 1902: S3, G24), administrator of the Chilaw District in the Northwest Province of Sri Lanka, commented:

> Attempt to commit suicide – a rather prevalent offence – should be punishable with rigorous as well as simple imprisonment. Would-be suicides generally want pulling together by the tonic of hard work.

Yet there was a counter-discourse at the time, which later became dominant, proposing that the impulsiveness of homicide was better explained as the consequence of excessive self-control. During the late 1950s, the American sociologist A.L. Wood conducted a study of homicide, suicide and economic crime in Ceylon to discover their 'social and cultural determinants' (Wood 1961: 6). At that time homicide was still considered a major problem, and suicide, with rates now increasing, an emerging problem. Wood worked in partnership with the Ceylon Police Department, from whom he gained access to homicide and suicide records and to whom he presented his findings. As a sociologist interested in deviance, Wood was an advocate of the then popular 'frustration-aggression' hypothesis. This predicted that pent-up frustrations would erupt as inwardly or outwardly directed aggression – suicide or homicide – depending on the psychological and sociological status of the person.

Through Wood's work, the frustration-aggression hypothesis directly influenced the thinking of the police force. For example, Wood's impact on Sir Richard Aluwihare, Inspector-General of Police and native of Ceylon, could not have been more striking. In 1954, Sir Aluwihare (*Administration Report* 1954: S3, A15) echoed the theories of his colonial predecessors when he attributed the causes of both homicide and suicide to a lack of 'self-control and moral inhibition'. Nevertheless, by 1958, by which time Wood had submitted his report, Sir Aluwihare (*Administration Report* 1958: S3, A183–184) demonstrated a considerable change in his thinking:

> In the majority of violent crime the causes have been attributed to sudden quarrels. The cases are instances of behaviour in which a tremendous amount of aggression suddenly explodes, apparently without sufficient cause. Although such cases are superficially somewhat puzzling and therefore conveniently categorised as sudden quarrels, a closer examination might reveal that the quarrel was not so sudden after all. Minor conflicts tolerated with difficulty over a period of time can suddenly summate to a strong aggressive intent beyond the capacity of a man, subject to frequent frustrations, to resist.

The theory of frustration also came to inspire other government policies. In 1967, the Ceylon Parliament published *Youth in Ceylon*, a two-part assessment of education, youth underachievement and national development. The first part of the report addressed the issue of a growing population of schoolchildren who held aspirations to further and higher education but who were denied the chance to participate. The report argued that:

> Once the individual youth is denied the social supervision of the school, he [has] nowhere to turn. The young person is abandoned by society as a failure. He does not enjoy the care of organised institutions, instead he is exposed to the influences of negative elements.
>
> (*Sessional Paper III* 1967: 29)

The report criticised a culture of achievement that had led to examinations becoming 'ends in themselves' (ibid.: 18). Furthermore, universal aspirations for capitalist progress had meant that 'the families of labourers and farmers [were] no longer at peace with their destiny' (ibid.: 30):

> The majority of families in Ceylon today are affected to a larger or smaller extent by modern frames of reference. Technology and modern communications have reached almost every remote village in Ceylon. With schools in every village traditional social frames of reference are replaced by new ones. The caste systems are giving way to modern concepts. The traditional acceptance of predestined social roles is weakening. Education has brought about new aspirations.... The expectations cherished everywhere are changes in status through education.
>
> (Ibid.: 29)

Failure to achieve in education meant that those who did not 'make the grade' experienced 'frustration' (ibid.: 29). In turn, this was said to lead to 'anxiety and, consequently ... aggressiveness of one form or another' (ibid.: 31).

'Youth frustration' subsequently became one of the major challenges seen to be facing the island, was cited as the cause of Sinhala youth insurgencies between the 1970s and 1990s that left more than 60,000 dead, and has frequently been blamed for suicide (Kearney and Miller 1985; Silva and Pushpakumara 1996; Hughes 2013). In fact, 'youth frustration' became an explanatory model for much social scientific writing on Sri Lanka between the 1960s and 1990s (Nissan and Stirrat 1990; Spencer 1997), as well as a master trope within popular discourses of suicidality (Widger 2012b) and youth discontent (Hughes 2013) more generally.

Equipped with sociological and psychosocial theories of change and development, suicide for the post-colonial state became a problem of social welfare that should be tackled through youth programmes. When in 2004 I interviewed the director of a local research and development organisation, she summed up the causes of suicide with a simple knowing statement: 'Ah, yes, acute frustration!' The development of specific government policies on youth affairs led to the creation of the National Youth Service Council (NYSC) in 1964. The NYSC became responsible for the formulation and oversight of government policy on youth and its administration through a network of regional sub-offices. Faced with ever-growing suicide rates across the country and the intensification of youth-led conflict in the north and east, in 1983 the NYSC established the Sri Lanka Federation of Youth Clubs (SLFYC), consolidating whatever youth groups had existed at the time into a network of 5,500 youth clubs island-wide. The SLFYC had a starting registered membership of over 600,000 members (National Youth Service Council 1999, June: 1). By 1999, across the 310 Divisional Secretariats of Sri Lanka, 7,749 youth clubs had been established or had affiliated themselves with the SLFYC (National Youth Service Council 1999, July: 7).

During my fieldwork I interviewed police officers and coroners working in Madampe, Kuliyapitiya and Chilaw, and also reviewed case files held at MPS ($N=61$) and Kuliyapitiya Coroners' Court (KCC) ($N=68$). The historical threads of state-generated suicide theories ran through their verbal accounts as well as the police reports and coroners' verdicts that I read. For example, the chief police officer in Madampe, a forty-two-year-old man from a *pura:ŋə* class village in the south of the division, told me that 'frustration and hopelessness' caused by 'family problems' were the main causes of suicides that his station dealt with. The Chilaw City coroner, a fifty-six-year-old retired government servant, also cited 'frustration, anger, and mental problems' arising from family quarrels. Around two-thirds of the case files I reviewed at Madampe police station and Kuliyapitiya Coroners' Court reflected these sentiments in one way or another. Principal verdicts included 'mental frustration' (*ma:nəsikə asəhane*), 'mental problems' (*ma:nəsikə praʃnə*) and 'mental hopelessness' (*ma:nəsikə kaləkiri:mə*), in the context of 'love problems' (*a:dərə praʃnə*), 'family problems' (*pavul praʃnə*), 'economic problems' (*a:rtikə praʃnə*), and, in men, of being an 'alcoholic' (*be:badda*).

The processes through which police and coroners came to a verdict of suicide reflected the culmination of their own investigations and assumptions drawn from these generating theories. In the vast majority of cases the means of death dictated how an investigation would proceed and intersect with the investigating officer's assumptions. Deaths caused by poisoning usually occurred in hospital, as the demise was slow and allowed time for discovery and transport. In those cases, investigating officers would rely on the testimonies of hospital staff and family members, in front of whom the act would often have taken place. However, deaths involving methods like hanging, drowning or lying down in front of a train were usually immediately fatal and committed in isolation, meaning that investigating officers had less information to go on. Therefore investigating officers would interview family members, neighbours and perhaps work colleagues, as well as draw more fully from what they assumed would lead to such a death. Importantly, coroners rarely had suicide notes or letters to review; of the sixty-eight coroner files I reviewed, only two contained such items.

Investigating officers find themselves confronted, then, with varying degrees of chaos. Under these circumstances, they look for 'evidence enough' to warrant a classification of death one way or the other. The police officers and coroners I interviewed agreed that a 'family problem' causing 'anger' or 'frustration' leading to the consumption of poison was 'evidence enough' to classify a death as self-inflicted. Simply, 'common sense' dictated that those ingredients – family problems, anger, frustration and poison – when put together inevitably meant suicide. Indeed, in many of the cases I looked at and followed, the relative quantities of those ingredients mattered less than them all being there at least to some degree. Even weak evidence of family problems or anger or frustration would carry through to a verdict of suicide if the victim died after swallowing a kind of poison strongly associated with suicide, such as pesticide. However, when the ingredients were changed, for example, pesticide for a more ambiguous method, investigators lost their confidence, and then they would search for stronger evidence of family problems. Drowning posed a particular challenge, as while drinking poison and lying down in front of a train were difficult to accomplish accidentally, drowning was considered an everyday risk, especially among children and youth. Thus Ravi's death could be classified as an accident even though villagers reported strong family problems, and I know of at least two more cases where the same thing occurred.

Table 2.10 provides a list of 'causes' of suicide identified by MPS and the official classifications used by the Sri Lanka police to tabulate suicide rates at national level. As can be seen, there are differences between the two. This is

Table 2.10 Discrepancies in lists of causes of suicide recorded by MPS and the Sri Lanka police

Motives recorded by MPS	Motives recorded by the SLPS
Love problems (*a:dərə praʃnə*)	Economic problems (poverty, indebtedness)
Family problems (*pavul praʃnə*)	Employment problems
Economic problems (*a:rtikə praʃnə*)	Problems caused with the elders
Health problems (*asanepa*)	Harassment by the husband and family disputes
Suffering because of a death in the family (*mala dukə*)	Disappointment and frustration caused through love affairs
Drunkard (*be:badda*)	Subjection to sexual harassment/rape
Mental problems (*ma:nəsikə praʃnə*: implies a range of problems, including suffering [*dukə*], frustration [*asəhane*], and anger [*tarəha*])	Addiction to narcotic drugs
	Aggrieved over the death of parents/relatives
	Loss of property
	Failure at examination
	Ill treatment by the children
	Sexual incapacity
	Mental disorders
	Chronic diseases and physical disabilities
	Exposure of illegitimate relationship
	Other reasons

Source: MPS, unpublished data and Sri Lanka police (2009).

interesting for at least three reasons. First, assuming that protocol has been followed, the Madampe data have been reported to the Sri Lanka police, and even though MPS used its own system of classification, the local data must have somehow been incorporated into national data. Second, neither the local nor the national data have been produced using a universally adopted system, raising obvious questions about the validity of both. Third, the discrepancy shows how despite efforts at creating a nationally coordinated system, MPS nevertheless produces data that is rendered contingent by the actual practices and processes of policing and suicide investigation operating at the local level. Thus, we can see how police officers and coroners (who locally record causes of suicide in line with those used by MPS) generate theories of suicidality that hover part-way between the village and the state, transforming village-generated theories into state-generated theories through the investigative and reporting process. Both sides produce a subjective ontology of suicide, and in the spaces of overlap generate an epistemology claiming an objective status that quantifies, for the purposes of national tabulation, the level of suicidality in Sri Lanka.

Clinics: Galmuruwa and Chilaw

The Sri Lankan health service is radically transforming the ways in which it treats self-harm and suicide patients, the effects of which began to appear in Madampe during the period of my fieldwork. Historically, mental health professionals in Sri Lanka had been relatively uninterested in suicide and their theories tended to reflect those of police officers and coroners. As Sri Lankan psychiatrists interviewed by Jeanne Marecek (1998: 74–75) as recently as the 1990s suggested: 'Here, suicide is just something people do.... For us, suicide is just an impulsive thing.' The mental health community, small as it was at that time, appeared to see only a limited role for itself in the prevention of suicide. Despite spiralling suicide rates during the 1970s and 1980s it was not until 1997 that a national policy was adopted, on the basis of a Presidential Commission urgently convened to deal with what was becoming a 'national embarrassment' (anonymous informant). Revealingly, the national policy had little to say about the development of mental health services, with recommendations focusing instead on practical and not-so-practical measures, including (Report of the Presidential Committee on Prevention of Suicide, 3 December 1997):

1 Reduce easy access to lethal methods.
2 Promote research on reducing the lethality of pesticides in use.
3 Educate the public on less harmful use of pesticides.
4 Create a culture which discourages suicides.
5 Ensure survival after poisoning.
6 Remove legal barriers to the correct handling of those at risk.

Then, on 24 December 2004, the northern, eastern and southern coastlines of Sri Lanka were devastated by a tsunami that spread across the Indian Ocean from its epicentre near Sumatra. In Sri Lanka, tens of thousands were killed and many more left injured and homeless. The international response was swift, leading to what some have called a 'third wave' of relief and rehabilitation efforts (Gamburd 2013; McGilvray and Gamburd 2013; Silva 2009). One effect of this was increased funding and support for the development of mental health services in Sri Lanka, which were assessed as being unlikely to be able to cope with the aftermath of the tsunami. In 2005 the Sri Lankan Mental Health Directorate (2005) with the support of the WHO, World Bank and a local mental health charity, published *The Mental Health Policy of Sri Lanka, 2005–2015*, a fourteen-page document outlining the government's mental health plan for the next ten years. The preamble to the policy explains that:

> The Government of Sri Lanka acknowledges that the country has one of the highest suicide rates of any country in the world and increasing substance misuse and psychosocial problems. Also after years of civil conflict, the 2004 tsunami and an estimated 2% of the population suffering from serious mental illnesses, it recognises that the need for an effective policy has never been greater.

Although instigated by the tsunami, the authors of the policy evidently saw a greater need coming from the suicide epidemic as well as the civil war. In any case, the policy led to the roll-out of specialist training for general medical practitioners and nurses, the yearly recruitment of 500 unemployed graduates as health and social care workers, and the development of community-level mental health services across the island.

In Madampe itself, the impacts of the policy have been limited. Several public health[3] options exist for the immediate medical treatment of people who self-harm in the Division. These include Peripheral Health Units (PHUs) – community health and medical emergency centres – at Silva Town and Galmuruwa – and larger District Base Hospitals at Marawila and Chilaw. However, as no emergency service exists to transport patients to hospital, the choice between them tends to depend as much upon the reputation of the place as it does ease of accessibility. Thus while the closest options for emergency medical treatment are the PHUs, the Silva Town PHU had something of a bad reputation and so people either chose the Galmuruwa PHU (GPHU) or to travel to the District Hospitals at Marawila or Chilaw instead.

Regardless of the facility to which patients were admitted, the assessment and treatment process was much the same in each. During my fieldwork at GPHU, I observed the admissions and treatment procedure for self-harm patients many times. Upon arrival at GPHU, all patients suspected of committing self-harm were given a medical check to ascertain the cause of injury and proper course of treatment. If the patient was uncooperative or unconscious, the person or persons who admitted them were interviewed to discover the circumstances under which the act took place, determine the method used, and establish the time lapse between the act and submission to hospital. Depending upon the patient's health, the attending medical officer either decided to keep the individual on the ward for treatment or recommended transfer to another hospital, most often Chilaw.

During the time of my research, patients suspected of committing acts of self-harm received no psychological or social assessment or aftercare from GPHU. Although some patients were referred to the new Mental Health Clinic at Chilaw (CMHC) for assessment and counselling, there were no established means for doing so. As such, the vast majority of patients returned home without any kind of follow-up support in place. The most that self-harmers received at GPHU was some kind of informal counselling from the medical officer or, more often than not, a stern reprimand from the ward nurse or orderly. For example, the GPHU doctor, a young man on his first posting since qualifying, told me that he urged people not to attempt suicide because it rarely solved the problem they were experiencing and that they were using up valuable hospital resources and staff time for no good reason. One orderly, a man in his fifties, would wag his finger and 'blame' (*baninəva*) self-harm patients for 'time-wasting' and causing their family members unnecessary 'worry and expense'. The aim of these interventions was to 'teach people that it is bad to commit suicide', as one staff member put it, rather than to identify or address any kind of underlying causes.

The Mental Health Clinic at Chilaw (CMHC) first opened its doors in 1999, at which time it was staffed by just one part-time health officer with basic training in mental health issues and a couple of nurses. Following the tsunami, CMHC received significantly increased funds and this enabled the recruitment of a consultant psychiatrist from Colombo, a graduate mental health trainee, and the full-time employment of two medical officers undergoing training in psychiatry. CMHC also opened a weekly field office in a village thirty kilometres north of Chilaw, and began a mental health awareness-raising programme in villages and schools, and with community groups across the area. The immediate consequence of this was a huge increase of patients overall, and of self-harmers in particular, so that by 2006 the clinic relocated to premises three times its original size. The service now being offered to self-harm patients admitted to CMHC could be described as a 'voluntary condition' of discharge. Hospital regulations stated that all self-harm patients should present to the consultant psychiatrist and/or one of the medical officers prior to their return home or transfer back to a local PHU. Failure to do so would warrant a record in their file as having 'left against medical advice', even if deemed physically fit.

My research at CMHC was conducted at a time when patient numbers were reaching breaking point, before it located to new premises. At that time, the two medical officers shared one small room while the consultant psychiatrist worked from an office further along the corridor. To manage the flow of self-harmers, inpatients referred from the emergency ward (which comprised the vast majority of consultations) and outpatients referred from elsewhere were restricted to Mondays and Wednesdays only. To meet with clinicians, all but the sickest patients queued in the hot, dark corridor outside the consultation room alongside those waiting for other services, from blood investigations to measurements for prosthetics. Internal referrals that were still heavily under the influence of medicines such as atropine were chaperoned by ward orderlies directly into the consultation room, where they were usually seen immediately.

Once in consultation clinicians usually spoke to patients for no more than fifteen minutes at a time. During consultation, clinicians would seek to ascertain the cause of self-harm, offer some kind of counselling, and if a prescription was given, explain the regime to be followed. Patients would be interviewed either by themselves or more often with a family member present. While the interview was going on, nurses and orderlies gathering patient files and prescriptions and other patients seeking to jump the queue would often hover at the clinicians' desks or interrupt the conversations taking place.

A review of patient files dating from the early 2000s up until 2006 showed how clinicians' assessments of self-harm had changed pre- and post-2005. Pre-2005 the clinic was staffed by a part-time medical officer, Dr Herath, and a male nurse, Mr Weerasinghe, whose reports tended to use non-medical languages of the kind found in police and coroner files. Thus, for instance, the causes of self-harm were often recorded as 'sudden anger' or 'impulsiveness', and consequently patients were recommended to attend 'anger management counselling'. However, post-2005 these diagnoses disappeared and psychiatric terms such as 'depression' and 'adjustment reaction' took their place. Although by 2006 anger management counselling was still being recommended, 'problem-solving skills' were also advocated and courses of anti-depressants were almost always prescribed. Nevertheless, like police officers and coroners, clinicians' professional verdicts of suicide causation continued to overlay a more mundane set of proximate causes. Columns 1 and 2 in Table 2.11 illustrate the kinds of mundane and professionalised diagnoses used by clinicians to describe the self-harm cases they saw, and column 3 illustrates the various interventions they recommended.

Table 2.11 Transformations from mundane to formal categorisations of self-harm and recommendations for treatment at CMHC

Popular terms used	Formal diagnoses	Recommendations
Educational problems	Depression	Medication (anti-depressants, anti-psychotics, etc.)
Employment problems	Schizophrenia	
Financial problems	Post-traumatic stress disorder	
Disputes with household members		Psychological counselling (depression, anxiety, PTSD, etc.)
	Adjustment reaction	
Disputes with other relatives	Alcohol dependency	
	Drug dependency	Anger management counselling
Disputes with friends, neighbours, villagers	Impulsive act	
	Severe grief reaction	Alcohol/drug addiction counselling
Domestic violence	Acute stress reaction	
Sexual abuse	'Copycat' (imitative case)	Problem-solving skills
Romantic problems	Psychotic disorder	Life skills
Somatic problems		
Other problems		

Source: CMHC, unpublished data.

At the interface between the village and the clinic, ontological subjectivities of suicidal practice generate from different arenas. However, the arena of the clinic is distanced further again from the village than is the arena of the court, and this has been especially so since the 2004 tsunami. After decades of relative disinterest the ontological work of the clinic has only just begun, seeking transformations in how suicide and self-harm are to be understood and managed. In place of the local theories of suicide – of how the village and the court understand such practice – we find a growing concern with the universal languages of mental health. While the language of the court has, I would argue, fused and cycled with the language of the village, there remains a gap between the clinic and the village. The implications of this are discussed in Chapter 8.

Integrating causal theories

The causal theories generated from and circulating among villages, courts and clinics reflect social status and professional concerns, and may be read in two ways. The first is as *evidence* of suicide, and the second is as an *ethos* of suicidality. In the former reading, the narratives of suicide causation generated by villages, courts and clinics may be understood as empirically accurate renderings of individual cases that say something quite straightforward about the lives and reasoning of suicidal people and the legal and health professionals tasked with their treatment and management. In the latter reading, those narratives can only ever be read as highly subjective stories that instead of being approximations to the truth are better understood as signifiers of, for example, class or gender positions that tell us more about the philosophical and moral bent of villages, courts and clinics than they do why someone 'really' tried to kill themselves, if indeed such intention can be ascribed at all.

Both approaches are limiting. The positivism of the evidence model fails to account for local ontologies of suicidal practices and suicidal knowledge, and the 'subjectivisations' attempted by the second model ultimately offer little by way of insight into causes and prevention. In a recent study of suicide case files generated by coroners and health workers, Fincham *et al.* (2011) grapple with the same challenge: Are the materials taken from the sources they deal with evidence or ethos? The answer they come up with is that they are both. Fincham *et al.* urge us to read them as 'a *topic* and a *resource*' (ibid.: 43, emphasis in original): as a subject for sociological critique (how coroners' and health workers' accounts are constructed) as well as a form of valuable data on suicide to excavate (a way of gaining insight into the actions and intentions of suicidal people). This 'dual paradigm' approach recognises that files relating to suicide represent two different levels of reality, one 'objective' and one 'subjective,' the lines between which are of course blurred.

With my own study, the records of courts and clinics form only a secondary layer supporting an extensive ethnographic record of practices and representations of suicide that I collected from surrounding villages. My 'three-way' reading of suicide – from the perspective of villages, courts and clinics –

Table 2.12 Generative arenas of suicidal practice in Madampe

Villages		Courts (MPS and KCC)	Clinics (GPHU and CMHC)
Pura:ŋə	*Estate*	Courts and clinics are usually staffed by *pura:ŋə* class people	
High caste	Low caste	Theories of suicide begin with concepts of family problems overlain with theories descended from their own institutional histories	
Middle class	Working class		
Buddhist	Buddhist, Catholic		
Low rate of female employment	High rate of female employment		
Globalisation/modernisation are wholly negative – cause family problems and suicide	Globalisation/modernisation have benefits – a cost is family problems and suicide	Anger (colonial theory) > frustration (post-colonial theory)	Anger/impulsiveness (pre-tsunami theory) > depression (post-tsunami theory)

provides not only a particularly strong set of evidence from which to develop statements about suicide in Madampe. It also provides a system for conjecture and refutation (Popper 1962) through the comparison of materials generated that can halt overstating the evidence obtained from any single source and apply a break on outlandish interpretations about suicide, either specific or general. As each chapter progresses, this method will become apparent in the ways in which individual cases contribute towards an inductive account of suicide in Sri Lanka that I build, wherein the specificities of individual kinds of evidence (from villages, courts or clinics) are combined.

Table 2.12 summarises the three practice arenas in Madampe within which theories of suicidality are developed. As the table suggests, court and clinic theories may be understood as professional elaborations of village theories. However, the table may also be read horizontally, and backwards and forwards. Even though historically village theories came 'before' court and clinic theories, today they are mutually generative and the representations they produce cycle between one another. I have shown elsewhere (Widger 2012b) how theories of suicidality in Sri Lanka have flowed back and forth between villages, courts and clinics, even all the while maintaining their own ontologically subjective identities and trajectories. Table 2.12 summarises the landscape created by arenas of social practice where suicides are formed, interpreted and broadcast as cases to the rest of world. In the next two chapters we explore these processes in detail, with a major focus on the village arena.

Insights for prevention

Summary of the argument

- Practices of suicide are *constructed through the interaction of generative arenas of social practice* – in Madampe these include communities, coroners' investigations and health interventions – *each producing their own theories* about why people die by suicide.
- None of these arenas has a primary *claim on the 'truth' of suicide*; through their mutual development *each shapes the other*.
- Understanding suicide means *understanding how a single case passes through social contexts* of practice that bestow suicide with meanings and give suicide its character.
- Prevention practitioners do not stand apart from the suicide process but are *an integral part* of the process. Their claims help shape the problem they wish to prevent.

Practical applications

- Dominant narratives of suicidality may *obscure more fundamental realities* so it is important to *consider alternative viewpoints* when designing interventions.

- Theories of suicide held by ordinary people are often very different to theories held by professionals and it is better to *use familiar and meaningful theories* than unfamiliar ones.
- Pay attention to the *ways in which different arenas of suicidal practice generate different theories of suicide* and the *implications of this for your own intervention paradigm*. For example, how does it relate to existing arenas and *are there clear pathways from one to the other?*
- Consider whether the process through which suicidal people pass from one arena to the next is *inclusive or excluding*. Does the programme *reflect local diversity characteristics?*

Notes

1 Real numbers are likely to be much higher, especially with regard to suicide. Divisional police only investigate cases occurring within their jurisdiction, and so patients transferred out of Madampe who subsequently died were not included in their data.
2 Not to be confused with tea, coffee and rubber estates that were populated by immigrant Tamil populations elsewhere on the island.
3 Private medical facilities were also available in Silva Town and Chilaw, although due to time constraints I never had the opportunity to visit them. However, from conversations with informants across villages, courts and clinics it became apparent that these were used more for specialist services than routine outpatient care.

3 Suicide *there*, suicide *here*

People in Sri Lanka commit suicide. It's become a fashion.
                                     Alutwatta resident, male, aged forty-seven

'Suicide in Sri Lanka is a very famous thing', my informants liked to tell me, and could quite understand why I had travelled to the country to study it. Throughout my fieldwork across villages, courts and clinics I was offered many different explanations for Sri Lanka's suicide rate, and in time I came to understand how they followed several predictable narratives. However, a central theme of my informants' accounts also concerned how suicide was a problem '*there*'. In Sinhala to say that something is '*there*' (*ehe*) can operate as a subtle linguistic device that when used in appropriate contexts and with an accompanying flick of the hand or head and critical facial expression, allows people to distance a subject from the self. This distancing implies not just a social and moral one but also a geographical one, so the phrase 'that is *there*' (*e:kə ehe*) becomes a way of saying that some issue or problem is a negative feature of a particular community in Sri Lanka, but fortunately and importantly not one found in one's own community.

When I asked people in Madampe whether suicide was a particular problem in their own village, they would often respond, 'no, that is *there*'. This would be followed by an explanation that suicide was only a significant problem in farming communities of the central and eastern provinces, and especially the Mahaweli Ganga Development zones: areas of the country frequently said to report the highest suicide rates. However, by dismissing suicide as a problem *there*, my informants were also stating a categorical difference between those areas and Madampe – *here* (*mehe*) – that by contrast was considered developed, modern, and so relatively free from suicide.

The distinction between *there* and *here* also corresponded with a distinction in how people tried to make sense of suicide. Suicide *there* was often explicable: geographical and social distance seemed to provide a separation and objective space that allowed people in Madampe to speak about suicide in the north-central and eastern districts with a degree of clarity. However, that same clarity was not found in their accounts of suicide *here*. For many people I spoke to, the geographical, social and often relational proximity of suicide in Madampe rendered the problem inexplicable. Lacking the same separation and distance from suicide *there*, suicide *here* was difficult to define precisely because it was *too* familiar. Put another way, suicide *there* was rarely just taken for granted because it formed a social phenomenon that people sought to account for, while suicide *here*, deeply embedded in the everyday sociality of individual, family and communal lives, was taken for granted and so rarely subject to the same kind of explicit discussion and analysis.

Moreover, expressions of suicide *there* and suicide *here*, understood as a generalised place elsewhere and a specific village of one's own, derived also from concepts of place and belonging described in the previous chapter. For my informants suicide *there* must by definition be distinct from suicide *here*, because *here* people have particular traits consequent from their relational ties to land and locality. If people in general are understood as being different from one another by the fact of where they come from, then their thoughts and behaviours must also be distinct, including their suicidal thoughts and behaviours. Insofar as Madampe people see it, suicide *there* and suicide *here* may be understood as quite different things – that is, of having an ontological subjectivity. A disposition of suicide *there* is acquired differently and involves different kinds of practice to a disposition of suicide *here*. This chapter explores how people in villages, courts and clinics in Madampe described suicide *there* and suicide *here*, the repercussions of which will be followed throughout the rest of the book.

Suicide '*there*': distancing the suicidal nation

Almost everybody I spoke to in Madampe had an opinion on why suicide was such a problem in Sri Lanka. During the course of my fieldwork certain themes often recurred, and these included 'the struggles of farmers', the consequences of economic reforms implemented in '1977', the rise of 'youth frustrations' and 'the problem with Buddhism'. Significantly, and as discussed in Chapter 1, Sri Lankan anthropology and sociology have also been concerned with the first three of these themes, and it is quite likely that over the decades popular and academic explanations of the suicide rate have informed and reinforced each other (Widger 2012b). But after telling me how 'famous' the problem of suicide in Sri Lanka had become, many of my informants would then quiz me as to why I had chosen to locate my study in Madampe. 'You know, suicide is not a problem *here*, but *there*, in Anuradhapura and the Mahaweli villages', several people told me. The overall impression was that suicide is a particular problem of remote farming communities rather than of peri-urban or urban communities like Madampe. For people living in peri-urban Madampe, most of whom were several generations removed from agrarian pursuits, the hardships faced by farmers were extreme but alien. Shehan, a twenty-two-year-old man living at Udagama, summed up the prevailing attitude well when he commented:

aiyo [my god!], the farmers have so many problems, that is why they kill themselves! They have cultivation problems. If the rain does not come, the rice does not grow. Then they will have economic problems. They cannot repay loans they took to buy seed and fertiliser. After that, they will have family problems. The wife will blame and then the farmer begins to drink to cope with his problems. That is when he might drink poison also. We cannot imagine the problems they face!

As I have mentioned, the Mahaweli Irrigation Development zones were considered by Madampe people to be especially at risk of suicide. The Mahaweli Irrigation Development Programme started in the 1970s and was aimed at colonising dry land in the east of Sri Lanka and providing peasant Sinhala families with tracts of irrigable land for paddy and other farming uses. Kearney and Miller (1987) have extensively examined the social consequences of the programme and its association with high suicide rates, as have Silva and Pushpakumara (1996) and others (for an overview see Muggah 2008). The view from Madampe also suggested that suicide was a problem in the Mahaweli colonies because farmers had been uprooted from their natal villages and lost kin and social support, leading to alcoholism and violence in the male population and suffering and abuse in the female population. Expressing a very similar narrative that accompanies international migration today, suicide was said to occur because of a breakdown of social and moral values in the context of separation (see Chapter 7).

So common has the assumption become that farmers commit suicide many informants questioned the incidence of suicide in other parts of Sri Lanka like Madampe, where farming was uncommon. Mary, a forty-seven-year-old woman living at Alutwatta, expressed incredulity that suicide could be a problem outside of farming communities because by definition they did not suffer from the same kinds of hardships:

I do not think suicide is a problem in other places [than the farming communities]. Elsewhere people have jobs and money and they do not have debt problems. Even if they do, they might have a rich relative who can help them. The problem is that *there* [in the farming areas] everyone is poor so no one can help. But *here* [in Alutwatta] if we have a problem we can ask our relatives. So I do not think people here drink poison because of a money problem. Maybe sometimes it is youth and their love problems, but suicide is not really a problem here.

Despite Mary's claims to the contrary, rates of suicidal behaviour in Madampe, while being 'average' by national standards, were still 'high' by international standards. However, her insistence that financial problems could not cause suicides in Alutwatta because families support their poorer relatives signalled an important difference in how people imagined the causes of suicide at the national level compared with the local level. During my research in Madampe, this issue arose repeatedly, and formed the second narrative by and through which people made sense of the national suicide rate.

Along with the problems of farmers, scholars have often argued that the negative effects of modernisation, urbanisation and development on local social and cultural ways of life (e.g. Gombrich and Obeyesekere 1988; Straus and Straus 1953; Wood 1961) aggravated the suicide rate. Similarly, people in Madampe of various social classes and backgrounds explained that in 1977 the United National Party (UNP) implemented a programme of economic reforms referred to locally as 'the open economy', as a result of which the country diverted from its path of state socialism and embraced market capitalism. The effects of those policies on 'traditional culture' (*sanskrutiyə*) have been agonised about and worried over ever since, with probably the overwhelming view in Madampe being that the policy was catastrophic for 'traditional' ways of life (cf. Spencer 1990b, 1992). In Madampe, '1977' was commonly held responsible for the breakdown of traditional caste and kinship structures, the rise of love marriage and youth frustrations, and the growth of unsustainable and, for most, unachievable consumerism. In reflection of this, '1977' was often offered as a catch-all explanation for a wide range of problems faced both locally and nationally, from youth love affairs through family breakdown to the national suicide rate.

The problems caused by 1977 threaded through the opinions of Don Appuhami, a high-status Udagama resident. Don Appuhami was not unusual in how he related the causes of the national suicide rate to social changes caused by the 1977 open economy policy. When I visited his home during my village census, Don Appuhami responded to my questions about family history with a diatribe on the decline of old or ancient (*pura:ŋə*) agrarian modes of life and the impact of class mobility and consumerism. Don Appuhami particularly lamented the passing of what he called the 'calm and quiet' (*səhane*) society, and its replacement by one that has 'lost respect' for the naturalness of caste hierarchy, is witnessing the 'breakdown of family life' and extended kinship bonds, and is characterised by the hedonistic 'pursuit of material things'. Reflecting a broader social narrative held by many *pura:ŋə* people in Madampe, Don Appuhami suggested that these changes were producing discontent, hopelessness and frustration (*asəhane*) in the village. Don Appuhami told me:

> In the past people were calm and quiet; but today they are always wanting more. They are not happy with their lot in life. Today people are always running after material things [*salli passe duvənəva*], and you cannot tell a person's level [social standing, status; *tatve*] by the things they own. Our family was the first to have a television in the village, and people would travel from miles around to watch it through our window! But today everybody has a TV.... Young men and women go abroad so they can buy washing machines. So now I have to buy a washing machine to show my level!

When I asked Don Appuhami to describe 'the past', he talked about the administrative and agricultural system under the British. According to Don Appuhami, that system was a reflection of pre-colonial society and ordered economic and social life on the principles of caste and sub-caste. For example, Don Appuhami suggested that when the ra:jəka:riyə, a system of caste-based service to the king derived from feudal times, was implemented by the British to develop the outstations and rural areas, people were subsequently ruled according to the principles of ascribed status which functioned to keep people in their place (cf. Gombrich and Obeyesekere 1988: 68; Peebles 1995). Don Appuhami also mentioned the close connection between the native colonial administrators and the communities they served. Under the British, village headmen were recruited from a locally influential high-caste family, under whose authority people 'naturally' fell. However, nowadays, Don Appuhami complained, the system of village headmen had been bureaucratised and populated by 'faceless individuals with no legitimate [caste] authority'. The distinctions between people had blurred, and the traditional (pura:ṇə) order was lost.

In a separate interview, I spoke with two men also of pura:ṇə status who lived in a neighbouring village. During our discussion, we visited the subject of suicide, and the elevated number found within the Sinhala Buddhist community. Like Don Appuhami, the men complained that social changes occurring since 1977 had eroded natural hierarchies like caste and created an unhealthy materialism in its wake, and the particular problems faced by the farmers. However, they also felt responsible for protecting the caste and class status of pura:ṇə villages like Udagama, and for them the rise of 'love marriage' was of special concern. One man, Upali, a former Grama Niladhari (village administrator), complained that:

> The youth today do not care about our village traditions and culture. They watch western TV and listen to western music and want to do modern things. You have to understand, in the past people married according to their parents' wishes, because parents have a better understanding about who is a suitable marriage partner. But these days the youth like to marry whoever they wish, without knowing about their [partner's] true character. It is because of this that children argue with their parents and then drink poison, or because all these marriages are failing and the husband or wife then drinks poison.

For these men, the Udagama elite, the difficulties the older generation faced in protecting the 'ancestral' or 'generational' status (parampara:ven enə tatve) of families and villages like theirs against the excesses of the younger generation accounted for the suicide problem in Sri Lanka.

Over in the lower status estate of Alutwatta, however, people unsurprisingly expressed less concern with the loss of a traditional social order than they did the struggle in gaining opportunity and status in the contemporary economy. Nevertheless, 1977 still informed their accounts, and for them the date stood more for the loss of kin support and encroachment on workers' rights and trade unions' power (Widger 2012a). The national suicide problem was framed as a consequence of market liberalisation and the frustrations that has caused for youth and working people. As Mary, quoted above, suggested, suicide became a problem *there* when people could no longer rely on their relatives for help: '1977' was understood as creating a selfish and individualised population in which material success was dependent upon competing against one's own kin and neighbours. Mary further commented:

> Because of 1977 there is competition between parents and children and siblings these days. Everybody is jealous [*i:risiya:*] of everybody else. Even if you have the smallest success others will say bad things about you.

Concerns about the social and moral effects of 1977 were often framed within discussions about youth, and the challenges young people have faced and continue to face in contemporary Sri Lanka. So frequent was the allusion to youth and their economic, social and political frustrations within narratives of 1977 that they formed an important explanation for suicide in their own right.

The study of 'youth frustration' (*taruṇa asəhane*) has been a mainstay of Sri Lankan policy and academic concern for many decades, through which it also entered state and court theories. Similarly, the problem of youth frustrations also threaded through Madampe people's narratives concerning the national suicide epidemic *there*, as well as certain accounts of the causes of suicide *here*. The popular opinion in Madampe seemed to be that the Sri Lankan suicide rate rose in direct correlation with a growing mismatch between youth expectations and realities in the fields of education and employment, as well as love and marriage. Often seen as a consequence of 1977, then, Madampe people's narratives blamed the suicide epidemic on the inability of youth to cope with the pressures of modern life, and the pressures put to bear on children and young people by their parents (cf. Chua 2011). Yet as with the struggles of farmers, the problem of youth frustrations was often seen more as a problem '*there*'. Nishantha, a trainee doctor at New Town Peripheral Health Unit, told me:

> The main cause of suicides is youth frustration. They fail exams or cannot find a good job and so commit suicide because they think their future will be lost. Or sometimes else they have a love problem because their mother and father do not agree to a marriage.

When I asked Nishantha whether youth in Madampe commit suicide for these reasons, he qualified his statement:

> Actually not so much, especially because of economic problems.... Youth here can find jobs locally or go abroad, so I do not think they swallow poison because of this problem. Love problems, yes, but economic problems, no. Boys in Colombo might kill themselves because they have failed exams and their parents are blaming them or boys in the farming districts because they want education so they do not become farmers. That is *there*.

Here there are more opportunities, and because so many go abroad to work they always have money to spend from somewhere.

Nishantha was himself a Colombo resident, having been posted to Madampe during his medical training. Like many people in Madampe, he did not consider the area rural but instead part of the urban sprawl of the west coast. He regarded educational aspiration a concern of either upper-class Colombo youth who competed to get into overseas universities, or rural youth who competed to leave the land behind, but not peri-urban youth for whom educational success was just one of several opportunities for advancement. Madampe youth born and bred expressed similar views. Surangi, an Udagama woman and recent sociology graduate of the University of Colombo, explained:

> Yes youth frustration is a big cause of the suicide problem in Sri Lanka but not here.... My batch mates [at university] came from all over, but you could tell the ones from the villages. For them university was a big deal, which it was for us, but for them it was the only chance to get away from the village. Maybe if they had not passed their exams they would have killed themselves. But for others university was important but not the only option ... we have relatives in good positions who can sometimes get us jobs, even without a degree.

The sense that university was not the only career option was especially strong among young men in Madampe. Starting a business or a spell of overseas migration was often preferable. Ranil, Surangi's younger brother (*malli*), did not do particularly well at school but passed his A levels. He was nevertheless driven to 'do business', he told me, like his father who had run a small *kaḍe* before his death. Ranil was at that time a sales executive working on commission for a mobile service provider, and hoped to start a phone repair business. For him, a spirit of entrepreneurship was characteristic of Madampe youth:

> Youth suicides are common elsewhere in Sri Lanka because they do not want to do business. They think that going to university is the only option. They come from farming villages but because of the education they have had at school they do not want to become cultivators. It is hard work and there is no money. Then they do not win a place at university and so become frustrated and kill themselves. But in Madampe boys want to do business or go abroad. Even if you go to university there is no guarantee that you will find a job. Actually, most do not. Suranga [a classmate] went to university but now he is back home living with his parents and being blamed by them!

While many narratives concerning youth frustrations were sympathetic in tone, those of older people were sometimes more critical in nature. Madampe parents and grandparents explained the risk of youth suicide as a consequence of 'youthfulness' (*taruṇəkamə*), a state of immaturity and inability to cope with problems and challenges in life due to a lack of moral education and discipline. Don Appuhami, for example, told me:

> Youthfulness is a problem because boys and girls face many educational and economic challenges but do not have the mental peace [ma:nəsikə səhane] to deal with them. They lack mental maturity and rush into decisions before thinking about the consequences.

Although Sinhala youth in Madampe thought of economic and educational frustrations as largely being a problem *there*, for the few Tamil youth I interviewed such hardships seemed to be much more pressing. I met Vishan, a twenty-four-year-old Tamil Hindu, at the Chilaw Mental Health Clinic after he had been admitted for counselling following a suicide attempt. While Vishan's own suicidal act has been precipitated by a love problem, he explained the high rates of suicide in the Tamil population using different terms. Speaking in 2006 when a fragile ceasefire between the LTTE and Sri Lankan government was in place, Vishan explained:

> Suicide among the Tamil people is caused by a lack of educational opportunities, and a lack of good jobs. The Sinhalese, they have taken everything, and we are treated like second-class citizens. In the past, we could go abroad but now it is very difficult to get a visa. We cannot get permission to go to UK or USA because the [Sri Lankan] government tells your countries Tamils are not oppressed. I myself had a visa rejected. But we have no chance to live here [in Sri Lanka], so what can we do?

For Vishan, the high rate of suicide in the Tamil community was directly attributed to the oppression Tamil people have suffered at the hands of the Sri Lankan government.

The fourth narrative I encountered in Madampe concerned the role of religion and what many non-Buddhists saw as the 'problem with Buddhism'. Most people I interviewed assumed that the suicide rate was much higher in the Buddhist community than it was in the Catholic or Muslim communities. While my Buddhist informants sometimes struggled to explain this, non-Buddhists pointed to the clear deterrents to suicide found within Catholicism and Islam that Buddhism was said to lack. As such, non-Buddhist narratives tended to focus on what was 'wrong' with the Buddhist/Sinhala community and what was 'right' with the Catholic or Muslim community. In so doing, their narratives displayed understandings of religion that drew from both 'great traditions' and 'little traditions' of Buddhism, Catholicism and Islam. Their accounts contained aspects derived from the great textual traditions of each religion that were refracted through and interpreted within the specific local contexts in which they lived.

Just as Buddhist theologians and religious scholars debate the ambiguous stance of Buddhism towards suicide (Becker 1990; Keown 1996; Wiltshire 1983), both Udagama and Alutwatta Buddhists struggled to tell me whether or not Buddhism contained any specific sanction against suicide. When I asked the head priest at the Udagama temple whether Buddhism contained any formal textual position on suicide, he replied that priests often remind their congregations of the first precept of Buddhism – non-violence (*ahimsa*) – and that this also applies to suicide. The monk told me that he stresses suicide causes problems for the family left behind, and pointed to the causes of suicide as increasing attachment to material things brought about by social change: both factors which good Buddhists should seek to avoid. However, the monk could not point to any doctrinal sanction specifically:

> We know that suicide is a problem in our community, and that it is caused by this consumerist society we are living in these days. People are forgetting that Buddhism teaches there is no need to run after material things. I teach that to develop a good mind we have to stop running after things, and also that Buddhism requires non-violence. We should not kill anything, even ourselves ... I also teach that suicide causes such problems for our families.

Likewise, no lay Buddhist I interviewed in Madampe claimed that suicide was explicitly condemned in Buddhism, although most did repeat the monk's objections that because Buddhists believe in non-violence they should not kill themselves for fear of bad karmic consequences. However, other informants pointed out that the moral and therefore karmic consequences of suicide depended on the kinds of intentions lying behind the act. If suicide was committed without violent intent, negative karmic consequences would not accrue. Deepal, a twenty-seven-year-old Buddhist man living at Udagama, explained the position thus:

> In Buddhism, suicide is only a sin [*pav*] if you have the wrong intentions. If you commit suicide to hurt another, then that is a problem. But if you commit suicide because you are facing unresolvable problems then it's not much of a sin.... Maybe then the sin is no more than stealing.... Of course usually we should try and face our problems and solve them, that is the better way.... But if we have tried that and failed, then maybe suicide will be okay.

This view accords well with the general scriptural principle, for example, as described by Narada Mahāthera (1988), that only an 'intentional action whether mental, verbal, or physical is regarded as *kamma* ... involuntary, unintentional, or unconscious actions do not constitute *kamma*'. Suicidal practices in Sri Lanka are often said to arise 'impulsively' or 'spontaneously', in which conscious, rational agency is often assumed to be absent (Marecek and Senadheera 2012). Deepal further explained:

> If I swallow poison but not blame another person when doing so, it is obvious that I am not trying to hurt another. Yet if I was to swallow poison and say that I did this because *ayya* [elder brother] blamed me, then people would know that I am trying to hurt *ayya*.

Thus, the presence of conscious intent implies an intent to blame another, which in turn implies negative karma. By disavowing intent, one can seek to avoid negative karma. The logic of karma thus complicates even further the problem of intent and the ways in which we might try to define suicide.

A related issue was whether *causing* somebody to self-harm led to negative karmic consequences for that person. Jonathan Spencer (1990a) has suggested that suicide has negative karmic consequences for people whose actions are deemed to have caused an injury or death, and that this may be understood as a significant motivation *for* suicide, as it becomes a way of committing karmic violence against others. Although in Madampe the idea that specific people can and should be held to account for causing another to self-harm was extremely popular, I rarely heard this explained in karmic terms. Rather, the negative consequences of causing self-harm were explained in social terms, either because that person was assumed to be subject to public shame (*læjja*), and/or because quite straightforward risks of physical assault were assumed to pertain.

Despite the fact that many Madampe Buddhists believed suicide was not a sin if one's intentions were non-violent, this did not translate into believing that the cause of the high suicide rate among Buddhists was Buddhism itself. The situation was quite to the contrary, in fact, as many Buddhists I interviewed claimed that Buddhism provided a very effective cure for suicidal impulses and 'mental problems' more generally. The temple was regarded as a chosen refuge during troubled times, allowing a space to meditate and achieve a state of mental peace to counter mental frustrations caused by 1977 and its aftermath. Many Buddhists suggested that the high suicide rate within their community was entirely coincidental. Buddhist informants reminded me that 'most suicides' were committed by youthful farmers, and because farmers were uneducated they could not be expected to follow the rules of Buddhism correctly. 'Good education' thus implied a general moral and religious disposition to the world that prepared people for their problems and thus overcome the risk of suicide.

Madampe Catholics and Muslims, on the other hand, had very definite views on the sinfulness of suicide. For my Catholic and Muslim informants, suicide was impossible owing to clear sanctions against self-killing found in the Bible or Koran. Mrs Perera, a middle-aged Catholic secondary schoolteacher, told me:

> The problem with the Buddhists is their religion. Because I am a Catholic, when I have a family problem or another problem I can read the Bible and get strength to face my problems. The Bible says not to kill yourself because of your problems. It is a sin, so I would never do it.

However, Mrs Perera could not point to any particular passage in the Bible condemning suicide, suggesting her belief was based on a more general assumption than specific theological knowledge. Another Catholic, a forty-five-year-old man named Siripala, gave a very familiar sociological explanation for the different suicide rates among religious communities in Sri Lanka. Echoing Durkheim, Siripala suggested that the regular opportunities to attend church or mosque and participate in collective worship meant that Catholics and Muslims had much greater scope for dealing with their problems than Buddhists, while increased surveillance in everyday life meant that suicidal people were quickly spotted:

> The Catholics and even the Muslims do not commit suicide because they have their congregation to support them. Catholics go to church once per week but the Muslims go to their mosque five times per day! Even if they feel suicidal, they will not have the chance, as people will see there is a problem and help. The Buddhists only go to temple on *poya* day [full moon], and even then half of them do not manage it!

While providing a fascinating example of a folk sociological theory of suicide akin to Durkheim's, Siripala's claims were hardly substantiated by his own practice. Although Catholic, Siripala did not once attend church during the almost two-year period of my fieldwork, yet he never displayed any suicidal impulses that I knew of!

In Madampe Old Town, Mr Irshad, a thirty-five-year-old Muslim teacher at the Muslim school, combined both social and religious explanations to account for the historically low suicide rate in his own community. On the one hand, Mr Irshad suggested, Muslims continue to live in extended households, with a number of families under one roof: something he said that the Sinhalese no longer do. He explained that Madampe Muslims are matrilocal, which is to say married couples live with or near the wife's parents, who have provided a house or part of their own house as dowry. For Mr Irshad, this meant that children and young people were never denied proper care and moral direction: 'Even though many mothers migrate abroad to work in the Middle East,' he told me, 'the children always have another mother to take over.' By contrast, when Sinhala mothers migrate 'they abandon their children and this is a huge cause of problems in their community'.

Ernest Gellner (1983: 1) wrote that 'Islam is the blueprint of a social order', and for Mr Irshad the clearly structured nature of Muslim society in Madampe was key to understanding its apparent immunity to suicide:

> We live according to the Koran. All family matters are ruled over by the man. All family and public matters pass through them, and in the event of a dispute that cannot be settled within the family the mosque authorities are called in. But in the Sinhala community fathers take a back seat in domestic matters, and when matters cannot be settled internally they do not go to the temple. When we have any problems we can always get an answer from our religion.

Buddhists and Catholics in Madampe often echoed these views about why their Muslim neighbours did not commit suicide. As indicated by Siripala's comment, many non-Muslims assumed that Muslims attended the mosque five times per day. They also assumed that Muslims lived in large, extended families. But perhaps the most important difference was that the Muslims were assumed to engage in business, and so did not suffer from the economic problems that troubled farmers or the negative impacts of 1977 that affected non-farmers, but in fact benefited from them. Shyamalie, a twenty-six-year-old Sinhala Buddhist woman, explained:

> The Muslims all do business and so this is why they do not commit suicide. Why would they? They do not face the economic problems that we Sinhalese people do. Some day they [the Muslims] will take over the country because of this!

Buddhist, Catholic and Muslim understandings of the Sri Lankan suicide rate issued from their own beliefs about how and why their own religions condemned or provided barriers to suicide, as well as stereotypical understandings of each other's religions and ways of life. As highlighted by Shyamalie's comment, these understandings were often of a prejudicial nature, and so indicated more than just a concern with why Buddhists seem to commit suicide more than any other community. For many Madampe Buddhists, their understandings also intersected with broader narratives concerning the fate of Sri Lanka as a 'Sinhala Buddhist nation' that was deemed to be under threat from internal and external forces, one of which was their own penchant to suicide and others' apparent immunity.

Such descriptions may be understood as reflecting both the 'evidence' and 'ethos' of suicidality in Madampe. On the one hand, what we might call 'practices of concern' – the humanitarian expressions in people's accounts of why remote farmers were especially prone to suicide – helped generate reasons for suicide that would later come to define their own actions, and the actions of others in Madampe. On the other hand, those same 'practices of concern' became a way of making political comments and criticisms about the state of the country today, including perspectives on the war, national identity, and ethnic and religious differences. Thus in this way the ideological work of suicide spreads far beyond the question of why people might die by suicide to encompass some of the most pressing challenges facing the Sri Lankan nation today. Yet, as will now be seen, such certainties proved difficult to translate simply back into Madampe itself, where the complexities of suicide *here* called for different approaches altogether.

Suicide '*here*': the ambiguities of language and practice

In Madampe, narratives of suicide *there* distanced the national suicide epidemic in geographical, social and moral terms. The kinds of problems that people said caused Sri Lanka's suicide crisis were not considered endemic to Madampe, and neither were the kinds of people found *there* found *here*, both of which meant that Madampe was largely untroubled by high rates of suicidal behaviour. Of those cases of suicide that did occur, most of my informants believed they were likely to be caused by certain kinds of 'family problems' (*pavul praʃnə*): disputes between parents and children over love affairs; marital problems between husbands and wives; material inequalities among extended kin. However, when I asked people to account for the patterns of self-harm and suicide found in their own communities linked to these issues, many explanations lacked the same certainty that accompanied their discussions of suicide *there*. Because the rest of this book provides an examination of suicide *here*, in this chapter I will focus on one subtle but far-reaching difference between how people spoke about suicide *there* and suicide *here*. This may be found in how suicide *there* was talked about using the term 'suicide' in both English and its Sinhala equivalent, but how suicide *here* was most often framed in terms of 'poison drinking' (*vaha bonəva*).

In spoken Sinhala, there is no direct equivalent of the English term 'suicide', but the written phrase '*siya divi nasa: gæni:mə*' translates as 'to take one's own life'. This was the phrase I used when I first arrived in Madampe, and many informants seemed to use the terms '*siya divi nasa: gæni:mə*' and 'suicide' interchangeably. However, it was when using these two terms that I was told 'that is there', and I became aware of the difference between suicide *there* and suicide *here*. After a few weeks of fieldwork it became clear that a much more popular spoken phrase existed which people used when describing suicide cases occurring around them: '*vaha bonə ekə*' ('poison drinking'). When I too began using the phrase 'poison drinking', I was no longer referred to Anuradhapura farmers but engaged in debates about the causes and representations of suicidal practices in Madampe.

This rather sudden turnaround in my fieldwork fortunes was of course revealing. I came to understand how people imagined suicide *there* through a mix of high-level, abstract terms including a textual Sinhala form and an English word descended from global suicidology. Both portrayed suicide as the result of a definitive act of self-harm that was unambiguously supposed to result in death. As the victims of particular economic, social and political circumstances, farmers, the casualties of 1977, youth and (uneducated) Buddhists were all known to commit suicide with a clear and unproblematic 'intent to die'. If understandings of '*siya divi nasa: gæni:mə*' and 'suicide' descended from textual or institutional authorities emanating from outside of Madampe, those of poison drinking arose from everyday practices experienced within Madampe. By referring to poison drinking instead of a more deterministic practice like 'attempting suicide', village-level terminologies were rooted in the sociality of such behaviour and not its intended or inevitable finalisation in death. Rather than forming set causal narratives of suicidality, descriptions of suicide *here* stumbled on the confusing relationships between discourse, practice and action on the one hand, and what might be the conscious or unconscious intentions of the suicidal person on the other.

According to my Udagama and Alutwatta informants, many suicidal practices in Madampe were not 'intended' to result in death. Rather, they were better understood as functioning to put the idea of death into other people's minds, as part of a longer process of exchange making up and responding to 'family problems'. It was often stated that the aim of raising the spectre of self-inflicted death was to make a family problem a highly public affair, the shame and *pav* of which would force an antagonist to back down, change their minds, alter their behaviour or whatever. Importantly, this understanding of suicide did not correspond with the theories generated from courts and clinics. Thus Dr Herath, a Chilaw mental health clinician, expressed exasperation at how threats to drink poison had become simple everyday expressions of suffering or sorrow following the activities of others. As a mental health professional, the lack of fit between the theories of suicide he had learnt during his allopathic training and the cases he encountered through his clinical practice led him to dismiss them as 'just talk':

> Suicide has become normalised now. People make suicide threats even when they have no intent to die but just to express sorrow. When you English might say 'I've lost my job, I feel depressed', we Sinhalese say 'I've lost my job, I'm going to drink poison'.

Nevertheless, among Madampe teenagers and young adults, verbal threats to drink poison formed a common part of negotiations in love affairs and were often used to advantage in attempts to win a heart. 'If I can't have you I will drink poison' was an established verbal threat among many of the young men I knew, while 'If you leave I will drink poison' might be deployed by either young men or women to stop attempts at separation. Many people in Madampe, and older adults especially, treated such threats as completely unserious, and often laughed whenever they heard of a case. They assumed that love-struck youths' threats to drink poison were part-and-parcel of courting games and highly unlikely to signal any 'real' wish to die. One middle-aged man living in Udagama complained:

> These bloody kids! They have all these ideas of love from the TV and movies and then demand the same here. However, in Sri Lanka, parents do not approve of love marriage and that is when they all start talking about suicide. Even over the smallest upset!

The ambiguities implied by poison drinking carried across into its performance, as well as those of other methods. Often I was told how men involved in family disputes could be seen outside their house, circling the base of a tree and looking up into its branches: 'You can always tell when a man has been arguing with his wife because he'll be in the garden finding a place to hang from!' the Chilaw City Coroner joked. According to the coroner, people who witness the act assume that the man is selecting a likely branch that could be used in some possible version of the future. The implication is that someone within the house, probably the wife or maybe one of his children, is behaving in a reckless fashion and 'playing with his life', as the coroner put it. Similarly, women might douse themselves with kerosene and then go to strike a match, while men or women may put a bottle of poison to their mouth and threaten to drink from it.

The common thread running between narratives of poison drinking and the myriad ways in which people threatened their own death was a 'management of deceit': the effort on the part of suicidal people to convince others that the idea of their death is tangible, and the risks that others are forced to take when judging how to respond. Argenti-Pillen (2007) has shown how deception and illusion are important features of Sinhala social life, wherein the telling of lies (*boruva*) closely followed by revelations of truth are used as a form of conflict or shame avoidance (cf. Spencer 1990: 177). In suicidal practices, *boruva* takes on an urgent dimension, wherein life and death choices have to be made. In Madampe suicide 'games' were often played by children, teenagers and adults, during which playful gestures and mentions of self-inflicted death existed alongside 'real' attempts, straying close to fatal actions and reactions (Widger n.d.). A case I reviewed at the Kuliyapitiya Coroners' Court showed how one man's repeated suicide threats had led his wife to dismiss them as so much attention-seeking. However, one evening the man did swallow poison, she did not believe him, and he died. When interviewed by the coroner, the wife said that her husband had normally threatened suicide 'to trick me'.

The ambiguities of suicidal language and practice and the relationships among suicide, people and place – of how people narrated suicide *here* and how they threatened and attempted self-harm and self-inflicted death as Madampe people – raise huge challenges in the conceptualisation and study of those behaviours. First, although I use the terms 'suicide', 'self-harm'. 'suicidal practice' and so on throughout the book, they have no straightforward parallels in spoken Sinhala. In suicidology, 'deliberate self-harm' is considered to be the ambiguous relative of 'suicide', in perhaps the same way as *vaha bonəva* could be considered the ambiguous relative of *siya divi nasa: gæni:mə*. However, that distinction is only found in language. In practice, performances of hanging, burning and drowning are also used to 'trick', even though, in Madampe at least, they rarely seem to be verbalised as tricks. Second, poison drinking accounts for the majority of deaths nationally, and half of deaths in Madampe. Clearly, the ambiguity of poison drinking only goes so far, and whether by accident or design can and often enough does result in death. Chilaw mental health clinicians used global suicide risk scales to try to ascertain the likelihood of intended death in self-harm patients they saw, in order to distinguish between acts of 'self-harm' and 'suicide attempts'. Meanwhile, people in Madampe used their own scales, drawing from victims' gender, age and social position, along with an idea about who was to blame, to distinguish deceitful from honest threats and attempts.

As I have already argued in the introduction, the ambiguities of language and practice make the task of setting formal definitions of suicidal behaviour impossible. Perhaps the closest we can come is to say that suicidal practices in Madampe function as a means through which the 'idea of death is put into other people's minds'. This may be to trick others into thinking that death is the intention, or, as I suspect is more often the case, to raise the spectre of death but leave eventualities unaccounted for. The registers people use to make sense of suicidal practice, be they the simpler theories of suicide *there* or the complex theories of poison drinking, unfold in relation to the generative practices of villages, courts and clinics, and the sum of traditions of suicidal knowledge offered by them. Dispositions to suicide, the processes through which they are acquired, and how people gain an understanding of the agentive self in so doing, are multifarious and discreet, slipping away just at the moment one has a grasp on them. Yet this too is a fundamental characteristic of suicide, and one without which the potency and allure of self-destruction may become rather less.

Living through suicide in different ways

People *live* through suicide and live *through* suicide in different ways. The same person may also live *through* suicide in different ways, depending upon their proximity to the case in question. Drawing from the work of the psychoanalyst Heinz Kohut, Clifford Geertz (1983) discusses the difference between 'experience-near' concepts and 'experience-distant' concepts used by the anthropologist. 'Experience-near' concepts are those used to describe the vast array of ideas, practices and explanations that comprise mundane cultural knowledge as recorded daily during the ethnographic encounter. 'Experience-distant' concepts are the formalised, abstracted, theorised concepts that anthropologists subsequently produce when translating 'mundane knowledge' into 'academic knowledge'. Thus, Geertz (1983: 57) describes the process through which experience-distant concepts are used to make sense of experience-near concepts:

> An experience-near concept is, roughly, one that someone – a patient, a subject ... informant – might himself naturally and effortlessly use to define what he or his fellows see, feel, think, imagine, and so on, and which he would readily understand when similarly applied by others. An experience-distant concept is one that specialists of one sort or another – an analyst, an experimenter, an ethnographer, even a priest or an ideologist – employ to forward their scientific, philosophical, or practical aims.

Yet it is not only specialists or anthropologists who seek to transform experience-near concepts into experience-distant concepts. When ordinary people are faced with crises in their lives, we might also expect them to perform the same operations, not only as a method of comprehension but also, and in what might amount to the same thing, as a method of coming to terms with the challenges they face. Thus, suicide *there* is understood using experience-distant concepts that literally distance the suicidal nation from Madampe. People come to live *through* suicide *there* in an abstract sense, the result of which transforms suicide into a problem rendered for 'other people'.

Suicide *here*, however, is kept within experience-near concepts. When people in Madampe seek to make sense of suicide, they do so not by transforming the ambiguities of experience-near concepts into clear experience-distant concepts but instead by delving deeper into the ambiguities of cases, approaching the problems of language and practice, and running into the problem of intent. Why so? Suicide is a traumatic experience, and forces us to confront, in the plainest kind of way, the ambivalence of our own existence and the limited corporeality of our lives. The questions 'what did I do?' and 'what could I have done?' present almost immediately. I am reminded of the social scientist whose life had been spent advocating social theories of suicide until her child died by suicide, when psychological theories came to offer comfort in the way Durkheim's theories did not. Comfort was gained from distancing the death in both relational and intellectual terms.

However, Ravi's family, friends and neighbours did not seek to distance the death as they otherwise sought to distance the national suicide rate. Meaning was instead to be found in the possibilities of explanation rooted in Madampe itself, which in fact brought Ravi's death very close to home. Instead of finding comfort in the clear but 'abstract' theories of suicide *there*, the confused but 'tangible' theories of suicide *here* were sought. Thus to live *through* suicide is to engage with the solid realm of what is certainly known *there*, while to *live* through suicide is to engage with the shadow realm of what may be known *here*. This difference raises questions concerning the representation of suicide in local knowledge, as without the benefit of long-term exposure to a place and its people the distinction between those two kinds of knowledge may never be known, or even acknowledged. It was only after some time that I learnt to ask the right kinds of questions to begin to explore, let alone make sense of, suicide *here*, as up until that point I had been eliciting knowledge about suicide *there*. Had I never managed to bridge that gap my understanding of suicide in Sri Lanka would only have ever been partial.

The existence of different kinds of knowledge, the one tangible and near and the other abstract and distant, highlights the importance of ethnographic studies not just of suicide but also of social life in general. I suggest that a large number of so-called 'cross-cultural' studies in suicidology, and the 'suicide and culture' movement more generally, are mistaking distant-knowledge for near-knowledge. This may be seen, for example, in the new wave of psychological studies in Sri Lanka where the theories and methods of Euro-American psychiatry are being put to use with little or no attempt at translation. The result is the measuring and 'proof' of distant-knowledge concepts like depression as if they were near-knowledge concepts. The remaining chapters of this book develop an account of suicide *here*, and in so doing illustrate the vital importance of understanding how living through suicide generates different kinds of knowledge, each particular to a different understanding of suicide.

Insights for prevention

Summary of the argument

- People often hold *different and conflicting theories* of suicide in their heads at the same time. These may be understood as deriving from *experience-near* concepts and *experience-distant* concepts.
- How people understand suicide as an *abstract problem* of human society may be very different to how they understand suicide as a *tangible problem* in their own lives.
- Many people recognise the *problem of intent* and do not necessarily assume any *fundamental* difference between 'intentionally' fatal or non-fatal suicidal acts. Ascribing intent is never a value-free act.
- All suicidal acts have the *potential of resulting in death*, and the use of suicide as a means of *putting the idea of death into other people's minds* is often the most significant immediate intention that may be discerned.

Practical applications

- Attempts at *measuring attitudes* towards suicide using *standardised methods* may only capture one set of beliefs about suicide ('abstract' or 'tangible') and so only provide a *partial picture*.
- Detailed qualitative investigation of the relationship between *language and practice* can provide a more *nuanced understanding* of the different beliefs people hold about suicide and how they relate to action.
- Prevention planners should be careful to formulate programmes that address the *different ways individuals think about suicide*, including those which may be *contradictory*.
- Ultimately it may be more effective to *focus on tangible beliefs about suicide* as these may be more directly related to suicidal practices (i.e. to focus on experience-near concepts rather than experience-distant concepts).

4 Relational flows

> *This not letting one another alone, it's at the bottom of nine-tenths of the crime and trouble.*
> *The Village in the Jungle*, Leonard Woolf (1981 [1913]: 147)

The passage above is taken from Leonard Woolf's *The Village in the Jungle*, a fictional account of rural life in late colonial Sri Lanka, drawn from his own experiences as a colonial administrator (Woolf 1997; Ondaatje 2005). The narrator is the local British magistrate, through whom Woolf speaks, and he is attempting to explain how an apparently sudden quarrel between two villagers led one to murder the other. Woolf's concern was more than literary, as rates of homicide were then considered extremely high in the colony (Rogers 1987; Straus and Straus 1953). Rogers (1987) has explained this as the result of status conflicts, during which apparently slight insults between kin and neighbours took on magnificent proportions in their contexts of action, and demanded swift and violent recompense.

What Woolf called '[t]his not letting one another alone' has since been widely discussed in the Sri Lankan sociological and anthropological literature. The proximity of relational violence (family, domestic, interpersonal and gender-based) to a range of social and political problems has rendered the concept useful for social analysis. Thus, we find the conflicts of everyday life used to explain village-level politics (Spencer 1990a, 1990b), joking relationships (Argenti-Pillen 2007), youth insurgency (Hughes 2013), and the gender politics of shame (*lᴂjja*) (Hewamanne 2003; Lynch 2007; Obeyesekere 1984; Spencer 1990b). Relational violence has also been strongly associated with shame and suicidal practice (Konradsen *et al.* 2006; Marecek 1998, 2006; Marecek and Senadheera 2012; Said 2014; Stirrat 1987; Widger 2009: ch. 5, 2012a, 2012b). If Sri Lankan post-colonial society has been one defined by violence at the national level through youth insurgency and civil war, it has also been mirrored at the local level through relational violence 'in and of' the domestic realm.

The previous chapter showed how narratives of suicide *there*, at the national level, and *here*, at the local level, manifest from particular understandings of suicidal practice. The aim of this chapter is to explore how suicide *here* comes to be practised and to obtain the representations that it does, through a close analysis of the relational violence of suicidal practice, within and under which everyday relational disputes and practices of 'blaming and shaming' – 'not letting each other alone' – come to hold extreme importance for protagonists. Across villages, courts and clinics, mundane representations of suicidal practice encompass 'family problems': a catch-all label linking relationships of dispute and conflict between intimate persons encompassed within the *ge:* and with the acts of violence generated by them. As noted by Jeanne Marecek and Chandanie Senadheera (2012), in Sri Lanka when somebody attempts to kill themselves or succeeds in doing so, the question that most often arises is not 'why' but 'who' (cf. Wolf 1975). By asking 'who', people in Sri Lanka try to establish who it was in the victim's household or kin group that acted in such a way as to drive the person to take his or her own life, and to single them out for public blaming and shaming accordingly. By establishing 'who', 'why' is also taken care of (Widger 2012b).

Passing into the relational worlds of suicide *here*, we thus come to consider the processual socialities of suicidal practice that generate representations of suicidal thought. In so doing the chapter introduces a core, recurring theme of the book: the relationship between suicide, gender and violence 'in and of' the family. This relationship is crucial for understanding the relational construction of suicide *here* but it also exists as part of a wider trope of Sri Lankan social life in which relational violence may be understood as being constitutive of the social. My approach stands in contrast to many models of relational violence that situate the appearance of violence as a consequence of social collapse (Harvey and Gow 1994: 11). Instead, I offer an analysis that is similar to other anthropological studies that deal with domestic and intimate partner violence and in particular works that explore the relationship between violence, gender and relationality in a 'generative' sense. For example, Wood *et al.* (2008) draw from long-term fieldwork in urban South Africa to show how the history of social and political violence in that country has permitted interpersonal violence to flourish. They argue that young men's violence against women may be understood as an expression of vulnerable masculinities in which violent acts may be seen to 'configure lives and subjectivities and to be productive of relationships' (ibid.: 43). Similarly, in a study of relational violence in Fiji, Christina Toren (1994) argues that violence committed against women and children is a key practice through which notions of kinship are constructed and understood.

In Madampe, the presence of violence at intrapersonal, interpersonal, communal and societal levels may be viewed as a crucial mechanism through which relationships between people are imagined, experienced and manipulated. This chapter introduces the everyday relational conflicts that generate representations not only of suicide *here* but also of kinship in Madampe in its entirety. The chapter begins by describing the moral frameworks that are used in Madampe to judge people and behaviours said to contravene good family lives, and then proceeds to discuss how suicidal practices in children, adults and elders generate theories of kinship through their suicidal practices that reflect the ideals of childhood, adulthood and old age 'lost' to the effects of modernisation and globalisation in Madampe today. The questions I am asking, then, are: How and under what conditions do certain kinds of relationship come to be valued so strongly that they are considered worth dying for? How and with what consequences do attempts to die make concrete certain kinds of relationship? In Chapters 6 and 7 I consider these and related questions with specific reference to young courting couples and older married couples respectively.

Blame, shame and suicidal practice

Descriptions of suicide *here* are often concerned with relational conflicts, and the on-going processes of claim and counter-claim of truth, lies and challenges to power and status that affect people's lives. Thus, while the story of people 'not letting one another alone' as the source of relational conflicts and social troubles is an old one in Sri Lanka, it is also one that cannot be understood apart from the contingencies of space and time in which they are made in the present. How relational crises are understood, experienced and responded to reflect the changing social, political and economic environment, and the kinds of everyday sociality and morality they manifest.

To make sense of this constellation of factors I focus down to the core concepts of personal and family 'honour' (*nambuva*) and 'status' (*tatve*) that regulate the lives of women and men, and the underpinning notions of 'good' (*hoñdə*) and 'bad' (*narəkə*) moral conduct which people routinely use to embrace or reject people, ideas and things. Gendered moral personhoods have recently been analysed in the context of Sri Lankan garment factories, which are widely understood as attracting or creating 'bad girls' (*narəkə kello*) by drawing them into the 'modern' (*nawi:nə*) world of industrial labour (Hewamanne 2008; Lynch 2007). In the village context, the gendering of 'good' and 'bad' locates ideals of femininity and masculinity in the domestic and public realms respectively, wherein women should be sexually and socially innocent (*ahiŋsəkə*) and subservient, and men should be 'honest' (*avankə*) and 'talkative' or outgoing (Widger 2009: 156–165). By failing to live up to these moral standards, one's own as well as one's family 'dignity' (*a:tmə gavurəve:*) may be brought into question.

The constant 'not letting one another alone' may be understood as the everyday processes through which good and bad character are expressed, judged, enforced or denied. 'I mustn't do that, I will be blamed!' is a common refrain heard throughout Madampe, from people young to old. The possibility of engaging in 'bad behaviour' that risks the pursuit of good family lives raised all kinds of fears in my informants, but the most important of these was of 'being blamed'. The Sinhala term used in this context is '*baninəva*', the more formal translation of which is 'scolding'. While *baninəva* certainly does involve scolding, it also carries an important element of blaming and ridicule. If to 'be scolded' is to be reprimanded for some kind of bad behaviour, *baninəva* is to be held responsible for something bad, and to be made subject to public embarrassment and shame because of it. Furthermore, *baninəva* often leads to 'shame' (*læjja*), although how this process takes place and the range of its effects depends on the social status of persons involved.

Shame (*læjja*), then, is the consequence of being scolded and blamed. The range of behaviours likely to be blamed and cause shame is vast. They include, *inter alia*: breaches of expected familial conduct like obeying those of higher relational status (elder siblings, parents, grandparents, mother's brothers), breeches of everyday social and moral conduct like lying, cheating, drinking, smoking, lazing around, and any number of activities that raise suspicions of sexual impropriety or drunkenness. Many kinds of behaviours that are likely to attract blame involve '*a:dambərə*' or 'excessive' or 'unjustified pride' (cf. Spencer 1990b: 169). In Madampe, unjustified pride was said to cause people to act out of turn, without proper thought for their own status or that of their family. The purpose of blaming is to challenge bad behaviour and draw attention to unjustified pride.

As both an individual and a collective interest, my informants told me that children are taught from an early age to fear their own blaming; that is to say, they are taught 'fear of shame' (*læjja-bayə*). In a famous passage, Obeyesekere (1984: 505) has described the means by which Sinhala children are socialised by the father to fear shame:

> Bad behaviour is corrected in the following manner: '*läjja nädda, mokada minissu kiyanne*,' 'aren't you ashamed; what'll people say?' When a parent, or other socializing agent, simply says '*läjja nädda*' the rest of the statement is implied, so that the reference to the 'others' is contained in it.... There is nothing unusual about these practices, which are found in many societies, except for one factor – the failure to conform is associated with ridicule and laughter by the parent, especially the father.

In Madampe, a cry of 'I'll blame [scold] you!' was used as often as an exclamation of 'aren't you ashamed?' to raise questions of moral character, for example, to challenge cheating and lying or sexual impropriety, reduce pride, and instil a fear of shame. Children and young people were especially conscious of what kind of behaviour might incur blame, be it a sibling, parent, relative, neighbour, teacher, or even a friend. 'If I try and speak with that girl elder sister [*akka*] will blame me', a young man told me; another said, 'because I can't find a job my parents are blaming me'. Similarly, men I drank with might refuse one more bottle for fear of being blamed by their wives for coming home late, while wives were conscious of the need to avoid confrontation with drunken husbands who were likely to blame them for no reason. When I realised that my enjoyment of the excellent rice and curry served at my lodging place was adding numerous pounds to my weight, I tried to diet. 'I'll blame [scold] you!' cried my host mother, who took my refusals of food as a personal slight and was concerned that if I began slimming, people in the village would think that I was not being fed properly, and thus cause shame for the family I was living with.

However, shame is never simply the result of blame but may also be used to blame: shame and blame often become caught in a spiral. Feelings of shame can cause people to react by blaming those who have blamed them, or perhaps another person. The aim in both cases is to deflect attention and thus shame from the self on to others. This process often played out among my male friends in Udagama, who spent a lot of time blaming and shaming each other, sometimes for laughs but also as a way of levelling differences among them and as a form of one-upmanship. As my unmarried twenty-something friends and I lounged on their front porches, a popular pastime was to joke about how one of us liked a particular young woman in the village, and had been seen 'speaking with her' – a euphemism for having a 'love affair'. 'Susantha *ayya* was speaking with *sudu*[1] yesterday', one might suddenly claim during a round of *carom*, at which Susantha would hurriedly reply, 'No, no! Him! Him!', pointing to another in the group. Exchanges like these provided my friends with opportunities to tease and ridicule, tell lies and counter-lies, and to reinstall a sense of shame.

Finally, however, for my informants there was nothing extraordinary about the ways in which blaming and shaming worked in Madampe. Not letting one another alone, whatever the motivation, formed a constant background hum to life in Udagama and Alutwatta. The everyday conflicts of status and shame were obstacles that people *expected* to meet, and when they did, they had strategies available to cope. One of these was to engage in 'telling lies', which obfuscated their own actions and motivations, and rendered simplistic 'good' and 'bad' moral dichotomies difficult to establish (Argenti-Pillen 2007). Insofar as blaming and shaming were taken for granted, the fact that they could lead to suicidal responses would appear extraordinary. Yet again, I would suggest that the obfuscation of intention and representation through the performance of suicidal practices that were *not just* lies and make-believe situates them as one more way of dealing with the accusations of others. Nevertheless, it was not others in general who could instigate suicidal responses through blaming and shaming, but specific kinds of others at different stages of life. Put another way, only blaming and shaming carried out by certain kinds of people could produce a suicidal response.

Relational flows of suicidal practice

Thus, the everyday conflicts driving on-going challenges to moral personhood and status change across the life-course from childhood, through adulthood, and into old age. Overwhelmingly the obligation of 'good behaviour' was expected of middle-class *pura:ṇə* unmarried women and middle-aged men: those in Madampe who are the most obvious vehicles of family honour and status and, in relation to teenage women and middle-aged men more broadly, display the highest rates of self-harm and suicide respectively. Conversely, those for whom the obligation of good behaviour was weakest was teenage men and middle-aged women, who display the lowest rates of self-harm and suicide. Drawing from an analysis of case files generated by coroners and

74 *Relational flows*

clinicians through their interviews with relatives and friends of the deceased and self-harm patients,[2] this section shows how only specific kinds of relationship were deemed likely to produce suicidal responses when they ran into problems. To illustrate this I map the 'relational flows' of suicidal practice in anthropological kinship charts, and create visual depictions of the relationships that people said caused unmarried and married men and women to commit suicide or self-harm. By using the term 'flow' to describe these processes, I wish to highlight how suicidal practices involved a two-way relationship, both being caused by the actions of others but also seeking to affect those others, and thus creating the kinship structures they wish to challenge or affirm in the process. Suicidal practices were rarely the last word in an argument, being one stage in a longer running dispute.

Relational flows of male and female suicides

Beginning with suicides, Figures 4.1 and 4.2 map the relational flows of male and female cases. Drawn from sixty-eight coroner files, they included fifty-six male suicides and twelve female suicides. Of these, twenty-three (42 per cent) male files referred to close relational problems with one or more individuals, compared with seven of the female files. Three-quarters of male and female suicides were associated in one way or another with spousal arguments. More than one-third of files referred to disputes between parents and children.

Relational flows of unmarried self-harmers

Turning now to self-harm, Figures 4.3 and 4.4 map relational flows in sixty-five unmarried male patients and sixty-six female patients who received treatment at

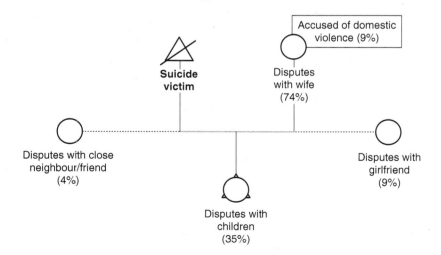

Figure 4.1 Relational flows of male suicides (source: KCC, unpublished data).

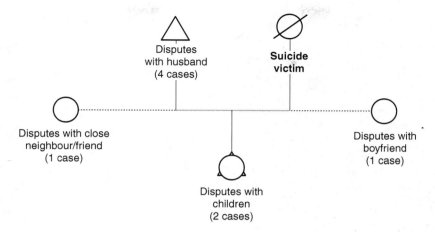

Figure 4.2 Relational flows of female suicide (source: KCC, unpublished data).

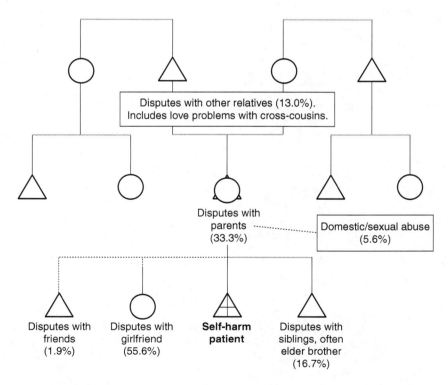

Figure 4.3 Relational flows of unmarried male self-harm (source: CMHC, unpublished data).

76 *Relational flows*

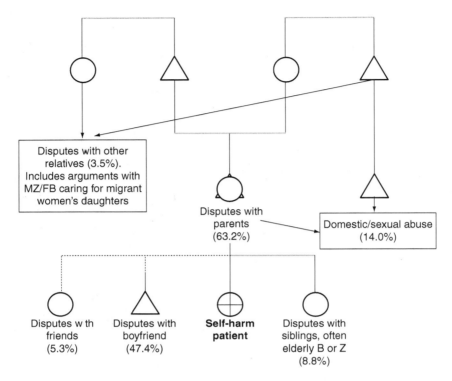

Figure 4.4 Relational flows of unmarried female self-harm (source: CMHC, unpublished data).

Chilaw Mental Health Clinic. Of the males, around one-third of files cited parental disputes, and around a quarter involved disputes with other relatives, including siblings, sisters' husbands and male cross-cousins (*massina*), and mothers' brothers (*ma:ma:*). The largest single category of relational disputes included quarrels with girlfriends or would-be girlfriends, a small proportion of which also included female cross-cousins (*næ:na*). As with male suicides, quarrels with friends accounted for a very small number of cases.

Relational flows in unmarried women suggested different trends to their male counterparts. Disputes with boyfriends or would-be boyfriends accounted for almost half of all cases, but quarrels with parents accounted for double those of males: one-third for males compared with two-thirds for females. However, disputes with older siblings accounted for less than half of cases as they did for males, while disputes with friends accounted for more than double as they did for males. Domestic and sexual abuse also accounted for around 14 per cent of cases – again significantly more than they did for males.

Relational flows of married self-harmers

Figures 4.5 and 4.6 map relational flows of self-harm in 106 married men and eighty-seven married women. Of the men's files, the vast majority – more than three-quarters – reported disputes with their wives, and almost half reported disputes with the mother-in-law and wives' brothers or sisters' husbands (*massina*). Only a small proportion included disputes with parents and siblings, although a larger number – 17 per cent – included quarrels with their own children.

Of the women, some 58 per cent of files reported quarrels with husbands, and 13 per cent quarrels with their own children. As with men, disputes with siblings and friends accounted for only small proportions of self-harm, but while almost

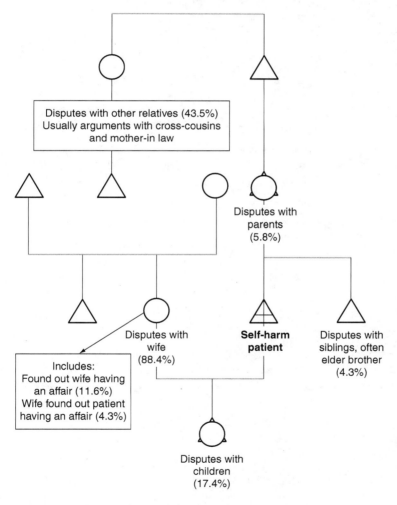

Figure 4.5 Relational flows of married male self-harm (source: CMHC, unpublished data).

78 *Relational flows*

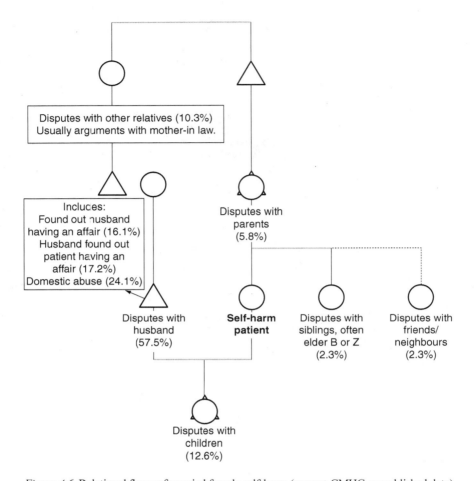

Figure 4.6 Relational flows of married female self-harm (source: CMHC, unpublished data).

half of men's files reported quarrels with other relatives, only around 10 per cent of women's files reported the same.

The files generated by coroners and clinicians show how for men and women of unmarried or married status (which may also be read as childless and parental status), different kin relationships are more or less likely to produce suicidal responses. For example, relationships more likely to be associated with suicidal practices included:

1 Unmarried children, and especially daughters, in disputes with parents, and especially fathers.
2 Unmarried males in disputes with older siblings, and especially brothers, or older kin outside the *ge:*, especially *ma:ma:*.

3   Disputes between boyfriends and girlfriends or husbands and wives.
4   Married men in dispute with wives' parents, wives' brothers, sisters' husbands and male cross-cousins (*massina*).

Conversely, relationships that seemed infrequently to produce suicidal responses included:

1   Friendships.
2   Unmarried women's relationships with older siblings and extended kin.
3   Paramours.
4   Married men's and women's relationships with their own siblings and parents.

When I showed similar charts to my informants in Udagama and Alutwatta, several different explanations were offered. However, they all tended towards one general causal theory: that of conflicted notions of kinship. The obviously much greater frequency of interactions between parents and their unmarried children, husbands and wives, and some extended kin such as *massina* (male cross-cousins, wives' brothers, sisters' husbands) and *ma:ma:* (mothers' brothers) was one explanation for their elevated suicide and self-harm rates. Put simply, increased levels of social interaction led to increased scope for disagreement and dispute. People often told me that suicidal practices increased at the time of *Aluth Avurudu* in April and *Wesak Poya* in May, when families came together to celebrate the Sinhala and Tamil New Year and birth, Enlightenment, and death of the Buddha respectively: events which often included excessive drinking ending in violent quarrels. This explanation was also to some extent supported by the suicide and self-harm data I collected from courts and clinics, which indeed showed that the incidence of self-harm and suicide increased during April and May. However, this did not occur consistently year-on-year, and increases were observed at other times of year not associated with important dates in the ritual calendar, family gatherings and drinking parties.

I suggest that the correlation goes beyond the simple fact that members of *ge:* happen to associate most often and so are more likely to come into dispute with one another. After all, unmarried sons presumably interact with their parents at approximately the same degree as unmarried daughters, but daughters engage more often in suicidal behaviours when their relationships run into problems. Jonathan Spencer (1990a) sought to explain the relational characteristics of Sinhala suicide in terms of status inequality, with suicide being a means of action for those otherwise powerless to resist or react against higher status members. Although status and power differentials are certainly an important part of the story, they are not the whole story. What appears to be the important issue is not the frequency at which people interact or asymmetries of power and status but instead the kinds of moral investments associated with different relationships. Put simply, only certain kinds of relationship are considered worth dying for.

In Madampe, suicide representations cluster around problems of kinship and the attainment of 'good family lives': the stresses and strains of families struggling in the current economic moment, and the specific issue of overseas labour migration. These problems are lived through suicide in different ways by children, youth, adults, and elders and *pura:ṇə* and *estate* people respectively. In children, suicidal practices in the form of 'play' and 'real' acts of self-harm provide an idiom for making moral claims about their lives, either in relation to the actions of friends or in relation to the failures of parents. In youth, adults and elders, suicidal practices are taken up in similar ways to make claims concerning the proper functioning of *ge:*: principally, the duties and responsibilities of children vis-à-vis their parents at different stages of the life-course, and those between specific other kin with whom one is believed to owe a customary obligation of responsibility.

The value of these relationships never simply exists prior to the suicidal response. The suicidal response marks them as valuable. When villagers, coroners and clinicians identify specific kinds of relational dispute in contexts of 'social breakdown', they are making a value statement concerning the ideal family and its apparent absence. It is in the very spaces of villages, courts and clinics that concepts of 'good family lives' are imagined and tested, in this context against the empirical facts of suicide cases. It is not that certain kinds of relational disputes 'close off' non-suicidal responses and 'open up' others. Rather, it is that kinship structures are made to fit the facts.

Suicide play and suicide practice in children and teenagers

In Madampe, the use of suicidal practices as a means of understanding and expressing relational forms and demands begins in childhood. For many people the idea that children may have suicidal thoughts or try to commit suicide is horrifying. Commenting on prevailing attitudes in Western societies, Pfeffer *et al.* (1993) suggest that childhood is widely construed as being a period of life that is relatively free from the stresses and strains that motivate older teenagers and adults to kill themselves. The thought of child suicide was equally horrifying for most adults, including some medical practitioners I knew in Madampe. Many also dismissed the possibility of child suicide, claiming that if acts of self-harm or suicide did occur in children then it was the result of accident or thoughtless imitation, or possibly simply lies and make-believe (*boru*). However, according to court and clinic records, self-harming practices began to appear from around the age of seven in both boys and girls, and the youngest suicide I recorded was of a girl aged just twelve years. Even according to records generated by courts and clinics, then, children demonstrably engaged in suicidal practices.

It was while collecting these data that I happened across a number of apparently 'accidental' cases of self-harm committed by children aged between four and seven. According to the notes I reviewed, the children had acted individually, in pairs or in groups of up to four, and in all cases consumed either *kane:ru* seeds or *niyəngəla* roots. Fortunately, in none of the cases had any of the children died or suffered lasting injury. Further interviews with the attending medical officers suggested that the cases occurred in the context of a simple imitation of the youth and adult cases of self-harm that the children had probably witnessed or heard about in their families, villages or schools. But upon my own investigations of the cases, during which I spoke to some of the parents and children involved, it became clear that the children had acted with a great deal more thought and intention than the medical staff granted them, and in that sense could be better understood as kinds of 'suicide play' which included explorations of 'good' character and conduct, the management of blame and shame, and ultimately expressions of family life. Children's suicide play may be understood as spanning what Goldman (1998: xviii) called 'mimesis and mythos': imitation and creativity. Suicide play, functioning like play more generally, provides a medium through which children imitate and innovate social and moral roles (Widger n.d.).

When I followed up cases admitted to hospital I was very careful in my questioning, as I did not want to lend 'legitimacy' to their behaviour and so perhaps encourage repeat acts.[3] As part of a more general discussion concerning the children's experiences of hospital treatment, I carefully inquired as to how they had come to be admitted. My interviews revealed how children's suicide play may be understood as kinds of practice exploring the manners and means of suicidal performances in Madampe. In some ways, the games I encountered were imitative of wider notions and understandings of suicidal practice, including which methods to use and how youth and adults should perform suicidal practice. In several of the cases the children had mixed *kane:ru* seeds with water and sugar, which is popularly believed by adults to make the toxins contained within the seed more potent: 'that is the correct way to prepare *kane:ru*', many people told me. Then, children had subsequently gone on to tell a parent or older sibling what they had done, in much the same way as older self-harmers do when they wish to lay the blame for their actions on a specific third party.

In other ways, children's suicide play diverged from youths' and adults' suicidal performances. Swallowing poison formed part of games and play exploring issues to do with the moral codes of friendship and family, from the children's own perspectives. For example, three girls and one boy, aged between four and eight years, swallowed *niyəngəla* roots apparently as part of a game in which one half told lies and cheated and the other half expressed sadness over their inability to trust others. In a second case, two children – a boy aged eight and a girl aged seven – had apparently been playing 'families', during which father came home drunk and shouted at mother; following this the children adopted the roles of the parents' children who swallowed *kane:ru* to stop the parents fighting. Equally, a common cause of young women's self-harm in Madampe was the violent abuse of the mother by the father, wherein the daughter swallowed poison to express solidarity with the mother. In these examples, children were clearly engaging in kinds of suicide play which explored social and moral problems often encountered by adults and teenagers, and which often led to adults' and teenagers' suicidal practices.

Throughout my fieldwork in Udagama and Alutwatta, I observed similar kinds of games to those I recorded in the hospitals, although ones that did not include actual self-harm. Many of these included play-acting some kind of self-harm in response to the failure of friends or family members to live up to (often gendered) moral ideals. Others were commentaries on the lives of older peers who landed up in situations the younger child assumed could lead to self-harm. Importantly, too, some did not legitimise self-harm but instead made fun of or ridiculed suicidal practice. For example, when one young man told me about his love problems, a younger boy aged eleven began imitating the older youth's despair through a suicide routine. The boy swiped his finger across his neck, clutched it, and then fell to the floor, tongue hanging out. Although I only ever came across one such case of neck-slashing in reality, the act was enough to have the other youth present doubled up in laughter. In another case, a young girl aged seven imitated somebody taking poison because of a love problem. She ran out of the room laughing hysterically at the thought of it: '*I* would never be so silly,' she said.

Just as suicide play allowed children to explore contexts and methods of suicidal practice more generally, their games also reflected gender constraints. For example, boys' play tended to involve situations wherein retribution of some kind was being sought, or alternatively as a game of dare or a form of playground bullying. Conversely, girls' suicide play concerned the regulation of intimate friendships and domestic relationships, as well as rejections of activities unsuitable for their gender such as involvement in love affairs. In these ways, children's suicide games, play and jokes re-created stereotypical expressions of gender and their impacts on the agentive self – issues I explore at greater length in Chapter 6.

My school-based research using a mix of psychometric survey and open-ended survey questions backed up by a smaller set of interviews also revealed how the causes of suicidal thoughts and acts of self-harm were often associated with problems of gendered moral character. Youth participating in the study ($N=964$) pointed to the moral and social causes of moral problems leading to suicide, including attempts at leading what students referred to as 'a good family life' (*hoňdə pavul ji:vite*), treating others with love and respect, avoiding gossip, and telling the truth. Often, students complained that their friends had let them down, or did not return the love and care they had showed towards them. Others complained that friends could not be trusted to keep secrets or tell the truth. Disappointments such as these were assumed to lead to suicidal practices as a way of seeking others to behave more appropriately – that is, as a way of generating forms of relationality and morality of which children wished to be a part.

The survey included space for open-ended written statements, which my assistants later translated. Statements were then matched to students' responses on suicide items, allowing for a greater understanding of suicidal youths' social and emotional worlds. Young people expressed their suicidal sentiments along gender lines and with reference to different kinds of relational groups. For example, Sampath, a seventeen-year-old male student, wrote: 'I want good friends. I will do anything for my friends', indicating a clear desire for improved social relationships, even though this desire was often thwarted. This theme was echoed throughout my research at Udagama and Alutwatta. Young men's social worlds were built around the friendship groups they formed, and from which they drew support across a range of areas of life. Yet because trusted friendships were not forthcoming, a fear of 'cunning' (*kapəṭi*) boys or men loomed large. Asanka, aged seventeen, wrote:

> There are many reasons I do not associate with my classmates. The main one is because I do not trust them. Therefore, I always keep separate from them. I see weaknesses in them.

Although not forming friendship groups akin to those of their male peers, female students displayed a greater concern with the moral conduct of friends and whether or not others should be trusted. Dilini, aged fourteen, explained:

> I like to get along with others and be friendly. This school is not a bad school but I do not like it. Some people in the school do not like me and I do not understand why.

Echoing Dilini, Thilini, aged seventeen, was concerned that: 'Sometimes I am sad. I believe others when I shouldn't and that causes me problems.' Similarly, Annurudika, aged eighteen, wrote: 'Others are selfish.... The problem is that I always trust other people. I hate this society.'

Another area of concern included jealousy. Female students expressed fears that other women were liable to become jealous of academic success or physical beauty. Samadhi, aged seventeen, suggested that for this reason she preferred the company of boys to girls:

> Everyone is selfish. I do not trust many people ... but I am kind to others. Many of my friends are boys because boys are not jealous of others. They do not have any problems.

Often the causes of suicidal practices were associated with unstable family lives and especially parental separation in the context of desertion, migration or death. That is: fathers' or mothers' failures to live up to the normative categories of kinship that define 'good' (*hoňdə*) or 'bad' (*narəkə*) men or women. Both male and female students indicated such concerns. Bandara, a 16-year-old male student, commented:

> I have no parents.... My father died when I was young and I live with my auntie and grandmother. My younger sister's look after my mother, she is ill. My mother does not come to see us.

For him, feelings of abandonment and loss of 'mother's love' was the source of emotional and social disruption in his life. Similarly, Keerthi, an eighteen-year-old man, wrote:

84 *Relational flows*

> Quarrels in my family cause me mental problems. My parents' illnesses also cause me mental problems.

For Keerthi, troubles stemmed from a perceived disorder within his *ge:* and his parents failing to fulfil caring responsibilities due to domestic strife and ill health. The female students I worked with expressed similar concerns. Harshani, aged seventeen, was worried about her family life:

> I cannot forget some problems. I think that my mother and brothers do not love me, I want to go forward with life, but it is very difficult to do it. I feel very lonely because my father is dead.

These written statements provide succinct expressions of youths' narratives of the relational contexts of suicidal practices. In childhood, suicide may be understood as a means for constructing a view of family and friendships that hold significance on *their* terms. Thus, we find children 'innovatively imitating' the pressures put to bear on their lives, their parents and their relationships with others, with suicidal responses interwoven as a method of rebutting or reconciling violence. The implications of children's suicide play are thus extraordinary, both in terms of the way self-harm has manifested as an acceptable and consequential trope through which relational violence may be challenged, but also through which self-harm itself becomes a kind of generative violence that has meaning for the children involved.

Demands of kinship and affinity: suicidal practice in adults and elders

Children's and teenagers' formative experiences of suicidal practice, developed through processes of imitation and innovation, may be understood as establishing the suicide causal frameworks deployed, changed and contested throughout life. In young women and men suicidal practices arose during the transition to married life, and later in older men in response to stresses placed on their role in the *ge:* and in relation to certain kin and affinal relationships. In this section I use four case studies to illuminate relational flows as they relate to violence in and of the home. As with children, and indeed as will have been learned in childhood, the relational violence of suicide stands as a means through which kinship can be stated, claimed, acted, contested and reclaimed.

Case 1: Sidath

The first case concerns Sidath, a thirty-nine-year-old Sinhala Buddhist labourer who swallowed poison after a quarrel with his daughter. The case was investigated by a Kuliyapitiya coroner whose report reflects the shared understanding of suicide as a result of 'family problems', in this case reasoned in light of reports of arguments between Sidath and his nineteen-year-old daughter. The coroner's explanation runs thus:

Daughter (19) said that one day she told father to shave. At that incident, he blamed her and went outside. After a short time, he came back inside and they had another fight. Then he hit her and went outside again. He came back home at about midnight. In the morning, she saw that he was dead after having drunk poison.

Perhaps the most 'remarkable' feature of this case is the 'unremarkable' way in which the coroner reports it. A short series of arguments, with their roots in the daughter telling her father to shave, leads to his death by drinking poison. The significance of the dispute clearly stems however from the subversion of normative rules of *ge:* – a daughter remarking on her father's untidy appearance and the challenge to patriarchy that entails. If we were to apply Spencer's (1990a) theory of suicide and kinship here, wherein the lower status actor is supposed to respond to suicide because direct confrontation with a higher status actor is considered to be impossible, then we would expect the daughter, not the father, to swallow poison. That in this case it was the higher status actor who swallowed poison signals an important feature of suicidal practice: it may be the resort of a patriarchal figure whose status has been subordinated, challenged, contradicted or lost, as much as it may the resort of victims of patriarchal violence. In Sidath's case, the challenge of the daughter laid bare the fact that, in his eyes at least, masculine and paternal norms had been upset. The act of suicide allows Sidath to have the 'final word' on the matter and, even though it comprises his own death, asserts the status of the patriarch once again.

Case 2: Jeromis

The second case concerns Jeromis, a seventy-eight-year-old Sinhala Christian belonging to a local evangelical church. The coroner took two statements, one from his 43-year-old daughter Kamala, and the other from his forty-seven-year-old son Chandra:

> KAMALA [DAUGHTER]: We live separately [from father]. Every day I gave him food and what he wanted. Yesterday we had an argument about some problem. He blamed me badly and told me to leave. After that, I sent his dinner with my son and daughter. Daughter came back and told me that grandfather was hanging from the main beam of the house. I went to see and shouted loudly. The neighbours came.
>
> CHANDRA [SON]: The dead person is my father. His house is about 200 metres from my house. There were no problems between my father and I. I go to see him whenever I am free and he comes to see us. I heard a shout from father's house at about 7 p.m. I went there and saw that there were a few other men near the house. When I got there, my father was hanging from a beam inside the house and was dead. Before this case, he had taken poison to commit suicide but at that time, we could save him. I do not know why he hung himself.

For Kamala, Jeromis' suicide was the result of a quarrel between them both, during which Kamala said Jeromis blamed her. The subject of the dispute is not mentioned, and neither is whatever Kamala may have said to Jeromis and vice versa. Chandra begins his statement by denying any quarrels with Jeromis – indeed, he paints a picture of a good family life in which son pays proper respects to his father – but does go on to report that Jeromis had in fact swallowed poison in the past. From the evidence available, the case would appear similar to that of Sidath: a dispute between father and daughter upsets the status relationship between them and it is the higher status of the two, who feels his position has been attacked, who commits suicide.

Case 3: Mary

In late 2005 I heard about the hanging of a seventy-two-year-old widow Mary, who lived in Udagama. People in the village narrated the story of her suicide through the lens of labour migration, quarrels between Mary and her son Harsha, aged forty-five, and Harsha and his sisters and sister's sons, and the stresses and strains of the *pura:ṇə ge:*. However, the ways in which people made sense of these relationships and the ways in which people said they contributed to Mary's suicide were not uniform, but fell into two camps. One camp explained Mary's suicide as the result of her own failure to care for Harsha, while the other camp explained Mary's suicide as the fault of Harsha's remarriage. From neighbours and friends I was told that Harsha himself blamed both his mother and his sisters' sons. These differences were also expressed by Mary's own relatives, with Harsha's second wife, Stella, blaming Mary, but Harsha's sisters and sisters' sons blaming Harsha. In this way, the disputes which were said to have led up to and caused Mary's suicide continued after her death, where they created further arguments and divisions among family members. During my fieldwork I spoke to Stella and one of Harsha's sister's sons about the events, as they saw them, leading up to Mary's hanging, as well as to fellow villagers who, as usual, were keen to share their theories as to what happened.

Stella's narrative began with the history of her relationship with Harsha, whom she met while working in Kuwait. Stella explained the circumstances of their relationship:

> My husband [Harsha] had been married once before me.... After he married he went abroad for a job and she [the first wife] had an affair. When he found out about it he divorced her. He gives her money every month for their children. When I was working in Kuwait I met him and we became friends. He told me his problems and told me that he liked to marry me. I accepted, and after a few weeks we came back to Sri Lanka to get married. Our parents supported our marriage. We lived here in Mary's house. We started a chicken farm.

Stella's account describes a common situation in Madampe, where migration is seen to lead to marital breakdown due to one or both partner's infidelities.

However, according to Stella's version of events the breakdown of the first marriage had not been especially fraught, and Harsha maintained his responsibilities towards the children. But things became more complicated when Mary admitted to having known about the affair and, instead of telling Harsha, gossiped to neighbours:

> When my husband was not at home his mother told me about his ex-wife and children. She told me that she had had another affair with a different man but she didn't tell this to my husband. She did tell our neighbours and they told my husband. He was angry with his mother for not telling him about his ex-wife's bad behaviour. It was a shame for [Mary] not to tell my husband.

Stella explained how Mary had failed in her motherly responsibilities towards Harsha by allowing the affair to continue, and helping it to become public knowledge. Harsha only learned about the affair because his neighbours had told him. Because of this the relationship between Mary and Harsha soured, and became increasingly confrontational. Stella described an apparently quite trivial argument between Mary and Harsha the day she committed suicide:

> [Mary] blamed my husband because he picked some coconuts from her tree. [His] elder sister came and also blamed my husband. She warned him not to blame their mother. Then sister's sons came and argued with my husband. They hit husband with a bar and his mother and I tried to save him. Mother fell down and then the neighbours came and solved the problem. Mother was very upset and was crying. At about 7 p.m. I was watching TV and sister came and asked where mother was. I told her that mother was at home. We tried to find her but couldn't and she didn't answer our calls. Then we saw her hanging from a tree next to the well.

According to Stella's narrative, Mary hanged herself simply because Harsha had taken a coconut from her garden; a perfectly reasonable act that led to a full-blown family row culminating in an attack on Harsha by his sister's sons. Stella told me she thought Mary hanged herself because she was afraid her grandsons would kill Harsha. Thus, while the precipitating event that spiralled towards Mary's suicide was a very minor discretion (and in Madampe minor discretions were often cited as the cause of suicide), what seems clear is that the event worked to bring into focus a long history of family conflicts centred upon Harsha that finally boiled over into a significant family feud that Mary sought to dampen down through her own death.

Contrasted to Stella's narrative was that told by Mary's grandson Kasun, aged twenty-one, Harsha's sister's son. Kasun stressed that although the family knew Harsha's first wife was having an affair, Mary didn't know about it. While Stella suggested that Harsha had heard about it when he was still in Kuwait and separated from her then, Kasun told me that in fact Harsha hadn't known until he returned to Sri Lanka – by which time, of course, he had met Stella:

> Mother's brother [ma:ma:] married a lady from Galmuruwa [a local village].... This was his first marriage and he had two children. All of them lived at [grandmother's] house and uncle had gone abroad to do a job. Meanwhile we got to know that uncle's wife was having an affair but [grandmother] didn't know about it. After uncle came back to Sri Lanka he quarrelled with his wife. He hit her and blamed her and told her to leave the house. [Grandmother] was upset about this because she loved his children. Then uncle quarrelled even more with grandmother.

Kasun's depiction of Harsha's marital problems was less favourable than Stella's, indicating a series of quarrels with Mary. Kasun also told me about the immediate circumstances leading to Mary's suicide, which differed substantially from Stella's account:

> Yesterday uncle quarrelled with [grandmother]. My mother went to uncle's home and blamed him. Uncle quarrelled with my mother and my younger brothers quarrelled with uncle. The neighbours then came and solved the problem. [Grandmother] was very upset about all this. She came to our home at about 6.30 p.m. and asked for mother. I told her that mother hadn't come yet. She asked me to keep something for her but at that time I was working and so asked her to put it on the table. When mother came home I told her that [grandmother] had left something on the table. I then saw that it was some money and earrings. Then mother went to try and find her. After a while when mother had not come back I went to uncle's house. When I got there, mother was crying and said that [grandmother] had hung herself.

Kasun's story omitted any mention of the coconut or the assault on Harsha by the sister's sons. Instead, Harsha is depicted as a confrontational man who argued with everyone, including Mary, until she could bear it no longer. If Stella sought to lay blame ultimately with Mary, Kasun laid blame with Harsha. Yet beyond this, both narratives centred the causes of Mary's suicide on family disputes with a genesis in labour migration and marital breakdown, and ideal kin relationships comprising the 'good family life', including the roles of the 'nurturing' mother and mother's brother, and 'dutiful' roles of the son and sister's sons. In their own ways, Stella and Kasun both accused individual family members of acting out of turn, of exhibiting unjustified pride and lack of shame. Stella's version depicted Mary and the sister's sons in this way, while Kasun's story suggested that it was Harsha who behaved inappropriately. As such, both chart spiralling quarrels as the cause of the suicide.

Case 4: Pradeep

This case concerns Pradeep, aged forty-two, who had migrated from Alutwatta to Italy for work for a couple of years. I was able to interview Pradeep directly, and also heard several different stories from other Alutwatta villagers. Both sets of narratives explored the problems that are said to arise between wives' brothers and sisters' husbands in the context of a sudden and rapid improvement in one party's financial status and standard of living. Pradeep explained that he had been working in Italy for a number of years in various menial jobs, but had managed to save a large amount of money by Alutwatta standards. Unlike other men, Pradeep told me, he resisted the urge to fritter away his money on expensive liquor and visits to brothels but instead saved what he earned, so by the time he returned to Madampe he had built up a large amount of capital. However, upon his return Pradeep began quarrelling with his wife's brothers (*massina*), who complained that Pradeep was failing to share his new-found wealth with them:

> When I came back to Sri Lanka everyone thought I was a rich man. My wife's brothers [*massina*] began asking me for help [*udav*]. In Sri Lanka when you have even just a little money your relatives will ask you for help and it's difficult to say no. So because of that I did help them. But then they blamed me for not helping them more. They said, 'you are our sister's husband [*massina*] you should help us'.

Although apparently semi-teetotal when he was in Italy, like many men in Madampe, Pradeep came to spend a large part of his spare time in the local bar ('Chinese Restaurant'), 'giving parties' to select male friends. For Pradeep these parties were an important source of social, emotional and moral support, providing a space to discuss his problems with trusted acquaintances in an area of exclusive male sociality. The parties represented a significant drain on his finances, but Pradeep valued them for the opportunities to relax and 'solve my problems', as he put it. However, Pradeep did not invite his wife's brothers to these parties, and because of this, Pradeep said, they became jealous:

> Those men started to blame me for spending my money on parties rather than helping them. They wanted to start a garment business, selling clothes in Chilaw. But how can I help them? They want four lakh [Rs.400,000, about £2,000]!

Despite Pradeep's apparent wealth, he felt unwilling to give his *massina* the money, even as a loan. I often heard men in Madampe lament how their own male relatives – and wives' brothers especially – are 'uneducated' and 'can't help', which implies not only a financial burden but a contravention of the assumption that *massina* support one another. Pradeep was no different, telling me that the reason he did not want to help his wife's brothers was because he could not believe they had the business acumen to spend his money wisely, or to make a profit.

The quarrels continued, until one day, some six months after his return from Italy, Pradeep's wife's brothers came to him and blamed him for wasting his money on parties that produced no good, and for risking their sister's financial livelihood as a result. That day Pradeep had been drinking at lunchtime with his friends in the local bar. Pradeep told me he felt angered by their accusations, and after his wife's brothers had left he swallowed nine or ten tablets of paracetamol. The dose was low but hospitalised him for a couple of days. Pradeep told me that he swallowed the paracetamol because he had grown tired (*mahansi*) of his wife's brothers' badgering of him, which was making him feel shame, and of being a bad *massina* to them. But Pradeep also told me that in fact he did not feel he owed any duty of care to his wife's brothers; they were poor (*duppat*) and unable to reciprocate: because of this there was no requirement for Pradeep to give them any more support.

Pradeep's self-harm may be read through the axioms of the *massina* relationship: a subject of much anthropological interest in Sri Lanka (Leach 1961; Tambiah 1965; Yalman 1967). Madampe people spoke about *massina* relationships as if they were defined by a relationship of equality, and the slang term of *massina*, '*maçaŋ*', used to refer to close male friends, also applies to strong amity and egalitarianism. In practice however, true *massina* relationships are rendered unequal by the nature of the marriage relationship (Stirrat 1975, 1982). Marriages are never, or are at least very rarely, between equals. Some extent of caste and class hypergamy is always assumed to exist, if only by virtue of the unequal relationship between 'wife receivers' and 'wife givers' that is created by the understanding of marriage as an exchange of daughters directed by material concerns.

These status differentials are complicated by the on-going duty of care that is supposed to be shown by brothers to married sisters. On the one hand, and resembling 'true' hypergamy, sisters' husbands are perceived as being of higher status than wives' brothers. On the other hand, sisters' husbands not only owe a duty of care to their wives, but also a duty of respect to their wives' brothers. In this way, the deference typically shown by wife givers to wife receivers is reversed, and the structural logic of hypergamy breaks down. This duty comes in several forms, the most important of which involves providing economic, social and political support. Under such circumstances, disputes may arise between *massina* if the higher status sisters' husband does not provide for their lower status wives' brothers, which is exactly what happened in Pradeep's case.

The argument between Pradeep and his *massina* was sparked and exacerbated by the fact of Pradeep's migration overseas. Like many of his Alutwatta neighbours, migration provided Pradeep with a means to new sources of wealth and this was transforming material relations and expectations in the *estate*. Therefore, when Pradeep returned from Italy an apparently wealthy man, it was incumbent upon him to provide for his higher status *massina*, the wife givers. Yet, in Pradeep's eyes it was he, not them, who had risen in stature and thus Pradeep felt little obligation to help his poorer relatives, who he felt would be unable to reciprocate in any meaningful sense. While Mary's suicide was aimed at 'preserving' what is an assumed social order of middle-class respectability and individualised *pura:ṇə ge:* in Udagama, Pradeep's self-harm was an attempt to counter the assumptions of *estate ge:* relations and extended kinship prevalent in Alutwatta. The conflicts that arose in the wake of Pradeep's return to

Madampe may all be read as attempts to remake the kinship order in two opposing ways: the first for the desire of Pradeep's *massina*, and the second for the desire of Pradeep himself.

Suicide and violence 'in and of' the family

In this chapter I have described the relationship between suicide, gender, generation and violence 'in and of' the family. In so doing I have written against the trend in Sri Lankan anthropology and sociology that situates violence as caused by kinship to situate violence as a cause of kinship. As people in Madampe live through suicide, the world is created around them. When suicidal practices are used to put the idea of death into other people's minds, it would 'make sense' to do so – or at least would only be the most effective – when those other minds are significantly related to suicidal ego. The relationships identified by suicidal people are the relationships considered worth dying for.

Relational flows of suicidal practice are shaped by everyday conflicts that arise in response to 'big' questions concerning 'good family lives'. Across the life-course and between middle-class and working-class households in *pura:ṇə* and *estate* communities, the kinds of relationships likely to produce potentially fatal conflicts differ for women and men, and children, youth and adults. In children and young teenagers, strong moral demands and expectations are placed on friends, siblings and parents. By adulthood, however, friendships lose their importance to be replaced instead by marriage relationships, *ge:* relationships, and the demands made by specific kin and affines. Always holding in mind an image of what was once or should be the 'good family', theories of suicidality generated throughout the village arena and regenerated in the records of courts and clinics reflect both evidence of, and ethos for, kinds of suicidal practice rooted in the struggles of children, parents and elders seeking to make sense of the changing world around them.

Thus, the forms of violence surrounding and encompassing Mary's suicide were imagined by Mary's family through an idiom of social breakdown. Yet what also stands out is the ways in which violence is also integral to family life and of realising idealised kin relationships. Quarrels and blaming are the standard currency of relationality, being used to set and test limits of kinship in various ways and to press into existence preferred ways of living and relating. The cases of Sidath, Jeromis, Mary and Pradeep each illustrate how suicidal acts can be used to state and restate one's own position and the position of others in the *ge:*. The more socially, morally, historically or financially valuable the relationship is supposed to be, the more troublesome and violent it becomes as struggles to make kinship escalate into suicidal acts. Violence is not destructive of the relational order but constitutive of it; suicide 'makes' the relationships the act is supposedly rejecting. Thus, suicidal practices generate kinship fictions, which come to pass as kinship facts.

The linkages between suicide and kinship pose important questions for the understanding of kinship more generally. Anthropological kinship studies come with a long and complex history and a summary is beyond the scope of this chapter. However, the recent work by Marshall Sahlins (2011a, 2011b, 2013) has sought to both condense that history into a digestible argument and to pose new possibilities for theoretical and empirical development. Sahlins's main idea is that kinship should be approached in terms of a 'mutuality of being'. That is to say, kinship is what people say constitutes the core, valuable relationships between themselves and specific others – kinship constitutes what Sahlins (1965) had earlier called a form of 'generalised reciprocity'. This idea has been expressed by a range of anthropologists, including Meyer Fortes (1969, 1978, 1983), who through a series of contributions spoke of kinship in terms of 'prescriptive altruism' – a relationship of 'sharing without reckoning' – within an 'axiom of amity'.

Maurice Bloch (1973) provided a further theorisation of the idea that kinship constitutes a space of positive moral life in which selfish interests are cast aside for altruistic communality. Bloch proposed that what appears to constitute a relationship of 'sharing without reckoning' is often better understood as a moral gloss put upon what might be a highly unequal and exploitative relationship. Bloch (ibid.) argued that relationships seemingly defined by a morality of 'sharing without reckoning' often involve a high degree of 'take' by one party from another over the long term. Yet sentiments of kinship not only allow for the obfuscation of this fact but also provide the moral rationale for its existence: simply put, 'it's what family's do'. Thus, the moral implication of 'mutuality' is what legitimises in the relational context the exploitation of lower status members at the hands of higher status members. Even so, who owes what to whom and when such debts are to be repaid is a problem which in practice rests in the eye of the beholder. The patriarchal (or matriarchal) figure may equally feel hard done by, and be hard done by.

Thus, suicide stands in relation to the contradictions and violence of mutuality in different ways. First, suicide may in fact be understood as a 'denial of sociality' or mutuality in the sense that to take one's own life is to remove oneself from the axiom of amity, using methods of what might sometimes be called enmity. In Madampe, as we have seen, women and children may use suicide as a challenge to patriarchy and a way of seeking redress against some of the most violent excesses of kin morality. Second, and conversely, suicide exists as a way in which mutuality is affirmed and amity generated, again through methods of enmity. Just as kinship as mutuality and amity rests on a disguise of significant gender and generational inequality, suicide disguises the normative bases for violence through an act of violence committed against the self. Thus the suicidal practices of men, arising in contexts wherein patriarchal norms have been questioned, restate a demand for (women's and children's) 'sharing without reckoning', and the perpetuation of domestic servitude. The suicidal practices of women, arising in contexts of domestic violence or family breakdown, may make an equal claim for compassion, release or resolve. These patterns will be evident throughout later cases described in this book, and are found to be integral to the explanation of suicide processes across Madampe.

Insights for prevention

Summary of the argument

- Suicide is often linked to, and may be understood as a form of, *relational violence*, including gender and domestic violence. Suicide may arise as a *response to violent abuse* or as a means of *expressing violence*.
- It is important to consider how relational violence and suicide may not simply be the result of 'social decay' or 'loss of social institutions' but also as *a crucial practice through which social relations are defined and managed*.
- Relational flows of suicidal practice reflect and generate *normative kinship ideologies* and typically overlay only those relationships that are considered 'worth dying for'.
- Women and men, and children, youth and adults may *all be at risk* from relational violence and suicide. *Gender analysis* of suicide should focus on men as well as women and consider the power dynamics of each.

Practical applications

- Understanding the *local ideologies and practices of relationality* can help to configure which kinds of relationship may be *more likely to produce suicidal responses* when they run into problems.
- Some kin relationships may be considered '*high risk*' and others '*low risk*'. High-risk relationships may include those between *hierarchically unequal* family members in terms of gender, age and social status. Low risk may include *lateral relationships*.
- In contexts of rapid *social and political change* family and kin relationships are often placed under additional pressure as reconfigurations of gender, age and social status come about. This may *transform high- and low-risk relationships*.
- The meeting of 'modern' ideas around *gender and child equality* in the home or workplace with 'traditional' ideals of patriarchy and age grade may be a particularly important *flashpoint* in the generation of suicidal practices.

Notes

1 *Sudu* (white) is a term used by men to refer to attractive young women. The term implies 'purity' in two senses: sexual, and, because fair skin is considered to be the most beautiful, tonal.
2 In order to map relational flows I analysed case files according to the relationships identified between the suicidal person (ego) and those people in his or her network said to have been the cause of the act. Relationships were coded according to marital status of ego (unmarried ego = parent, male/female sibling, other relatives, friends/neighbours, boyfriend/girlfriend; married ego = parent, own children, male/female sibling, other relatives, in-laws, friends/neighbours, paramours). In some cases more than one relationship was identified (e.g. dispute with wife and dispute with children). Results were managed using Microsoft Excel and overall patterns constructed as kinship diagrams using Genopro.

3 This element of research proceeded through the same channels as others. I obtained parental approval to speak with the children but did not take notes as part of the process. At the time of my fieldwork, no special ethical approval needed to be sought for this kind of work, although I believe that this has now changed.

5 Suffering, frustration, anger

I felt anger and drank poison.
　　　　　　　　Female self-harm patient, Chilaw Mental Health Clinic

Relational flows of suicide *here* generate their own emotional flows, which in turn generate relational flows of suicidal practice and suicide representations. Evidence concerning the psychological basis of suicide in Sri Lanka has been subject to debate, with some researchers agreeing that deep-seated psychological illnesses like depression do not account for the majority of cases in Sri Lanka (Marecek 1998), and others arguing that it does (Samaraweera *et al.* 2008). This difference may be understood as one more example of a much wider and long-running debate in anthropology and psychology concerning what the nineteenth-century polymath Adolf Bastian called 'the psychic unity of mankind'. The resulting arguments among various schools of thought concerning the cultural specificity or universality of human cognition and psychological states like depression and the use value of psychiatry more generally have been a focus of sustained contention, as I have already described in Chapter 1.

In this chapter, I approach this controversy through an examination of the ontological grounds that give rise to particular theories of suicide in Madampe incorporating emotional and psychological practices. Rather than using the Sri Lankan example as a tool with which to support or deny one approach or another, my interest instead is to explore how practices of suicide and the violence of kinship manifest particular emotional and psychological states. Instead of asking, '*is* suicide an expression of psychopathology, the question becomes, '*under what conditions* might suicide become psychopathological, and for whom?' The answer, I will suggest, is when suicide comes to question dominant narratives of the family: that is, when suicide begins to expose the inequalities of mutuality in Madampe *ge:*, from the subject positions of male and female youth, adults, and elders.

Thus, the chapter examines how practices of suicide *here* are generated from particular kinds of emotional problems that correspond with gender, generational and status concerns. Drawing from accounts of self-harm and suicide collected from village, court and clinical arenas, my aim is to follow the explanations of my informants to develop the outlines of an emotional model of suicidal practice which links everyday quarrels to specific psychological states: 'suffering' (*dukə*), 'frustration' (*asəhane*) and 'anger' (*tarəha*). The model I present is an abstraction of disparate cases that by themselves demonstrate the high degree of crossover that I have already stressed is a crucial feature of suicidal practice in Madampe. In so doing, I am seeking to overlay a local theory of suicidality that starts to draw together those disparate threads and present a common logic: namely that states of 'suffering' lead to 'frustrations' which can lead to 'anger', at each point producing different kinds of suicidal practice. My case for doing so is not to deny the ambiguities of practice I have already described, but rather to show how shared experiences of economic and social life produce common stories of affect: that varied interpretations are held together by a shared 'cognitive map' of how social conditions produce emotional experiences and attendant suicidal responses.

In a short article on the emotions of suicidal practice among Sinhala speakers, de Silva (1989) provides a glossary of terms associated with different psychological states. De Silva's review points to the richness of Sinhala emotional languages, and of how I, being only conversant in Sinhala, had little chance of mastering them. This chapter explores the significance of three terms indicating emotional problems that are routinely associated with suicidal practice in Madampe: suffering, frustration and anger. Despite their commonality, however, I do not wish to suggest that these were the only terms people used to describe suicidal practices, or that they were the only important ones. I also do not wish to suggest that alternative interpretations to those I have given here do not exist. Rather, I aim to show how they point to particular emotional problems associated with particular kinds of suicide committed by particular kinds of people. In fact, they could be described as words standing for broader idioms that catch a range of other words and ideas, convening around emotional experiences that have a particular processual logic in Madampe.

That said, I also believe that the terms hold an additional significance with regard to understanding suicide because since the nineteenth century they have been taken up by successive governments as suitable words to describe and thus tackle the suicide epidemic. The interplay of folk and official discourses has, I suggest, given the model of suffering, frustration and anger developed in this chapter a particular coherence. On the one hand, the model reflects popular Buddhist and Ayurvedic concerns of bodily reactions to social experiences, including states of coolness and heat in their corporeal-emotional manifestations (Kusumaratne 2005: 179–185). On the other hand, the model reflects academic psychosocial concerns developed in the 'frustration-aggression' hypothesis that I described in Chapter 2. Any discussion of suffering, frustration and anger in Madampe thus needs to be contextualised within this broader national and international, governmental and academic, world. At the same time, the folk model needs to be recognised for its role in operations of power and inequality along gender, generation and class lines, and the academic model needs to be understood as a suicidological model developed in and for a very different social context (Widger 2012b; see also Chapter 8, this volume).

Emotional flows of suicide stories told in Madampe

Alongside the everyday conflicts that people report as causes of suicidal practice, there existed a set of folk suicide stories by which people in Madampe sought to make sense of, and lay claim to, the causes and consequences of suicide *here*. In their narratives of suicidal practice informants often turned to a well-rehearsed triad of phrases, including 'suffering' (*dukə*), 'frustration' (*asəhane*) and 'anger' (*tarəha*), when seeking to explain the emotional states associated with them. This was the case for suicidal people themselves, as well as those who dealt with the aftermath, either within the arena of the village or of courts and clinics. Moreover, the phrases also appeared within more general discussions of suicide, and existed as a means by which suicide threats, self-harm and self-inflicted deaths could be talked about in the abstract.

As a trio of 'popular' phrases, then, the terms 'suffering', 'frustration' and 'anger' peppered conversations and at that level they have had very amorphous representations. In some ways they were used interchangeably, as Madampe people knew that by referring to 'suffering' one's interlocutors would fill in the other two by themselves; the same may be said for when one is speaking of 'frustration' and 'anger'. As emotional states, suffering, frustration and anger were said to exist as feelings possible to experience individually, but also oftentimes cumulatively. Conditions giving rise to suffering, if left unaddressed, are said to flow into frustrations of two distinct kinds – 'mental' (*ma:nəsikə*) and 'sexual' (*lingikə*) – which can, if left to ferment and be suddenly provoked, erupt into 'sudden anger' (*ikmaŋ tarəha*). In fact, 'suffering, frustration and anger' may be understood as amounting to a total model of mental and physical health in Madampe. As will be seen, certain kinds of problems and misfortunes are assumed to set in motion predictable mental and physical consequences of suffering, frustration and anger along gender and class lines.

The trajectory from suffering to anger is understood as one of flowing from a state of relative mental and physical coolness and individual and social stability to one of extreme heat and individual and social instability (cf. Beck 1969). In Madampe, as indeed across Sri Lanka and South Asia more generally (Daniel 1984; McGilvray 1998; Nichter 1987; Obeyesekere 1984; Osella and Osella 1996; Trawick 1992), excessive heat is associated with temper, violence and impulsivity; coolness with calmness, peacefulness and steadiness. These are also qualities associated with women and the working *estate* class on the one hand, and men and the middle *pura:ṇə* class on the other hand. Cool behaviour is marked by quietness, reason and fear of shame: the qualities of 'good' *pura:ṇə* men and women. Hot behaviour is marked by loudness, irrationality, passion and the absence of shame: the qualities of 'bad' *estate* men and women. While by definition all suicidal acts are 'hot' to some extent, suffering suicides are considered cooler – and therefore calmer, more peaceful and more rational – than frustration or anger suicides – which in turn are considered more violent, more impulsive and more irrational.

The journey from suffering to frustration to anger may be viewed as one of increasing heat and of passing from a cool, male, *pura:ṇə*, middle-aged state to a hot, female, *estate*, youthful, even childlike, state. As heat increases, behaviour becomes more volatile and unpredictable, and so passes from one side of the set of gender, class and age binaries to the other. It is in this sense that the terms suffering, frustration and anger become more specific when used in relation to suicidal behaviour, and not only say things about the suicidal person's social status but also enable the suicidal person to say something him- or herself about social status – whether to affirm it or to challenge it. States of suffering, frustration and anger that are expressed through suffering suicide, frustration suicide and anger suicide become reflections of status positions within the social hierarchy, as well as ways of supporting or denying the hierarchy. Claims of suffering, frustration and anger are thus 'structured and structuring' claims standing for an absence or expression of agency.

Suffering suicide

The emotion of suffering is said by people in Madampe to be experienced widely, as an almost inevitable condition of 'modern' life. For Madampe people, the idea of suffering evokes a kind of mental distress arising from myriad everyday and more unusual problems. Suffering also implies a kind of 'sorrow' or 'hopelessness' at an inability to change things in the world, from interpersonal disputes to 'the rising cost of living' to the 2004 tsunami. Politicians have noticed this, often framing policies and initiatives as efforts to 'reduce the suffering of the people'.[1] In these more general contexts, suffering is said to be experienced collectively by the nation at large and to be caused by major impersonal forces such as 'the economy' or 'globalisation'. Such refrains are heard throughout Madampe, among both old and young: 'the cost of living rises every day, that is why we are suffering', said one thirteen-year-old boy I knew, echoing his parents' fears, but also those of his own.

Suffering in these normative senses is not thought of as being likely to lead to any particularly extreme social or emotional response. Everybody suffers; it is just the way of the world, and one must get by as best one can. In this way suffering, as the first of four Noble Truths of Buddhism, is a religious expression (Obeyesekere 1981, 1985, 1990), but one that is found too among the Roman Catholics. And indeed for some, release or salvation from suffering may be achieved through religion, in the ways that Obeyesekere (1985) and Stirrat (1992) have described. As Obeyesekere (1985) has suggested, through religious practices including possession states, suffering can be attached to and transformed by religious concepts, which offer a framework for understanding and so managing feelings of suffering, and thus 'getting by' in life. Stirrat (1992) recorded how some Sinhala Catholics similarly appeased their own suffering through participation in religious practices. In Madampe, however, resort to supernatural explanations and solutions for suicide was extremely rare, and I only chanced upon a couple of cases. The vast majority of suicides were understood as having mundane causes that required mundane solutions.

Sometimes, however, suffering exceeds normative expectations, and can then become excessive. The excessive (as opposed to populist-religious) experience of suffering is what people in Madampe say can lead to frustration and anger; excessive suffering is also said to be a cause of suicide. Excessive suffering includes a range of *unmanageable* negative feelings such as helplessness, hopelessness and worthlessness, and attendant somatic complaints such as sleeplessness, loss of appetite, and cold and flu symptoms. All of these complaints can be brought on by the actions or demands of others. In Madampe, it is men and the high-status *pura:ŋə* class, and *pura:ŋə* class men in particular, who are thought to be most at risk of such 'suffering suicides'. One reason that people in Madampe give for this is men's general lack of participation in religious activity and family life when compared to that of women, which people say means that men are less able to cope with their problems and so suffer excessively. As one mental health clinician commented:

> Men have so many problems, much more than women or children.... But they do not have any kind of support. They do not go to the temple, and they do not stay at home. They just go to the bar and drink.

There is, however, another reason for *pura:ŋə* class men's association with suffering suicide and this derives from the ways in which men may legitimately express excessive suffering at all. Men's absence from the temple is one indication of this, as is the way in which suffering suicides tend to be practised. Public declarations of excessive suffering, be it through religious expression or public acts of self-harm, are thought to be wholly inappropriate expressions for *pura:ŋə* class men to engage. As discussed by Gombrich and Obeyesekere (1988), devotional forms of Buddhism have been rejected by the middle class more generally and the *pura:ŋə* class in Madampe in particular, who have adopted instead a highly personalised and constrained approach to religious practice. The comportment expected by and of *pura:ŋə* class men, in both religious and social life, is one of 'calm and quiet' contentment (*səhane*). When problems or misfortunes do occur, 'respectable' men must deal with them without recourse to bother and fuss, but rather through a determined yet unstated action. This may be through a private act of worship at home or through an act of self-destruction that should also be subtle and leave little trace. Suffering suicides are, then, typically also 'private' suicides, a fact that makes them more likely to be lethal.

A final issue concerning the appearance of *pura:ŋə* class men's suffering suicides is that of men's status within the household (*ge:*). The normative structure of the bourgeois *ge:* places men in the position of patriarch, and this position is assumed to be unquestionable. But questioned it very often is, both by wives' status which makes them decidedly more powerful within the domestic realm than men, and also by children, whose own behaviours often run counter to the expectations which fathers lay down. Wives' power is especially important in terms of the domestic economy as it is she, and not the male wage earner, who decides how money should be spent, and this often causes considerable disputes.

However, when problems for men surmount as a result of their status being challenged, it is 'inappropriate' for them to react in any overt kind of way. As men in Madampe would see it, such a response would not only be accepting the premise of their lost status, but would also draw attention to it. Far better, then, to withdraw quietly, through an act of suicide. Patriarchy is, in this sense, a 'dead-end' that acts as a structural constraint on men's actions.

These three issues – a lack of social support, expectations of 'calm and quiet' responses to problems, and the 'dead-end of patriarchy' – conflate to encourage men to commit acts of suffering suicide. Suffering suicides are acts of desperation in that the causes of suicide are seen to exist beyond human manipulation. Reflecting this, suffering suicides are best understood as a means of escape from problems, rather than a means of engagement with problems. Two case studies illustrate this. The first suggests how suffering can become excessive and by itself lead to a 'quiet' and private act of suicidal behaviour; the second suggests how challenges to a man's status within the *ge:* lead to a withdrawn private act of suicidal behaviour.

Case 5: Roshan

This case passed through the Chilaw Clinic and provides an especially clear illustration of suffering suicide and, indeed, of suffering suicide's proximity with clinicians' own estimations of what causes 'depressive suicide' (see Widger (2012b) for an explanation). Roshan was one of the few patients who returned to the clinic for follow-up treatment and was regarded by clinicians as a shining example of how effective psychiatric and psychopharmacological interventions could reduce suicidality. Roshan's frequent visits to the clinic meant that I not only had the chance to observe several consultations but also, through the clinician, to direct some of my own questions as well.

Roshan was a twenty-two-year-old Sinhala Buddhist man who upon leaving school with three A levels obtained an apprenticeship under a welder in a garage. Although not of the same status as a government or private sector white-collar job, welding is a relatively well-paid skill in Sri Lanka, and as such Roshan's prospects looked good. This was all the more important, as a few years previously Roshan's mother had migrated to the Middle East to work as a housemaid, and had not been seen or heard from since. Roshan's father, who lacked any formal education at all and was already pushed to make a living good enough to provide for Roshan and his three younger siblings, subsequently became very distressed and began drinking heavily. With responsibilities for the three younger children now falling on Roshan, the four of them went to live with their paternal grandmother. However, she was ill and dying, and found it increasingly difficult to cope with caring for her grandchildren while also dealing with her drunken son, who often visited the house and, according to Roshan, 'caused problems'.

Roshan's apprenticeship as a welder ended and he subsequently obtained a full-time position in the same garage. In time, Roshan began a love affair with his employer's sister's daughter, an eighteen-year-old woman named Thilini. Roshan and Thilini conducted their affair for around six months before Roshan's employer, Thilini's mother's brother, discovered it. Thinking the relationship inappropriate, he demanded that it stop, and blamed Thilini for her indiscretions. He also threatened Roshan with unemployment if he insisted on pursuing the affair. Caught between his desire to show his love for Thilini and his equally important financial responsibilities with regard to his siblings and grandmother, Roshan told me that he felt to be 'suffering on all sides', and attempted suicide.

The suicidal act practised by Roshan was, as a suffering suicide, quiet and private. Roshan bought several packets of paracetamol from a local shop and returned home to swallow them in his bedroom. Somewhat incredibly, Roshan then went out again to play cricket with some friends. During that time, Roshan never told anyone about what he had done, but returned home just as he began to feel ill. He did not stop in the shared spaces of the house, and refused to eat any dinner, saying that he felt tired and wanted to go to sleep. However, during the night Roshan's vomiting (whether this was self-induced or not, Roshan would not say) woke his siblings, and upon discovering that he was ill they called a taxi and rushed him to hospital. According to the medical staff treating Roshan that night, he had tried to refuse help, saying that he wanted to be left to die. However, the intervention was successful, and Roshan survived. Before going into further analysis of this case, I present a second to add further illumination to the issues involved.

Case 6: Thilakarathna

A Kuliyapitiya coroner investigated this case. Thilakarathna, a Sinhala Buddhist male aged in his forties, committed suicide following a dispute with his wife. The local coroner collected the wife's statement, which I reproduce here.

> The dead man is my husband. We married sixteen years ago. I have two sons. My husband was an alcoholic. He had been addicted to arrack for five years. He quarrelled with me four days ago [four days before the suicide took place] because he asked me for some money [for drinking] but I didn't give him any. After that he took money by force and went out. He came back after four days and he asked for two sarongs and shirts. The doors of the house were locked but I didn't open them. I opened a window and gave him the [clothes]. After that he went away. I closed the window and went to sleep. Later I went to find him. I got to know he was working at the mine but I didn't go to meet him. I was afraid because I thought he would hit me. I went to the shop to buy some things. That was about five o'clock [in the evening]. Manju, who works with my husband, came and told me that [he] had hanged himself from a tree at the estate [in the coconut plantation]. At that time I didn't go and see his body, it is about half a kilometre from our house. I think that the reason for his death was our family problem [*pavula prashna*, marital quarrels] and his drinking.

While Thilakarathna's wife's statement is of course only a one-sided view, several key elements of suffering suicide are found within it. It was the wife, not the husband, who controlled the flow of household money, and Thilakarathna had to ask his wife for funds in order to go out drinking with his friends. In Madampe, wives' refusals to hand over money for drink often led to suicidal behaviours, although in this case Thilakarathna took the money by force. Nevertheless, in so doing he transgressed an important division of domestic labour within the *ge:*, and did not return home for several days. However, when Thilakarathna did return his wife refused to let him in, instead passing the sarong and shirts through a window. It was at this point that the wife mentioned she was afraid that Thilakarathna would become violent. However, it seems instead that Thilakarathna went to a quiet place in a coconut plantation and killed himself.

Roshan's and Thilakarathna's cases illustrate in different ways the relationship between suicide and kinship as they unfold in men's emotional and psychological experiences. For Roshan this was in relation to his emerging status as an employable young man with prospects, but nevertheless considered not good enough for his employer's niece. For Thilakarathna this was through his exclusion from the *ge:* and his wife's literal claim over the domestic realm. Both cases indicate challenges to the patriarchal order and the limits of 'respectable manhood', and how gender delineates the responses of men to what may be described as two extreme choices. The first would be to engage with the problem faced and in so doing to accept the premise of the challenge – ultimately, to 'give in' to the demands of those they consider have no claim on their actions (those whose visions for the 'good family life' they do not wish to see realised). The second is to play their final hand – to withdraw from the world, and in so doing to negate kinship altogether. In Roshan's case, the latter was taken following conflict with his employer and girlfriend's mother's brother: Roshan's superior by two counts. In Thilakarathna's case, it was the normatively inferior wife and *ge:* that were rejected.

Concerning women's suffering suicides, we find the same kinds of troubles, only this time reversed. If women enjoy a great deal of practical power within the *ge:* then husbands' attempts to challenge or deny it can lead to excessive suffering and suicide. This especially seems to be the case in circumstances in which men become violent towards women. In Madampe, abused women have very few lasting avenues of escape from abusive marriages other than labour migration, with formal separation and divorce very difficult to manage in financial, social and legal terms. While wives' families *will* temporarily take back a woman who has suffered at the hands of her husband, to do so as a final option is never undertaken lightly. A divorced woman's chances of (at least 'respectable') remarriage are low, especially if she already has children. Thus, it is not uncommon to encounter women who have self-harmed repeatedly because of domestic violence, each time returning home to the abusive context.

Case 7: Karunawatti

Karunawatti, aged forty-five, was married with three children. Karunawatti's husband, Gunarathna, was considered by many to be an alcoholic, and indeed he drank *kasippu*, the local illegal homebrew, on a daily basis. In Madampe village society the telling of lies and false gossip (*boru*) is considered something of a pastime, and people often have to deal with malicious stories about themselves or their *ge:* members. Karunawatti and Gunarathna thus were not particularly special; when stories began to be passed around that Karunawatti was having an affair with another man in the village.

However, Gunarathna had been diagnosed by Chilaw mental health clinicians as suffering from 'pathological jealousy', a neurotic disorder commonly found in alcoholic males, in which men develop unfounded suspicions that wives and partners are conducting affairs. In village terms Gunarathna was said to be suffering from jealousies associated with *Kalu Kumara*, the 'Black Prince', a malevolent spirit said to steal away women and more generally standing as an idiom for women's sexuality and the need for its control (see Chapter 7). However designated, Gunarathna's jealousy came to be fuelled by the village gossip he was hearing, and in time he came to accuse Karunawatti of having sexual relations with dozens of men in the village, including her own relatives and even her own father.

Over the course of several months Gunarathna's alcohol-fuelled behaviour became increasingly violent, with verbal abuse spilling over into physical abuse. Feeling trapped by her suffering, Karunawatti said that she began to contemplate committing suicide, and kept packets of painkillers and other medicines in the house. Eventually one day when alone in the house Karunawatti took the tablets, but was discovered by one of her children and taken to hospital. When Karunawatti left hospital, she returned home, apparently with no further attempts being made by herself or others to remedy the abusive home context.

In clinical records, Karunawatti's long-term sufferings are described as the cause of her suicide attempt. Her husband's violent behaviour, even if 'pathological' as Chilaw clinicians had argued, may be understood as an extreme example of how violent acts constitute the *ge:*. As will be discussed below, women's suicidal practices are often associated with 'anger' when they arise in contexts of dispute. In Karunawatti's case, the emotional status of the act was said to be one of 'suffering'. Bringing Karunawatti's suicide into orbit with 'respectable' *pura:ṇa* class and male suicides is the fact that the act of self-harm was conducted privately and quietly. Anger suicides are public suicides, but Karunawatti's act was committed when she was alone. As will be described below, people in Madampe often use this simple distinction to define suffering suicides from frustration suicides and anger suicides. As with Roshan's and Thilakarathna's acts, the suicide is intended as a withdrawal from the situation. The gendered process of suicide however further influences how this transpires. For men, withdrawal may be achieved because it is they who, ultimately, allow the presence or absence of themselves or others in relational terms. For women, withdrawal is never entirely possible, for at least the simple reason that women cannot separate from the *ge:* on terms of their own choosing.

Taken together, these three examples of what may be described as 'suffering suicide' register what might be called a 'depth experience' of suicide. For women and men whose suffering leads to suicide, catharsis cannot be found in the social world but instead in the world of 'cool' introspection and self-destruction. At the beginning of this chapter I asked under what conditions might suicide be associated with psychopathology. In formative terms suffering is arguably very similar to what psychologists might call depression (cf. Obeyesekere 1985), although ordinary people in Madampe would never use that phrase or recognise the biomedical theory associated with it. In any case, for those who perform suffering suicides the meaning of the emotion is not inevitability one of negativity; suffering suicides are not 'depressed' suicides. In Sri Lanka, there is no obvious tradition of 'honour suicides' as might be said to typify some kinds of suicide in other Asian societies, for example, Japan. Instead, suffering suicide may be understood to function as a 'shameless' death and in so doing bestow the actor with a similar reverence as bestows an honourable death. That is, they are cool, quiet and do not seek to disrupt the social order but in fact in many ways to preserve or extend it.

Frustration suicide

Excessive suffering does not always lead to suicidal behaviour, and if not, then people say frustration may develop. Excessive suffering is said to become frustration when it manifests in two distinct experiences of 'mental frustration' or 'sexual frustration', which are also often accompanied by the same kinds of somatic complaints as excessive suffering. Mental and sexual frustrations are therefore understood as the consequences of unchecked kinds of suffering in occupational life and financial matters on the one hand, and love or marriage on the other.

Concerning occupational lives, people in Madampe understand the concept of work and career broadly, encompassing both employment and housework within them. A man's (and increasingly a woman's) failure to find or progress in work is understood as having the same kind of emotional implications as that of a woman (and increasingly a man) who toils 'all day, every day' at her (or his) housekeeping and child-caring chores. Again, feelings of hopelessness and helplessness are paramount here. However, due to their prestige and financial reward, middle-class occupations are not thought of as being very likely to lead to frustration. Although people with respectable and comfortable middle-class jobs in the public or private sectors may have just as many worries as working- or labouring-class people, they would never talk about them in terms of frustration. Working-class people and labourers, however, do talk about their problems in such terms, and of those frustrations as being caused by the hard physical demands and poor financial recompense of their work.

As such, mental frustration and frustration suicides tend to be found most often among working- and labouring-class men and women. An often-crucial cause of frustration is said to be men's failure to make a living, and wives' responses through blaming them for being unproductive or wasteful of household resources. For example, many men practised suicidal behaviours due to financial problems, while others did so because of their inability to repay a loan. In other cases still, men practised suicidal behaviours in order to protest against or prevent wives' decisions to migrate abroad, an act which upsets the gendered division of domestic labour.

Love and marriage, as dependent on success in occupational life as they are on attraction, commitment and family approval, are also understood as carrying risks of frustration should they fail. 'Love' (*a:dərə*) is so viewed because it is often unrequited, or else faces barriers to realisation in Madampe's strict environment that not only prohibits love affairs between youth but also mixed-sex socialisation of almost any kind. For Madampe people, romantic love can often turn into (or already just is) sexual lust; unreleased sexual lust implies sexual frustration. Similarly, marriages are said to fail precisely because they lack sufficient sex. Frequent sexual relations between spouses are considered the essential ingredient in any good family life: it 'provides the oil that greases the machine', men say. Men point out that if sex is removed from marriage, then all of the ordinary stresses and strains of married life, including mental frustration, can take over, and families flounder. For young people suicidal behaviours are especially linked to sexual frustration. The majority of suicide threats, acts of self-harm or self-inflicted deaths of unmarried people that I investigated involved unrequited or lost love in some way.

So, while suffering suicides tend to be practised as a means of 'escape', frustration suicides were more likely to be practised with a more specific kind of social function in mind. For these reasons frustration suicides may be committed either quietly or loudly, privately or publicly, depending principally upon the social status of the person, and how they may be constrained by social conventions that regulate emotional expression. Women and younger people are in positions of normative subordination vis-à-vis husbands and parents respectively, and so for them it is inappropriate to express forms of protest or complaint in direct ways (Spencer 1990a). However, just as in 'working-class' devotional religious practices (Gombrich and Obeyesekere 1988), expressive suicidal behaviours subvert this expectation, and the act gains social and political potency, and the ability to alter normative expectations. In the following cases, several features of both mental and sexual frustration are shown to develop in a married labourer living in Alutwatta on the one hand, and an unemployed graduate living at Udagama on the other.

Case 8: Priyantha

Priyantha had been married for around a year before he began thinking that his wife, Nishani, was becoming 'lazy' (*kammæli*). Priyantha complained that she was 'not cooking rice every day'; an accusation that usually only meant one thing: that Nishani was refusing to have sex with him. This in turn implied that

Nishani was unhappy with him, and probably for a financial reason. Priyantha was a labourer in a coconut fibre mill in the estate, and the meagre pay he earned was barely enough to support his growing family. To plug gaps in the household finances Nishani started talking about migrating overseas. Faced with the strains on his domestic and economic standing (*tatve*) posed by Nishani's plans, Priyantha said that he began developing feelings of sexual and mental frustration.

To relieve his frustrations, Priyantha embarked upon a love affair with a woman whose own husband was working in the Middle East. One day Priyantha arranged to meet his lover in Udagama, from where the two planned to take a three-wheel taxi to a cheap guesthouse. However, Nishani had learned about the affair and this particular meeting, and upon Priyantha's arrival at the rendezvous point she appeared and confronted her husband. Suranga said that Nishani shouted at both him and his lover using 'filthy words', and threatened divorce. The rendezvous point was a bus stand surrounded by a few small shops. Such a public as well as 'aggressive' display of emotion by a woman was quite out of the ordinary. Priyantha told me that as a result 'I felt shame and so drank poison' (*maṭə læjja hituna i:ṭə passe vaha bivva*).

With the episode played out in full view of local residents and passers-by, Priyantha feared that ever-increasing embellishments of the story would circulate around the area, and even back to Alutwatta, which was just two miles away. Priyantha also feared that he would become known as a philanderer and as a man whose wife was unruly and uncontrollable: an equally shaming charge. He ran over to a shop, grabbed a bottle of kerosene oil, and managed to drink about a quarter of it before a bystander intervened. In the commotion that followed Priyantha did not notice what had happened to Nishani, but it was apparently his lover who called for a three-wheel taxi and rushed him to the hospital nearby. There Priyantha received medical treatment and was kept on the ward for two days, upon which he was discharged in good health. After leaving hospital, he returned home to Nishani and ended his affair; a few months afterwards his lover travelled to the Middle East to join her husband. Since then, Priyantha told me, Nishani had become less 'lazy', cooked rice every day, and was now generally 'good' all round.

Although stories about the suicide attempt did indeed spread across the Madampe Division, there was little by way of criticism as far as Priyantha's own conduct was concerned. Priyantha's philandering was routinely described as an unfortunate but still perfectly understandable consequence of his frustrations. On the other hand, Nishani's angry outburst at the Udagama bus stand was seen as an entirely unreasonable response to Priyantha's indiscretions, in that her punishment of him far outweighed the apparent crime. For that reason, many people agreed, Nishani was far more 'at fault' than Priyantha, even if some people ultimately disagreed that Priyantha's suicide attempt was itself justified. Finally, some people viewed the matter as wholly ridiculous, and condemned both parties. Overall, by attempting suicide, Priyantha had not only been able to deflect attention away from his extra-marital affair and present himself as the victim, but to restore order within his *ge:*. Priyantha gave up his mistress;

Nishani began cooking again, and no longer entertained notions of travelling overseas.

Case 9: Chutaka

When I interviewed him, Chutaka, aged twenty-two, was unmarried and living with his parents, having recently returned home from university. Chutaka had been educated at the Herath Gunarathna Vidalaya to A level standard, and subsequently obtained a place on a management course at Peradeniya University. As part of his degree, Chutaka had gained ten months' work experience in the Wayamba Development Bank. He graduated in 2005 with a lower second-class Honours degree, although he told me that he felt disappointed by his grade and should have done better.

Following graduation, Chutaka, like many of his cohort, could not find employment within the field for which he had been trained. Consequently, his mother and father were blaming him. To improve his chances of employment, Chutaka proposed to undertake further studies in IT, but his parents, thinking that this would make little difference, told him he should take any job he could find. Chutaka disagreed with their suggestion, and preferred to remain unemployed. He claimed that following this, he developed low self-esteem and this manifested in feelings of anger:

> Because I am unemployed and have no money, I have no feelings of self-worth. I can't do anything. I think why should I live? Parents ask their children 'why don't you do a job, why don't you give your family something?' When they say that, I feel angry because I can't help them. If I cannot help them how can I develop self-confidence [*a:tma:bima:nəyə*]?

The stress of unemployment, uncertainty and parental expectation led Chutaka to develop mental frustrations that manifested in abnormal behaviour. Chutaka told me that he became angry and confused when his parents blamed him, while his friends reported that he would sit on the bus and talk in a loud voice about inappropriate things and without seeming to care that other passengers overheard. As Chutaka's unemployment reduced his chances of marriage, and as those of his age began to marry, Chutaka's friends teased that he would develop sexual frustration. Although Chutaka denied it, his friends said that he would use boys' legs to release his unfulfilled urges, in an act locally known as 'cutting the stones' (*gal kapənəva*).

To earn money, Chutaka engaged in a range of activities that included drawing on his passion for art and his knowledge of mathematics. Chutaka had once told me that he would have liked to have been a professional artist, and was employed by local businessmen to design and paint billboard advertisements. He also gave tuition lessons in mathematics to students preparing for the GCE and A-level examinations. Chutaka found both of these activities to be cathartic. In relation to his tuition work, he told me: 'Teaching is a marvellous experience.

When the students get happy I also get happy ... their minds are pure unlike adults.' With this statement, Chutaka was implying that children did not place the unfair expectations on him that adults, and in particular his parents, did. The nature of the work, too, was fulfilling, as it provided a distraction and self-confidence:

> My experience of frustration is to feel not wanted [*epa: vuna:*] because I cannot find any work. This makes me think that the value of my life is not so important. I can feel better by doing a job. It gives me something to think about and then I can forget my frustration. We are encouraged by our own actions and after that we feel more motivated.

Chutaka's interpretations of his frustration, and the solutions he found for it, were rooted in Buddhist ideals. Although normative Buddhist values state that frustrations are developed because of attachments to the material world, followers are nevertheless encouraged to engage with the world. In this sense, Chutaka's 'Buddhist' understanding of his frustration was confined, as it were, to the ritual space. The monk at Udagama *vihara* advised Chutaka that 'all things are empty, so don't dwell on them. Thinking is not the solution, working is the solution.' Chutaka found solace in this advice, which encouraged him not to dwell on his negative thought processes but to find employment. Even so, Chutaka continued to visit the temple to put his mind to rest:

> [Buddhism] gives me relaxation to my mind. It gives the real way to solve problems. Meditation is also important to keep our mind in one place. When I am fed up with my life, I think about Buddha's way and I feel relaxed. When I get tired with working my mind asks for relaxation [*sæhællu*]. When I want relaxation, I go to the temple. It's a quiet place and that helps me to keep my mind in one place and on one aim.

Thus, Buddhism, meditation and the temple grounds provided Chutaka with explanations for and routes to solving his frustrations. However, the refuge did not offer a lasting solution, as Chutaka estimated that the relief gained from each visit would last 'little more than a week'. On the other hand, finding self-confidence through work and the material well-being that work provides did offer a lasting cure. It was for these reasons, Chutaka suggested, that he never felt the need to resort to suicide.

Priyantha's and Chutaka's cases describe two different perspectives on frustration suicide in Madampe, which, as we saw in Chapter 3, alludes to the problem of frustration that has been so integral in discussions of suicide *there*. While the cathartic effects of religion and employment – classic sources of social integration in Durkheim's theory (see Chapter 1) – should not be dismissed, they may also be understood as signalling the significance of frustration suicides in another way. Compared with the cool, quiet 'depth experience' of suffering, frustration is imagined in more tangible terms, but also with 'practical' solutions on offer. This is not to suggest that frustration is a 'shallow experience' and thus frustration suicides are 'shallow suicides', but rather to point to the socio-emotional bases of different kinds of suicide in Madampe and their relationships to different kinds of people and different kinds of problems. In the case of Priyantha's suicide in the face of public shaming, there was little 'honour' or 'shamelessness' attached, even if he did transfer shame from himself to his wife. In the case of Chutaka, a suicidal response would perhaps have attracted more sympathy and therefore may have existed closer to the suffering suicides described above. What all this points to is the transitory nature of frustration suicide between suffering suicide on the one hand and anger suicide on the other, as conditions pass from 'coolness' to 'heat'.

Anger suicide

In Madampe the 'external' suppression of 'internal' desires for changes or successes in matters of work and love are said to cause frustration. When released, the reverse force of long-suppressed frustrations results in eruptions of what is called 'sudden anger' (*ikmaŋ tarəha*). Often, people say that only apparently 'trivial' things can be enough to spark a burst of anger; typically, they involve encounters with others that have directly affected self-esteem and public standing, and caused shame. For example, a twenty-four-year-old man called Pahansilu told me that he became 'suddenly angry' after he felt that his girlfriend was not listening to him. Roshan, a twenty-six-year-old man, claimed that he 'suddenly got angry' after telling a young woman that he loved her, only to be rejected. My informants explained that suicidal responses occurring in the context of sudden anger appear to be 'impulsive', and to have arisen with little or no prior warning and no prior planning. It is also extremely common to hear people speak of feeling 'hot' (*rasne*) immediately prior to and during an anger suicide. Reflecting their passion and heat, anger suicides are unpredictable.

It seems that young women in particular, who report the highest levels of self-harm, associate themselves with anger suicide. Patient histories held at the Chilaw clinic provided dozens of insights into women's anger suicides, with almost none found in male self-harm records. The following illustrate a selection of these: Charmali, aged twenty-seven, swallowed poison following an argument with her husband during which she said she became 'suddenly angry'. Anusha, aged twenty-five, swallowed hairstyling gel after her mother-in-law told her that people were criticising her husband, about which she became 'suddenly angry'. Harshani, aged seventeen, swallowed poison having become 'suddenly angry' after her grandmother blamed her for some moral indiscretion. Nishani, aged twenty-seven, swallowed fertiliser after becoming 'suddenly angry' at her husband, with whom she had been arguing.

Anger suicides, like suffering and frustration suicides, exist as idioms by which the structural constraints limiting action may be challenged, circumvented or transformed. In this case, it is not just the class position of working or labouring men and women or the love problems of youth that cause suicides; it is also the subordination of women in the domestic realm, paradigmatically by men or mothers-in-law, which is at stake. Expressions of anger directly challenge higher status actors as such expressions collapse the hierarchy between the angry person and his or her superiors. In so doing, higher status family members may be forced to bend their rules and allow women to open up new spaces for action in their lives. The following case illustrates how one woman used anger as a way of negotiating troubles she was experiencing in family, love and work.

Case 10: Padmini

Padmini, aged nineteen and unmarried, swallowed kerosene after experiencing a range of familial and romantic problems that had caused her to experience excessive suffering and frustrations that erupted in a burst of sudden anger. During an interview at the Chilaw clinic, Padmini explained that she lived in a reconstituted household: her father and mother had separated a few years earlier and since then her father, who had retained custody of the children, had remarried. Neither Padmini nor her sisters had ever enjoyed a good relationship with their stepmother, and the problems between them were exacerbated by the financial troubles the family was experiencing. Padmini said her stepmother had demanded that instead of going on to university as she might have done, she was to find a job in order to contribute to the household income. As such, but against her will, Padmini found a place on a vocational course in nursing. This combination of factors led to Padmini's suffering:

> I feel sad [*dukə*] when I think about my sister and father. I couldn't do further education because my father and mother are not living together and sometimes there are problems with our stepmother. Also, father has some economic problems. Because of these things, I couldn't do further education.

Padmini graduated from nursing college in February 2006, after which she obtained a job in a private hospital at Chilaw. As the journey between Padmini's home and the hospital was too long for daily commute, she lodged at a house nearby. Padmini found her new job and home disappointing. She claimed that her work colleagues treated her badly, she started to feel isolated. Padmini told me:

> Although I decided to be a nursing officer, I am disappointed with the situation. The people I love don't love me. I feel lonely [*matə taniy*]. I am troubled [*matə karədərəyək wage*].

Padmini was conscious that her maltreatment, suffering, and frustrations could lead to anger. She tried to cope with her problems and not get angry. One way of doing this was to observe the *pansil*, the Buddhist precepts for living a peaceful (*səhane*) life. Padmini told me:

I don't get angry with anyone. I want to be friends with others. I always try to cope with my problems, my mental problems and harassment from others. I try to live life happily even while I am suffering. I help anyone who asks me. I always believe what others tell me. I am always open. I observe *pansil*. Therefore, I think that I am not doing anything wrong.

Soon afterwards, Padmini met a married man and they began an affair. The affair provided Padmini with a source of happiness in her life, and she said that for a while her situation improved. Yet Padmini's respite did not last long, as soon afterwards colleagues and her landlady found out what had been going on. Following this, Padmini's sufferings grew and came to a head one day after the landlady blamed her for having an affair. Padmini said that she became angry and swallowed the kerosene in front of her landlady in order to make her feel afraid and shamed, and so that her colleagues, too, might suffer in the same way. Yet the act of anger suicide also exposed Padmini to further shame, highlighting her not just as a 'loose woman' but also as a woman who suffers from angry and impulsive outbursts.

Anger is an idiom used by suicidal people in Sri Lanka to express powerlessness and achieve recognition, but it is also one that runs against strong social imperatives to avoid the expression of anger (Marecek 1998, 2006; Marecek and Senadheera 2012). In Madampe, men and the middle classes, and middle-class men and women in particular, say that anger is a sign of poor morals and social backwardness, and is especially so when exhibited by young people, the working or labouring class, and working- or labouring-class women in particular. The stigma of anger is so great that even suicidal people, when talking about their own anger, do so apologetically. Thus, for example Nayanathara, aged fifteen, who experienced suicidal thoughts, told me: 'I am a good child but sometimes I can get angry.' Piumali, aged seventeen, who practised self-harm, said, 'I can't control my anger. I would like to get along well with my friends but I can't do it. As a result of my anger I have a lot of problems.' For these young women anger is a shameful emotional state they work hard to suppress but ultimately find impossible to avoid when faced with certain pressures. Yet it is also this that can make anger suicides so powerful: they challenge the assumptive foundations of social order and gender roles and usurp power relations within households and communities.

As we consider anger suicides we find that compared with the shamelessness of suffering suicides and the in-between status of frustration suicides, anger suicides are thought of as being more obviously 'pathological'. The pathology of anger suicides is of course a function of the association of anger with passion, heat and impulsivity – all 'female' qualities found also in youthful and low-status men. However, anger suicides also seek to bring about change, and in this sense they may be understood as acts that undermine the social order and challenge ascribed gender roles. Thus to ascribe 'pathology' to anger suicides is an exercise in social control. On the other hand, the 'negative' associations of anger suicide are all well known and those who perform anger suicides expressly play upon the shameful nature of anger. The public nature of anger suicides – which overwhelmingly take place in the presence of those assumed to have caused the suicide – leaves little doubt of whom in the *ge:* the angry person wishes to blame and shame.

Developing an 'ethnopsychiatric model' of suicide in Madampe

For analytical purposes, I have overdrawn the distinctions between suffering, frustration and anger on the one hand, and gender, age and class on the other. As the examples mentioned throughout the discussion have suggested, 'real life' is rather messier. Nevertheless, there are also visible trends, and these are created by the social structures of gender, age and class within which Madampe people are acting. These tend to funnel middle-class people and men towards suffering suicide, and working- and labouring-class men, women and youth towards frustration or anger suicide. The ways in which suicidal people tell their own versions of the emotionality of each thus have consequences for how their claims against others – accusatory or not – will be heard. Middle-class men tell stories of suffering which seek to consolidate their position within family and community as the patriarch, while working-class men, women and youth tell stories that challenge their subordinate status. Drawing from the material presented in this as well as in previous chapters, Table 5.1 summarises these patterns.

In this way, suicide creates as much as it negates. Suicidal practices help people to construct and live their own understandings of the world as much as it enables them to challenge or escape the world, the ramifications of which also of course come to reshape, in a piecemeal way, the social order. Proposing a cognitive map that framed my informants' understandings of middle- and working-class, old and young, and male and female suicidal practices, I showed how popular ideas of coolness and heat underpinned descriptions of suicide. Suffering suicide is cool, and in the main is practised by middle-class men with the aim of preserving the patriarchal order; frustration and anger suicides are increasingly hot and practised by working-class men and women and youth with the intent of undermining it.

Table 5.1 An ethnopsychiatric framework of suicide *here*, formalising linkages from ontological grounds in the village through social status and corporeal affect to social effects

Suffering suicide	*Frustration suicide*	*Anger suicide*
Male	Male/female	Female
Middle-aged/elderly	Middle-aged/youth	Youth
Middle class/*pura:nə*	*Pura:nə*/*estate* class	Working/*estate* class
Cool	Warm	Hot
Private, quiet	Private, quiet/public, loud	Public, loud
'Conserves' social order	'Conserves' or 'challenges'	'Challenges' social order

The conflations of class, gender and age with mental and physical states predicted by Ayurvedic ideas established a set of ideal binaries along the lines illustrated in Table 5.1. Although existing as formal categories that shape people's preconceptions of, say, what kinds of suicidal behaviour middle-class men were most likely to perform, in practice they were regularly confused, as, for example, men practised hot and passionate anger suicides and women practised cool and calm suffering suicides. Moreover, frustration suicide, existing as the logical bridge between suffering and suffering suicide on the one hand and anger and anger suicide on the other hand, inevitably contained elements of each.

The emotional and psychological status of suicide in Madampe is double-edged. On the one hand, the emotions of suicide are practised as part of the suicidal act and it is through particular emotional expressions that social practices are made and communicated – they represent an 'ethos' of suicidality. On the other hand, the emotions are 'real' in the sense that they prefigure suicide and give suicide its cause and its character – they exist as 'evidence' of suicide. The cognitive map I have proposed provides what I view as an 'ethnopsychiatric' model of suicide in Sri Lanka. I suggest that the core concepts of suffering, frustration and anger, their patterned distribution in the community, plus their clear associations with power and status concerns, provide a valuable starting point in what could be a broader examination of 'folk' psychological understandings of suicide, its causes, and ultimately its prevention. By focusing on the ways in which the emotional and psychological characteristics of suicide in Sri Lanka are generated in arenas of social practice (including how coroners and clinics have dealt with such problems – see Widger (2012b) for a discussion) we can move beyond older debates in cross-cultural psychiatry to develop new theories.

The argument concerning the language of psychological problems is pertinent here. Anthropologists and others have repeatedly stressed that mental illness exists at least as much, if not more so, in the discourses and narratives of psychological suffering as they do in any universal architecture of the human mind and its pathologies. Among those arguing against that claim is Vikram Patel, a chief advocate in the Global Mental Health Movement (GMH), who recently suggested that 'a rose remains a rose no matter how you call it' (quoted by Bemme and D'souza 2012). Thus, for Patel, mental illnesses like depression may be called different things by different cultures and even present themselves in different ways (for example, somatic complaints over emotional disorders), but they share fundamental aetiology and symptomatology.

In this chapter, I have argued that both narratives and emotions of suffering, frustration and anger emerge from contexts of social practice. In so doing I have privileged neither the relativities of language nor the universalities of human minds, but have sought to show how possibilities of both unfold in ethnographic situations. Asking *under what conditions* particular understandings of the emotional and psychological vectors of suicidality emerge, I have left open the question of whether suffering, frustration and anger mean identically the same things in English as they do in Sinhala. In fact, Sinhala speakers will know that there are no *direct* translations of *dukə*, *asəhane* and *tarəha*, with 'suffering', 'frustration' and 'anger' being close, but not the only, approximations. I have followed convention when translating those terms, but then of course convention may be wrong. For example, *asəhane* may also be translated as 'discontent' or 'unease', although in Sri Lanka it is most often translated as 'frustration'. Similarly, *səhane* may be translated as 'contentment', 'ease' or 'peace of mind'.

More important for my purposes, however, are the actual processes attendant to *being* in states of suffering, frustration and anger, and of committing suffering suicides, frustration suicides and anger suicides. Now words become less important than actions, and, from the actions around suffering, frustration and anger we see particular constellations of meaning that build our ethnopsychiatric theory of suicide. It is a processual model that demonstrates a certain logic. Suffering leads to frustration that leads to anger, depending upon the interaction of experience, social status and bodily affect. The coherence of the model derives not from the meaning of particular words but the larger corpus of Ayurvedic, Buddhist, folk – and I would argue increasingly allopathic – medical traditions. However, it is also a model under constant change and flux, both in time as well as space. The framework I have advanced here is both partial and transitory, but I also think it is insightful and ultimately hopeful concerning the formalisation of local logics of suicide into a model that will have therapeutic value.

Insights for prevention

Summary of the argument

- In Madampe popular languages of suicidal practice point towards a common '*ethnopsychiatric framework*' through which people come to understand and evaluate suicidal behaviour taking place around them.
- The psychological and social practices forming the framework are best understood as being *mutually generative*. Psychological and social states are related through gender, generation and class positions of suicidal people.
- The framework indicates both *ethos and evidence* of suicidality. Men and the middle classes are often assigned a psychosocially 'legitimate' status (suffering), and women and the working classes an 'illegitimate' status (anger). However, these do also seem to be states experienced by suicidal men and women, respectively.
- Emotions of suicidal practice exist in relationship with, and as a way of *experiencing and talking about*, relational inequalities and violence.

Practical applications

- Popular languages of suicidality can provide a route to *understanding psychological and emotional states* of suicidal behaviour. An analysis of how they relate to patterns of suicidal practice *can help to reveal* a locally meaningful 'ethnopsychiatric framework'.
- Like social practice, emotional practice is never *non-political* and the psychology of suicide often implies a host of gender, generational and class prejudices.

- Careful attention to these prejudices can help to further *reveal the causes of suicidal practice* and highlight important areas for investigation or intervention.
- Standardised psychosocial measurements are likely to only capture elements of ethnopsychiatric frameworks – the development of any such instruments can only proceed on the basis of *careful ethnographic research and linguistic analysis*.

Note

1 During my fieldwork, I was often intrigued by the extent to which Sri Lankan politicians as well as heads of state framed their policies and programmes in terms of reducing the suffering of the people rather than, as would seem to be more common in the West, increasing their well-being.

6 One life, one love

He's been speaking to a girl. Surely he will take poison now!
Udagama youth, male, aged twenty-two

This is the first of two chapters that explore how people in Madampe live through suicide in highly specific relational and emotional ways. We saw how practices of relational violence in and of the home constitute flows of suicide and self-harm, and in so doing generate kinship and emotion in the present. This chapter examines suicidal practices arising among teenagers in response to 'love problems' (*a:dərə praʃnə*), and in particular the high rate of self-harm in young women, as forms of 'self-discipline' first emergent in childhood and elaborated in youth as a method of navigating the difficult terrain of love. I perform a comparative analysis of the narratives of romance accompanying such acts on the one hand, and their often far from romantic abusive causes and consequences on the other. The chapter uncovers the village-, court- and clinic-generated stories lying behind general narratives of youth suicide *here*, which often gloss their actions as the result of 'love affairs' or 'disappointments in love', and how these rub against wider imaginings of the 'good family life'. As such, the chapter explores the ways in which violence and suicide are rendered with a romantic allure, providing a justification for young men's advances towards women and young women's acceptance or rejection of them, as well as women's advances towards men.

Although both men and women express narratives of romance and experienced coercion and abuse, they were deeply shaped by gender and status. On the one hand, young men performed suicidal practices to eulogise or stake a claim of love, often with the effect of causing the object of their love a huge amount of shame, guilt and suffering. On the other hand, young women rarely related the same kinds of romantic narratives as their male peers, but instead were motivated due to parental punishments brought about by questions concerning their sexual comportment. Yet for young women and not men, stories of being involved in a love affair and especially of responding to love problems with suicide was deeply problematic for future marriages, possibly foreclosing the chance for respectable marriage in later life. As such, the chapter applies the relational and emotional frameworks developed in Chapters 4 and 5 to explore how imaginings of the 'good family life' are sought by the unmarried to produce what might be called 'romantic suicides' of frustration and anger.

At stake here is the relationship between suicide and what people in Sri Lanka call the rise of 'love marriage' in the modern period. The paradigmatic marriage in South Asia is a union of two families, not two individuals. By all accounts in Sri Lanka today, love marriage, an ideal of the 'companionate marriage', is an entirely modern phenomenon, and one that is usually blamed on corrupting Western influences. In Madampe, youth suicides are often blamed on the conflicts caused by younger generations' desire for love marriages and the older generations' desire to maintain the social order of arranged marriages, and the rise in the suicide rate since the 1960s linked to it (Gombrich and Obeyesekere 1988; Straus and Straus 1953; Wood 1961; Silva and Pushpakumara 1996). Yet, as the 1950s ethnography reported in Chapter 2 suggests, marriages contracted on the basis of loose 'individual' preferences with no greater aspiration for familial advance was probably the norm *until recently*, when a preoccupation with 'respectable' arranged marriages came to the fore. This is not to say that those older marriage practices were 'love marriages' as they are imagined in the modern period, but rather to point out quite simply that the fact of people picking and choosing marriage partners without formalisation and ritualisation used to be very common, but not so today. Quite opposed from being caused by the breakdown of 'traditional respectable marriages' in Sri Lanka, the rise in the suicide rate over the twentieth century is probably better explained as the consequence of the *spread* of beliefs in respectable arranged marriages alongside the expansion of the middle classes, which came into conflict with the looser marriage practices of the peasant and lower classes of earlier decades.

Reflecting these interests, this chapter contributes to the growing body of work in South Asian anthropology and sociology which is concerned with romantic love and the 'rise' of the 'love marriage'. This literature shows how in Sri Lanka as well as across South Asia, love affairs and love marriages, especially in middle-class communities, occupy a particular social and moral space of ambivalence, at once increasingly common yet remaining often highly problematic for individuals, families and societies at large (Caldwell 1999; de Munck 1996; Donner 2008; Fuller and Narasimhan 2008; Lynch 1990; Osella and Osella 1998; Parry 2001). Perveez Mody (2008: 6–7), for instance, describes love marriages in middle-class New Delhi families as occupying a 'social space of moral ambivalence'; a 'not-community' providing a 'testing ground for the limits of community.' Mody (ibid.: 7) shows how love affairs and love marriages are routinely accompanied by questions such as: 'Will the couple be obstructed in their attempt to marry? Will they be pursued by the police and their families? Will the parents and families force a capitulation and welcome them back into the fold?'

In Madampe, love affairs and love marriages form spaces of moral ambivalence in which people enquire how and to what extent notions of the 'good family life' should be enforced. Such unions rouse strong sentiments and lead to assaults by parents on their children, especially daughters. Young women bear the brunt of families' efforts to regulate romantic relationships and control daughters' sexuality, and this can be considered a major factor influencing the high rate of self-harm found in that group. For young women much is at stake when embarking on a relationship, as, should any suggestion of impropriety become public knowledge, then young women's opportunities for arranging a respectable marriage in later years may be jeopardised. Equally so, young women's self-harm can raise important questions about their 'character' in the eyes of others, also risking future marriage chances. Thus, to become involved in a love affair, and to respond with suicide if the affair fails, poses considerable problems, and these are of far greater consequence for women than for men. By contrast young men are rarely if ever 'tainted' by past histories of love affairs and suicidal responses may be more easily shrugged off as an act of romantic bravado.

Love marriage in Madampe

In general terms people in Madampe speak about 'love marriage' (*a:darə viva:ha*) and 'proposal marriage' (*yojitə viva:ha*), which imply clear distinctions between two kinds of marriage ideal. However, these terms obscure a more complex set of practices in which no discernible line can be drawn between the pathways leading to marriages of one sort or another (cf. de Munck 1996; Fuller and Narasimhan 2008). The vast majority of what people in Madampe call 'love marriages' may be better understood as 'self-contracted proposals' – or 'self-arranged marriages' (Singh and Uberoi 1994: 101) – during which parental approval is sought and must be secured for the marriage to go ahead with the full trappings of a formal and public marriage ceremony. Similarly, 'proposal marriages' are often better understood as 'arranged love marriages' in which young people play a central role, have a chance to get to know one another prior to marriage, and also have the option to veto a match suggested to them.

The terminological ambiguities surrounding marriage make a study of incidence and practice difficult to negotiate. Following local conventions, during my village census taking I asked informants what kinds of marriage – 'love' or 'proposal' – they and other family members had contracted, and often received embarrassed laughter before a reply. My assistants joked that we ran the risk of 'being slapped' by asking the question: by enquiring whether people had contracted a love marriage or proposal marriage we were asking whether they had engaged in morally ambivalent behavior or even eloped – or whether they had experienced 'family problems'. Thus, by deciding to classify their own marriages or those of their ancestors or descendants as one form or another, informants were as much staking moral claims as they were reporting actual practice. Data pertaining to rates of 'love marriage' and 'proposal marriage' are therefore better understood as indicating informants' willingness or unwillingness to define a union one way or another, each of which says something important about how they imagine a 'good family life'.

Even with this bias on the research process, the responses I received tallied with other studies conducted in Sri Lanka. Bruce Caldwell (1999) was involved in a large-scale survey of marriage practices in the southwest of Sri Lanka, and found that reported proposals had dropped from 73 per cent of marriages before 1940 to just 32 per cent by 1980 to 1985, with reported love marriage becoming the norm. Sørensen (1993: 129, 136, cited by de Munck 1996: 700) compared marriage practices in a new Mahaweli settlement and an 'old village' in eastern Sri Lanka, and found that while around half of all marriages in the new settlement were classified as 'love marriages', only around 20 per cent were so classified in the old village. My own data collected from Udagama and Alutwatta – an old *pura:ṇə* village and new *estate* village respectively – show how informants in both places classified the majority of marriages before around 1975 as proposals, but after 1975 as love. However, the pace of change from proposal to love was apparently more rapid in Alutwatta than in Udagama, echoing Sørensen's finding that love marriage may have first been more acceptable, either in practice or as a label, in colonies than in *pura:ṇə* villages.

These quantitative patterns reflect a richer ethnographic context wherein claims of having contracted proposal or love marriages spoke to the class constitution of each village. Udagama people, as *pura:ṇə* people, were less willing to describe the marriages of their parents and grandparents as 'love' marriages, opting instead for 'proposal', even if they did not actually know, and perhaps my asking was the first time they had even thought about it. 'It was back then, it must have been a proposal', I was sometimes told when asking whether a parent or grandparent had contracted a love or proposal marriage. And as with the past, so with the present: if Udagama's history was thought of as a time of greater moral virtue, my questions concerning marriage type were considered more risky in Udagama than in Alutwatta. Udagama informants admitted somewhat reluctantly that they had arranged their own marriages, and sometimes I heard conflicting accounts of the same marriage. These problems were not nearly so evident in Alutwatta, where people were more willing to describe their own marriages and those of ancestors and descendants as love marriages.

Nevertheless, today the majority of marriages in both communities are still described as 'love marriage'. Given the moral ambivalence of that label, and given that those marriages could have as easily been called proposals if informants so wished, the reason Udagama people especially opted to describe their marriages in such terms is an important question. At least part of the answer lies in informants' desires to project an image of the 'modern' bourgeois 'companionate marriage', which the term 'love marriage' better conveys. Referring to love marriages in middle-class Chennai, Fuller and Narasimhan (2008: 751) describe companionate marriage 'an ideal of ... "emotional satisfaction" that is not premised on young people's unfettered personal choices', and which parents and children together arrange. In Madampe, the ethos of companionate marriage goes further to include only a minimal level of parental involvement, with many marriages simply requiring their agreement and almost no interference over the process of spousal selection, increasing the scope for 'personal choice'. That said, youth in Madampe have a very clear understanding of whom their parents would approve or not. My male informants were clear about the kinds of women they could marry, with caste, class, family background, educational level and 'character' all forming key issues to consider (Widger 2009: 244–248). Even though parental involvement was minimal, this was in many cases only because they had effectively brought up their children to fall in love with the 'right kind of person'. The extent of 'real' choice over marriage partners is probably not as great as many Madampe youth would like to believe.

Despite the apparent acceptance of love marriage and only indirect involvement of parents in the early stages of companionate relationships, actual practices of courtship remain severely limited in Madampe. The term 'love affair' brings to mind images of Euro-American dating practices, which is not the case in Madampe. Even being suspected of involvement in anything other than the most 'innocent' (*ahiŋsəkə*) platonic friendship with a member of the opposite sex runs the risk of expulsion if teachers find out, while being seen 'speaking with' a girl or a boy can result in strong parental reprimand, especially for females. In both Udgama and Alutwatta 'love affairs' meant little more than talking to a boy or girl on the road or in the bus to school, at sports meets, or other social events like religious festivals and life-cycle celebrations including funerals. It is not uncommon for love affairs in Madampe to be based on irregular meetings, a few times a week or even months, for perhaps no more than a few minutes each time.[1]

Thus, the ideal of companionate marriage and personal choice does not come without its consequences, three of which are especially relevant for the argument being made in this chapter. First, young women have come to hold a great deal more freedom over the choice of marriage partner, having virtually *carte blanche* to reject a match suggested to them. 'If I don't find anyone, my parents might suggest a boy, and then I'll be able to decide whether to marry him or not' was the common answer I received when asking young women about their marriage preferences. While arranged love marriages proceed through processes of negotiation which extend over a period of time and daughters are thus rarely faced with simple 'yes, no' choices, their increasing role as active players in those negotiations can and does challenge men's understandings of the marital relationship and the patriarchy it entails.

Second, and as an extension of this, men may be understood as responding with a range of behaviours, including sexual harassment and suicide, as a way of promoting their own interests. Just how young men might successfully approach and attract young women was a source of constant discussion among my unmarried male informants, who together set their evaluations of their own and others' masculinity against this benchmark. Third, the back seat taken by many parents only continued so long as their children were courting correctly, and transgressions of parental wishes or family interests – and daughters' sexuality especially – were swiftly dealt with. The following sections explore the effects of these issues on suicidal practices committed by young men and women in Madampe, respectively.

Narratives of romance

When I arrived in Madampe and started to ask about the causes of youth suicide the most frequent response I received was 'love affairs'. The answer seemed entirely obvious to my informants, both male and female, and young and old, and peppered conversations I had across villages, courts and clinics. Although no one knew whether such acts were intended to result in death, disappointments in love were assumed to cause self-harm as a way of signalling the level of one's devotion to a potential lover, and seriousness about a match to parents, by putting the idea of death into other people's minds. Romantic suicides were usually described as frustration or anger suicides: they arose in contexts of increasing heat and the breakdown of a 'traditional' social order, wherein romantic commitments and sexual attraction and lust caused youth to commit impulsive suicidal acts. However, upon deeper investigation it also became apparent that this dominant narrative only usually applied to young men's suicidal practices, although, as we shall see, it motivated a smaller number of women's romantic suicides as well.

A well-known romantic suicide in Madampe was that of Thaniya Vallabha, a Sinhala prince who reigned in the area during the late fifteenth to early sixteenth centuries. The story goes that Thaniya Vallabha had been engaged in battle against invading Portuguese armies when false news had spread that he had been slain upon the battlefield. After hearing of Thaniya Vallabha's death, his wife, who loved him deeply, committed suicide. When Thaniya Vallabha returned home to find her dead, he too was overcome by grief and killed himself. Because Thaniya Vallabha had been adored by his subjects and died for the love of his lost wife, he was deified as Thaniwelle *devol*. Today Thaniwelle *devol* is honoured at the Thaniwelle Devalaya, a shrine famous for its statue of a riderless horse, located on the Colombo–Chilaw road at the entrance to Madampe Old Town. The Thaniwelle Devalaya is visited by Madampe people who seek the deity's help with many aspects of their lives, for example, in examinations, at job interviews, and, fittingly, with love affairs and marriage proposals.[2]

No one in Madampe told me that they, or anyone else, engaged in suicidal practices because of Thaniya Vallabha's lesson. The story did not directly inspire similarly lovelorn youth to end their lives. Nevertheless, the romantic allure of Thaniya Vallabha's suicide was well commented upon by my informants, and for many was considered to be a reasonable response to tragic love, in the same kind of way that admirers of Shakespeare's *Romeo and Juliet* might also feel an affinity for the protagonists' star-crossed plight. This was especially so among my younger male informants, who shared a belief in 'one life, one love': an idea which in rhyme I am not entirely sure hadn't been borrowed from the Bob Marley song 'One Love', but which speaks to a popular Sri Lankan and broader South Asian fascination with the allure of (tragic) romantic love (Mody 2008; Osella and Osella 1998, 2006; Trawick 1990). My male friends in Madampe maintained that their commitment to 'Sri Lankan love' was unique, and this could be witnessed in the turbulence unrequited or lost love caused in their lives, which sometimes called for suicidal responses.

Madampe male youth explained the logic of 'one life, one love' in terms of a fatalistic ethic. Its defining feature, I was told, is the belief that in the world 'there is only one person you can truly love', and 'if that person is missed or lost, a second will never come along'. Some further argued that this one person is also that person with whom one has their first romantic relationship, which for most is experienced some time during their school or university career. As such, the belief in its extreme form maintains that the first love is also the one true love. The belief in 'one life, one love' thus creates plenty of scope for romantic failure, which of course is the point. My youthful informants rarely saw the path of 'true love' as running smooth, but instead as being marred by disappointments and frustrations. Nevertheless, relationships that exhibited those characteristics were assumed to be more romantic and more loving than those that did not. It was this belief that provided a tidy explanation for youthful romantic suicides, as the sheer inevitability of suicide in the context of failed love was 'obvious' for everyone to see.

However, youth in Udagama and Alutwatta did not invest in the promises of romantic love marriage to the same extent. Their acceptance of it was shaped by their experiences of growing up in a *pura:ṇə* or *estate* community, and by gender constraints. In 2005 I conducted a short marriage attitudes survey in each village, and found that Udagama and Alutwatta youth expressed different ideas about love marriage (see Widger (2009: ch. 6) for a full discussion of survey findings). Reflecting Udagama's more conservative and 'traditional' environment, almost 20 per cent of unmarried respondents in that village said they would prefer to contract a proposal marriage, compared with no unmarried respondents in Alutwatta, all of whom said they would prefer a love marriage. While youth in Udagama could well have been overstating, and Alutwatta youth understating, their acceptance of parental involvement in marriage choices, the findings support my claim that Udagama people were generally more concerned about the propriety of proposal marriage and impropriety of love marriage than Alutwatta people. Moreover, my interviews with youth in both villages suggested that Udagama females were the most likely to expect to contract an arranged marriage, while Alutwatta males were the least likely.

For young men, the dire consequences of 'one life, one love' were assumed to encompass a range of suicidal practices, from minor self-cutting through dangerous or lethal self-harm to a kind of 'social suicide' via 'loitering and drinking'. Each of these practices was said to be undergone because of romantic disappointment or loss, of men's inability to tell or convince women of their love using other means, and due to rising feelings of frustration or anger.

Case 11: Kumara

Minor self-cutting, a form of 'safe' self-harm rarely found in Madampe and never appearing in hospital records, only arose in the context of love problems. Kumara, a seventeen-year-old Sinhala Buddhist living in Alutwatta, explained how he had inscribed the name of a young woman he loved on his arm using a razor-blade. The cut was not lethal and required only minor medical attention. Kumara told me:

> I cut my arm to show my love. When boys are in love they can show their love by doing this. I myself know a few boys who did the same thing.... When a girl sees that a boy has done this thing she will know that he loves her.

Unlike poison drinking, the act of self-cutting comes with no ambiguity: the intent is not to raise the idea of death but rather to mark upon the body the extent of one's devotion. Drawing from interview research with youth who cut themselves in the UK, Helen Spandler (2001) has shown how self-cutting exists as both an intrapersonal and an interpersonal act with multiple meanings attached for the individuals concerned. Spandler argues that although self-cutting can sometimes be about communication, it is also about releasing psychological distress. According to Kumara, when Madampe boys cut themselves they never do so randomly or in lines or patterns, but instead write the name of a specific girl. Self-cutting is better understood as an expression of deep, longing love for a particular person and as a method of exploring feelings of sexual frustration.

If self-cutting was about eulogising 'one life, one love', self-poisoning may be understood as an attempt to stake a claim of love. Echoing popular sentiments, one twenty-one-year-old man told me: 'Boys will swallow poison when a girl tells him that she doesn't love him, because he knows he will have lost his one love.' Of the cases of romantically inspired poison drinking I encountered, the vast majority occurred when a love affair had recently ended. The belief among my young male informants was that by drinking poison a woman would be forced to take a man's declarations of loving devotion seriously. The act would set up an obligation on the part of the woman to show him loving kindness (*metta*) in return (see Chapter 8), which would then facilitate the realisation that he was indeed committed in his love. In practice, however, this rarely seemed to happen. When speaking to young women who had experienced a past boyfriend drinking poison, they spoke about the 'mental problems' this caused them rather than any reawakened feelings of love.

Case 12: *Thakshila*

I met Thakshila, aged twenty, in 2006 through a mutual friend. Thakshila had been in a relationship with a man called Prasad, aged twenty-six, for several years before he obtained a job in Japan and migrated. When Prasad learned he had the opportunity to move to Japan he asked Thakshila to marry him so that they could travel together. However, Thakshila was doing well at school and she was hoping to enter university, so she decided to end the affair. In response to this Prasad drank poison but survived. Talking to Thakshila about the event a year later, she complained that it had caused her problems and made her 'fearful' (*bayahitenə*) of love. At that time she had been courted by a man living in

Alutwatta and this was dredging up old feelings around the incident. Thakshila told me:

> I think about love very seriously. I have lost my first love, so I am fearful to love again because I'll have lost my love again. I can't bear it. I think I am very sensitive [*hari unuwenə*].

Thakshila's male cousin, Thilana, also knew about the case. Thilana told me that by drinking poison Prasad had 'abused' his cousin: 'He drank poison to abuse Thakshila because of this problem [of Thakshila not wishing to migrate].' According to Thilana, the consequence of Prasad's actions was to make Thakshila feel considerable guilt and pain, and lose her way in life. Even though Thakshila had previously been doing well in her studies her grades began to suffer and she missed out on a chance of going to university. A year after Prasad's self-harm Thakshila had only just begun to recover and was looking at applying to a private university in Colombo.

Moving into the realm of idiom and association, a third kind of romantic suicide is a form which threatens young men's 'good character' (*hoňdə çarite*). Men who have experienced romantic problems or loss are said to become 'loiterers and drinkers' (*ka:ləkanniya*) and 'village ruffians' (*ganaŋ ka:rəya*), usually as a way of dealing with the sexual frustration from which they are assumed likely to suffer. When my research assistant's love affair came to an end he told me: 'I'll start hanging around the junction and drinking *kasippu* now!' Although joking, he was playing up to a popular stereotype and in fact did start to drink more often in the local bar. I heard of young men responding to failed love affairs by loitering and drinking and becoming trouble-makers many times during my fieldwork, and in several cases people clearly thought it was an alternative to self-harm. In these cases, becoming a trouble-maker could be understood as a form of 'character self-harm': a wilful self-sabotage of men's 'good character' which has the same kinds of repercussions for the girlfriend as men's bodily self-harm.

Unlike self-cutting and poison drinking, however, becoming a trouble-maker has no obvious 'target'. When men engage in character self-harm the general assumption is that they have suffered from romantic disappointment but the woman in question is rarely singled out for blame or shame. Instead, social self-harm may be better understood as an introverted act: a behaviour which allows a love-struck youth a chance to express self-pity and perhaps win the sympathy of peers, but which has no other external consequences beyond ruining his public image. The consequences for family are even more limited, as parents are much less accountable for sons' troublesome behaviour than daughters', and in any case it is assumed that young men will 'grow out of it' and still be able to marry and become respectable householders. To that extent, social self-harm arises when men do not wish to cause the object of their love any kind of blame or shame, or when the barriers to love are considered beyond men's ability to control.

In young men, the dominant narrative of romance fuelled their suicidal practices. Framed as a consequence of 'one life, one love' (*panə vage: a:dare*), their actions may better be explained as a response to the changing field of marriage practices in Madampe, and in particular pressures to meet, court and propose to young women in a context where dating remains an impossibility. Reflecting the social and moral terrain of Madampe's 'not-community', men's romantic suicides were usually targeted at individuals: in the majority of cases young women and only occasionally parents. Referring to the barriers they faced, many of my male informants joked that love was 'dangerous' (*baya:nəkə*) and that poison drinking would be a likely outcome of any romantic endeavour. For them, however, romantic suicides spoke of moral and ethical virtues, even if in practice they had serious implications for the object of their affections.

Suicides of coercion

Narratives of romance did shape young women's suicides, but to a much lesser degree than men's. Young women I spoke to told me they also subscribed to the idea of 'one life, one love', but when it came to suicidal practice this explanation was offered less often. In contrast to young men, the barriers to love were more squarely identified with parental opposition, including when 'dispute with a boyfriend' was a cited cause. Women's repertoire of romantic suicides was much smaller and only included dangerous or lethal self-harm: self-cutting and loitering and drinking never arose. In some cases suicidal practices occurred owing to disappointed or failed love, but in the majority of cases due to parental opposition.

Case 13: Saduni

The first case involves Saduni, a twenty-one-year-old woman, and Jaliya, a twenty-three-year-old man, living in Kuliyapitiya and Alutwatta, respectively. Saduni and Jaliya had been in a relationship for three years before Jaliya decided to end the affair. Following this Saduni began to make suicide threats to Jaliya over the telephone, via text messages and through written letters. Saduni also told the couple's friends about her suicidal plans. Around twelve days after the affair was over Saduni telephoned one of Jaliya's friends, Aravindra, aged twenty-three, and told him that she had bought a bottle of fertiliser with the intention of drinking it. According to Aravindra, Saduni also asked him to 'apologise' to their friends for 'causing them trouble' by committing suicide, and gave every sign that she intended to do it. Aravindra responded by telling Saduni she was 'young and had plenty to live for', so she should not commit suicide. He asked Saduni not to drink the fertiliser until he had a chance to come and speak to her the following day, to which she agreed. Having brought attention to her sorrow, Saduni ceased to make suicide threats and as far as I know never carried out her plans.

This case mirrors that of Thakshila and Prasad described above. To that extent it may be understood as a romantic suicide committed within the dominant

126   *One life, one love*

narrative, and as such is reflective of a reality in which Saduni clearly felt she 'owned' the courting process in the same way as men do. However, while Prasad's self-harm greatly upset Thakshila, Saduni's threats seemed to have little or no effect on Jaliya. Of course, Saduni did not actually swallow poison and so Jaliya did not have to face the harsh consequences of his actions. Even so, Jaliya seemed unmoved by the events. When I asked Jaliya about the case he responded that he 'always knew' Saduni had never meant to swallow poison, and was simply acting out. Jaliya dismissed Saduni's actions as a ruse to get him back, but that this would never have worked. Like many of my male informants, Jaliya did not believe *women* could use poison drinking to re-create a romantic relationship, in the same way that *men* thought they themselves could. The threat did not work because Saduni, as a woman, could not 'own' the courting process.

Case 14: *Nayomi*

The second case illustrates how romantic competitions sometimes foreshadowed young women's self-harm, and shows the impact of adults' attempts to control young women's sexual comportment. During my research at the Chilaw clinic I met a fifteen-year-old Sinhala Buddhist girl called Nayomi, who had swallowed poison because of a 'love problem' and was briefly counselled by clinicians. Since the age of thirteen Nayomi had been involved in a 'romantic relationship' with a boy in her class. However, in recent weeks a friend had tried to come between them, which caused Nayomi to become sad (*dukə*). Nayomi regarded her friend's actions as 'not good' (*hoňdə næ*), and as transgressing codes of one life, one love, which stated that friends should not interfere in each other's love affairs. One day Nayomi saw her friend talking to her boyfriend and blamed her, calling her bad names with the intention of causing her shame. However, the friend's aunt learned about this and blamed Nayomi in return, saying that she should not be talking with boys or accusing her niece of doing the same. Later, Nayomi's father, who was drunk at the time, heard about what had been taking place and beat her. Nayomi's father was angry that his daughter had been speaking with a boy, that she had become involved in a public dispute with another girl over the matter, and that another adult had intervened to reprimand his own daughter for her bad behaviour. Nayomi told the clinician that she drank weedkiller after suffering from a day of quarrels that culminated in her father's violent response:

> All day people had been blaming me but I tried to solve the problem. When father blamed me, I could no longer stand it. I suddenly felt hot and sad and drank poison to make father afraid. At that time, I did not think about dying but just to make father afraid to blame me.

Nayomi's case demonstrates the interplay of several important features of young women's self-harm in particular. First, it shows how processes of blaming and shaming described in Chapter 3 spiralled in Nayomi's life, from a small argument between schoolfriends to a larger dispute with adults, and finally to a violent reprimand by her father. Second, when the dispute came to involve the girl's aunt and Nayomi's father another set of concerns came into play, including the implications of being blamed by an elder and also the questions raised over Nayomi's sexual comportment.

Case 15: Arsha

The third case echoes these themes and allows for a comparison of young women's and men's responses to love problems through a single example. Arsha, a fifteen-year-old girl living in Alutwatta, swallowed poison after quarrelling with her parents over a love affair. Arsha explained how she had become involved in a love affair with an eighteen-year-old man called Dinesh, of whom her parents disapproved because he was unemployed, but also because Arsha was still at school and they feared the relationship would jeopardise her education. Moreover, they were especially concerned that the affair would ruin her 'innocent character' (*ahiŋsəkə çarite*). One day Arsha had a particularly violent argument with her father, which other villagers said became physical, although Arsha made no mention of this; because of the argument she swallowed poison. Like other young women, Arsha stressed a close connection between an all-consuming feeling of love and the subsequent need to self-harm:

> When I met Dinesh I knew he was good (*hoñdə*; honest, innocent, trustworthy) and after some time we came to love. When my father told me to stop this affair I felt sad because I did not want to give up my love. That day [when I swallowed poison] father had come and told me that I can never speak to Dinesh again. I felt great sadness about this and saw the poison so drank some ... I didn't really think about it, I just did it.

Arsha told me that she swallowed the poison because her father's accusations questioned her innocence, and she wanted to make him feel 'afraid'. Yet although Arsha's parents did still not approve of the relationship, Arsha herself decided to end it. When I spoke to Arsha three months later, she said that with the benefit of hindsight it was for the better, although of course the whole experience had been very upsetting:

> My parents were afraid for me but even that didn't change their mind! But actually after that I was kept at home for several months and I came to realise that my love for Dinesh had changed. It was a very difficult period for me but I know that it is better if I concentrate on my schoolwork so maybe I can go to university. That is what I want now, and am working hard!

In contrast to Arsha's positive steps forward however, Dinesh was said to have become a drinker and a loiterer. Dinesh's less drastic response may be understood in two ways. First, as a man he was thought less likely to respond to love problems caused by parental opposition than he was to love problems caused by girlfriends' decisions. Second, the fact that it was Arsha's parents who intervened and not his own would have made a suicidal response largely ineffectual. As I argued in Chapter 4, suicidal practices emerge when those who cause problems are considered worth dying for, which Arsha's parents would not be. In this context, the 'lesser' suicide of loitering and drinking, understood as a manifestation of sexual frustrations, was a more likely outcome.

Young women, the victims of men's romantic suicides, rarely sought to inflict the same suffering on boyfriends. Reflecting their own position within the moral vision of the 'good family', they were instead more concerned with the effects of parental opposition and in particular questions of sexual comportment. Perhaps because of this, the range of women's suicidal practices was smaller than that of men's. Relatively unconcerned with convincing men of their love than they were of defending or deflecting challenges to sexual innocence, poison drinking arose because it was the only effective means of engaging relationships worth dying for: that between parent and child.

One life, one love: reconsidering 'romantic suicides'

Sri Lanka's suicide epidemic is often explained by ordinary people and academics alike as having roots in the introduction of love marriage to the island. The evidence suggests that the suicide epidemic as it relates to 'love problems' is better explained as a growing interest in 'middle class' proposal marriage and the expectations of 'respectable' courting practices. While the erroneous belief is dominant in narratives of romantic suicide and youths' expression of poison drinking in terms of one life, one love, a deeper reading shows how romantic suicides are integrally about gender and sexual politics, constitutive of relational violence in and of the home. In particular, they revolve around men's and parents' responses to women's demands for greater equality in the marriage contract, and to open up further space to explore heterosexual identities. The argument advanced in this chapter turns upside-down the accepted history of romantic suicides, and by extension the spread of romantic love ideals, in Sri Lanka. While particular social and cultural expressions of love in Sri Lanka are undoubtedly 'modern', the idea that a marriage is not simply a union between two families but also two separate people is not. That fiction comes from the middle-class fantasy of what makes a good family life and, according to the available ethnography it was the preference of landed classes and not the larger community of land-poor or landless peasants.

The 'personalisation' of the marital process is crucial here. In Madampe men are expected to find their own spouse while women are expected to have the ultimate say in who they will marry, but neither without agreement from parents. This leads not to a policing of youth love affairs by kin who might be driven to murder when wrong choices or demands are made, but instead an increasingly micro-politics of suicidal action in which lovers themselves engage in forms of self-harm to advance or negate their claims. Meanwhile, a core issue facing young women is a contradiction in the marriage process, which both allows for their involvement in the identification of a marriage partner but disallows their ownership of courtship, partly due to men's resistance and partly for fear of attracting sexual shame and reduced marriage choice. Parental surveillance and abuses committed on daughters when they are suspected or found to be involved in love affairs accounts for a large proportion of young women's self-harm. The high rate of self-harm found in young women may be explained by the social and moral terrain of youth social and sexual lives in Madampe. Young men and women may both be 'hurt' – emotionally as well as in social status – by love problems, but men have a greater range of responses from which to choose than women, who in turn have far more to lose from a failed love affair.

Thus the relational violence of romantic suicides exists as both a form of self-discipline and a form of dominance. The twin processes of power involved in romantic suicides renders them especially potent. The self-cutting of lovelorn young men conveys a medium of angst resplendent of the 'global teen', from the *Hikikomori* (self-confined) youth of Tokyo to the *Emo* (emotionally hardcore) youth of London. It also draws from the sacrificial logic of self-destruction of South Asian suicide and, for example, the withdrawal suicides of *pura:ŋə* men and women. Yet we also find the protest of youth and the anger of love when it is lost, suppressed or otherwise confounded. In this way self-discipline becomes an exercise of power or resistance, imposing or rejecting amorous advances. The multi-directional nature of seemingly linear 'romantic suicides' poses challenges for how the experience of companionate marriage is developing, intersecting 'traditional' and 'modern' elements at the nexus of local and global paradigms of love.

Insights for prevention

Summary of the argument

- Like many Asian societies, at rhetorical level Sri Lanka has witnessed a *transition* from 'traditional' forms of 'arranged' or 'planned' marriage to 'modern' forms of 'companionate' or 'love' marriage.
- Popular rhetorics of love and marriage disguise a more *complex history* in which ideas of arranged and companionate marriage may have always *coexisted* to some degree.
- In this context suicides may often arise due to clashes between *preferred marriage options* ('traditional' or 'modern'). Suicides may also arise as a means through which young people can *stake a claim of love or reject an advance*.
- However, what might be presented as 'romance suicides' may be *better understood* as 'suicides of coercion'. Suicides used in this context are often *acts of violence*, particularly (although by no means always) by men upon women.

Practical applications

- Youth suicide prevention programmes must be aware of the *complex histories and sociologies* of young people's lives, including, as the subject of this chapter points out, how love and marriage are understood.

- Despite overwhelming appearances, *few 'romantic' suicides are ever romantic*. Instead, romantic suicides are often *better understood as practices of coercion or protest*.
- Preventing romantic suicides may be particularly challenging and require a *broad focus on youth communication*, and in particular *awareness around gender equality and non-violence*.
- Parental interventions may require a focus on *communicating with children and youth*, including strategies to do with *talking about sex and relationships*.

Notes

1 During my fieldwork the spread of mobile phones greatly expanded the opportunities young people had to conduct love affairs, and since then the rise of Facebook and other social media sites has widened this further.
2 Edirisinghe (1999) records three versions of the story of Thaniya Vallabha's death. The first is that he committed suicide in the manner in which Madampe youth suggest. The second is that he was ousted from power and lived out the rest of this days in the 'wilderness' north of Puttalam. The third is that he was indeed killed by the Portuguese.

7 The Black Demon

A rumour had spread that his wife was having an extra-marital affair.
  Male self-harm patient's case notes, Chilaw Mental Health Clinic

Men hang themselves because they've got nowhere to go.
  Udagama teacher, male, aged forty-five

This chapter continues the discussion of specific lived contexts of suicidal practice to explore the high rate of suicide found in middle-aged men. This involves an analysis of the situations giving rise to male suicidal practices, and in particular men's perceived ability or inability to practise manhood, including labour migration, drinking parties, and the ability to satisfy, materially and sexually, wives and lovers. Thus, the chapter explores men's suicides and, in particular, the ways in which claims of suffering, frustration and anger are made and understood, including how the honourable slides into the pathological. As will be seen, the interpretation of men's suicides depends upon a range of factors that are not available to men who engage in practices that entail a 'pursuit of fun' when that fun questions men's good characters. While in Chapter 5 I explored men's suffering suicides as instances in which good character held, in this chapter I explore the processes through which character may be undermined, including the work of the clinic in such transformation.

Osella and Osella (1996, 2000, 2006) have explored constructions of masculinity in contexts of labour migration and modernisation in Kerala, southern India, and illuminate the complex ways in which manhood is perceived, learned, adopted, practised and transformed. On the one hand, Osella and Osella (2006) argue, stories of men's lives tell tales of individual development and progress through the successful pursuit of male 'breadwinner' roles: of men 'on the strengths of their wits, single-minded dedication and resourcefulness ... [transcending] ... initial disadvantages' (Osella and Osella 2006: 53–54). On the other hand, 'they reveal slippages, discontinuities and ambiguities in ... lived experiences of modernity, raising doubts about whether such a struggle against hardships and setbacks has been at all worth it' (ibid.: 54). Their analysis reminds us that constructions of male gender are never straightforward, and may only be understood through detailed examination of contexts of practice and action.

Studies of men and masculinity may be found throughout the Sri Lankan anthropological and sociological, but only specifically so in a handful of contributions (e.g. Gamburd 2000, 2008b; Jeganathan 2000). Michele Gamburd has been concerned with documenting the effects of labour migration on gender constructs. At the time of Gamburd's research, the rate of (documented) male migration was half that of females; thus, Gamburd (2000) was concerned to explore the effects of female migration on masculinity, which she understands as making men 'breadwinners no more'. The husbands of migrant women are left behind physically, socially and economically by Sri Lanka's absorption into the global economy, and Gamburd interprets men's suicides within the framework of 'challenged masculinities' created by the reversal of domestic gender roles heralded by female labour migration. In a separate study, Gamburd (2008b) has explored the role of men's drinking parties in creating spaces of male sociality and camaraderie, which may be understood as both being paid for, and a consequence of, wives' migration.

Pradeep Jeganathan (2000: 39) has described the emergent spaces of young male practices of masculinity as a 'space for violence'. In a combative essay, Jeganathan (ibid.: 52) argues against the 'anthropologisation' of violence in Sri Lanka that has categorised violence as a rupture associated with fear of shame (see Chapter 4), and proposes instead the counterpoint of 'fearlessness' (*bayanætikamə*) as a driver of male violence. Jeganathan suggests that fearlessness is epitomised by the village 'thug' (*çaṇḍiya*), who stands as opposite to those who are constrained by fear of shame. Both thuggery and fearlessness are practices of masculinity that produce spaces for violence by their exuberance and 'machoness' and the firm embracing of behaviours that would ordinarily attract blame and shame.

This chapter builds on Jeganathan's and Gamburd's work, and complicates the narrative of 'challenged masculinities' found in the Sri Lankan social science literature. Instead of regarding suicidal men as the product of inverted gender roles, I develop the idea of the 'dead-end of patriarchy' I first expressed in Chapter 5, which is a concept that men in Madampe were often aware of and with which they struggled. The notion of a 'dead-end' pulls in and builds upon the themes of movement and separation explored in this chapter. Thus, I show how movements experienced in both positive and negative ways define men's social worlds; that is to say, as experiences of both 'fear' and 'fearlessness'. Fear and fearlessness may be equally empowering and disempowering for men, but the common theme is the way in which men in Madampe define patriarchy and the freedoms of movement it entails, and the necessary pressures this puts to bear on their role as householders through idioms of strength, courage, zeal and entrepreneurship.

This sets up a paradox that can lead to suicidal practices. When men's movements are curtailed by the realities of *ge:* and the demands it can make, men literally and figuratively find 'they've got nowhere to go' (*ohe:innəva*), as one male teacher at Udagama told me.[1] For men in Madampe, to be physically, economically or socially 'going somewhere' (bæ:rakyanəva) exists as the converse of having 'nowhere to go': an oft-perceived cause of men's suicides. Opposed to that, in the court and the clinic, it is movement itself that is deemed to be a cause of men's suicide and the cessation of movement its cure: the consumption of alcohol and male and female migration are both considered to be direct causes of suicidal practice in men as well as their wives and children.

The way the chapter is constructed attempts to 'write a path through' this paradox. The first half of the chapter is given over to a sketch of men's pursuit of fun through movements associated with drinking and migration. The second half of the chapter explores the costs of these benefits, and as with previous chapters, the violence it entails. Now drinking and migration are viewed from the 'dark side', as behaviours with distinct and destructive social and emotional effects. As an overall contribution, the chapter situates suicide within this paradox and the wider debates concerning alcohol and migration, as they exist in the South Asian and anthropological literature.

Movement and the 'pursuit of fun'

People in Madampe in general, but men in particular, feel they are 'going somewhere' when they are free to pursue 'fun'. That is to say, activities that take them away from the humdrum of daily life and into unpredictable or uncertain waters where the constraints of shame can be thrown off and fearlessness embraced. For both women and men trips away from Madampe usually involved the breaking of core taboos, including those making demands on women's performance of innocence and men's of honesty. On a journey undertaken by the Udagama preschool to distribute aid in a southern village destroyed by the tsunami, two teenage girls spent the trip back home dancing provocatively up and down the hired bus to loud music played on the stereo. An unimaginable display in the village context, their dancing was even more extraordinary due to the presence of a Buddhist nun in the party. Similarly, when I accompanied my host family on a visit to the Kataragama *kovil* in southeast Sri Lanka, we stayed overnight in the Buddhist pilgrims' rest house. As usual, the men passed the time before the evening meal drinking arrack, but the women also drank beer: the only such time I observed this to happen.

Men in Madampe pursued fun (*hoñdə kalədasa:və*) in many ways. Trips on the back of a motorbike to the local town, going by bus or private vehicle on a longer sojourn, escaping for the afternoon in the local bar, sneaking off to a brothel with a couple of friends, or migrating abroad for a couple of years to work in the Middle East all counted as *jolly time*. Perhaps living up to the old cliché that it is not the destination but the journey that is important, it was also the simple fact of moving about that men seemed to enjoy, and which lent their otherwise morally inappropriate behaviours legitimacy. At base, 'going somewhere' to '*have fun*' or a '*jolly time*' with the intention of '*full enjoy*' – all phrases that people used in English to express the pursuit of fun – implied the means and reasons for doing so, and this suggests both financial well-being and social worth in the eyes of others. Thus, men's control over the means and reasons for movement and fun is highly valued and expressed in many forms, yet perhaps the most important of these is simply the ability to leave the *ge:* in order to participate in domains of exclusive male sociality. In this section, I explore two of these: the first, drinking parties, and the second, overseas migration.

Pura:ṇǝ *and* estate *drinking cultures*

For those who can afford it, the consumption of alcohol provides one of the most important ways in which men can express their ability to 'go somewhere' in Madampe. This is so not only because drinking implies a high level of economic worth but also because drinking stands in direct contrast to normative village morals that strictly forbid alcohol consumption and expressions of drunkenness. For Buddhists, the consumption of alcohol contravenes one of the five precepts, and even Roman Catholics can find sanctions in the Bible against drinking if they so wish. Thus the majority of men to whom I spoke would initially deny being a drinker, claiming it was against their religion, bad for their health, or, most often, would get them into trouble with wives, girlfriends, parents and children – drinking was not something that 'honest' (or *pura:ṇǝ*) men would do. However, after some time this 'façade of honesty' would crumble and it would turn out that they at least drank with a select group of male kin and/or friends, at weddings and other life-cycle events, and possibly at the local bar. Indeed, in Madampe all social events were for men by prerequisite drinking events. They were characterised by the heavy consumption of arrack, gin or brandy, and generally took place once a week. Depending upon the size of a *ge:* and its social network, men typically found themselves at drinking events several times a month, if not more often.

There is a large body of research that shows how drunken behaviour reflects socially ascribed values and norms (e.g. MacAndrew and Edgerton 1969; Marshall *et al.* 2001; Samarasinghe 2006), and in Madampe status constraints have significant impacts on the ways in which men speak about their own drinking practices and actually behave when drunk. Men of *pura:ṇǝ* standing seek to maintain the façade of honesty, and this means that when they drink at public events they try to do so with at least a veneer of respectability. Following the funeral of a friend's uncle, who was Roman Catholic and had been cremated at the Madampe cemetery, his kin and friends congregated at the funeral house (*maḷǝ gedǝrǝ*) for the wake. As was usual for such events, male and female attendees did not mingle, with the men setting up camp at the back of the house and the women inside. Having sat me down in the garden, my friend turned in a conspiratorial kind of way, and asked: '*api bomudǝ*' ('shall we drink?'). I was led to a van parked away from the house, wherein a few bottles of good arrack, mixers and a couple of glasses were laid out. We poured a slug, added some soda water and swallowed the drink in one go. By then, a couple of other men had arrived to take a drink, and we headed back to our seats to make way. Following this pattern of turn-taking, the men at the wake, who numbered around twenty in all, spent the evening getting progressively drunk, in a very obvious but nevertheless 'discrete' kind of way.

Similarly, *pura:ṇə* men also drink covertly when they are at home. My landlord, a retired bank manager on a government pension, typically drank at least a half-bottle of arrack every evening. However, his glass would be left on top of the fridge in the side room, with the arrack placed discreetly on a workbench and a bottle of soda water or ginger beer kept cool in the fridge. For him, the evening began going over the household accounts and those of some friends who paid a small fee for doing so. Every thirty minutes or so he would rise from his desk, saunter somewhat subtly to the fridge, take a shot, and sit back down again. At around 9 p.m., one hour before the evening meal was served, he would join his children to watch whatever teledrama was playing that night. He continued to drink covertly during this time, and only stopped when the meal was served, as is exactly appropriate to do. At other times, when I drank with my landlord and his son, we always did so around the dining-room table. As juniors, it was unsuitable for us to drink arrack at home in front of our elders, so we would drink beer, which was kept on the table, while the father would drink arrack that again was kept in the side room. In so doing a distinction was being made between 'hot' (*rasne*) and 'cold' (*si:tələ*) drinks, age and social status. Arrack, regarded as 'hot' due to its high alcohol content, was only considered fit for private consumption by the patriarch, while beer, regarded as 'cold' due to its low alcohol content, was consumed openly by his underlings.[2]

Concerned to maintain their status as a respectable household, my landlord and his sons never drank in local bars, although many men of means in Madampe often did so. When I first visited in 2001, the town had just three rather dingy bars, with the interior kept dark by closed windows preventing prying eyes from seeing who was inside. During the two years of my fieldwork, two more bars set up for business. Significantly, they were open to the light and thus reflected the growing trend for *conspicuous* alcohol consumption taking place in the town.

Sometimes men use bars to drink alone, perhaps stopping off on the way home for a quick quarter-bottle of arrack. Often, however, men drink with friends, acquaintances and colleagues, although always in groups with no internal age or status differentiation but strict separation from other drinkers. For example, the group of men I drank with were all in their forties with professional jobs, and several had spent some time working abroad. One of them was a teacher, and often his ex-pupils, now grown up and with jobs and families of their own, would come into the bar as well. When they did so there would inevitably be an uncomfortable atmosphere as the teacher was 'shy' (*læjja*) to be seen drinking before his pupils, and his pupils likewise 'shy' to be seen drinking before their teacher. Usually one party would opt to finish up and leave, and given that this sensitivity applied not just to teachers and their ex-pupils but also to senior and junior work colleagues, during busy periods public bars would become places of constant movement as middle-class drinkers shifted from one location to the next, seeking somewhere more appropriate to become drunk.

Standing in contrast to 'respectable' middle-class drinking practices are those assumed to be performed by the working class and labourers. These are epitomised by the local '*kasippu* man' (*kasippu miniha*), or village 'drunkard' (*bebadda*). Conversations about *kasippu* invariably invoke much laughter in Sri Lanka, yet *kasippu* men are nevertheless always regarded as likely 'dangerous' individuals who exhibit fearless and violent behaviour.

Kasippu is a generic name for homebrew, but the term is also used for an illegally produced spirit of varying and uncertain strength usually favoured by very low-income men. A decided aura of mysticism surrounds the production of the drink, with people speculating wildly on its usual contents. It is said to be produced in giant vats in the middle of paddy systems or in the depths of the jungle, where no one can see it. Mosquito coils (burning rings of mosquito repellent) and barbed wire are popularly assumed to constitute its main ingredients, as are any unfortunate creatures – snakes, spiders, bats, geckos and so on – that happen to fall in. This is in contrast to the contents of the more socially accepted *kasippu* homebrew, which is made from mangoes, bananas and other fruits, and, like homebrew in Europe and America, attracts a certain degree of folkish charm and discussion among men on the best recipes, fermentation techniques and times, and about how to create the highest alcohol content.

As consumers of mass-produced illegal *kasippu*, however, *kasippu* men visit the *kasippu* den (*kasippu gedərə*), typically a private house from which *kasippu* is sold. The police occasionally raid *kasippu* dens, and their owners and customers fined. More often than not, though, the owner of the *kasippu* den bribes the police to stay away. A relatively small *kasippu* den in Raja Watta, a low-caste quarter in Udagama, sold around five litres of *kasippu* in quarter-, half- or one-litre measures per day paid Rs.1,000 per month to avoid being closed down. As such, *kasippu* men are implicated in corruption.

Worse than that in local eyes is how *kasippu* men become drunk. Socially acceptable or middle-class drinking, except in special circumstances, is that which is accompanied by restraint: namely fear of shame. Drunkards are not expected to lose control of their speech or body, and men that do are often shunned as drinking partners by those conscious of shame (and because they can become rather boring). One characteristic of *kasippu* men is that they cannot control their behaviour, and make an exhibition that attracts shame upon themselves and their *ge:*. Padmisiri, the owner of the Raja Watta *kasippu* den, was also known to be a '*kasippu* man' (*kasippu miniha*). Together with his friends, Padmisiri would get drunk at School Junction and make a scene, for example, by shouting at passers-by and dancing in the road. With his 'bad characteristics' taken altogether, Udagama people regarded him as one of the fearless village thugs of the area, and not welcome in their *ge:*.

Despite *pura:ṇə* protestations that men of their standing do not drink in public or lose fear of shame when doing so, on several occasions I accompanied friends on day-long drinking sessions that started in the bar but finished on the beach at

Chilaw and once outside the local temple, and always with exhibitions of fearlessness. These occasions would often be accompanied by men playing loud music on car stereos and dancing in the street, in much the same way as *kasippu* men are blamed for doing. For my drinking friends, who were all engaged in respectable jobs and married with children, drinking and dancing in an open space was valued because of the sheer freedom it afforded. This was a freedom expressed most rudimentarily by their being able to urinate in the open air, which the teacher only did on such occasions and much relished when he had the opportunity.

For those who can afford it, these kinds of activities are first enjoyed during premarital years, and especially so by university students. A common sight around university campuses is a trishaw parked up on the side of the road, loud music blaring, a few empty bottles of arrack lying around, and four or five boys dancing enthusiastically. Batch-mates also often meet up during holidays for drinking sessions, and in Madampe this usually also involves a trip to the coast to swim in the often treacherous waters and to make amusing sand sculptures of human anatomy on the beach.

The pinnacle of middle-class drinking practices, however, is the drinking party, which due to their expense are always exclusive affairs. During my fieldwork, I attended dozens of parties, the majority of which were held by the same small group of men that included two *massina* (wife's brother and sister's husband) and three old schoolfriends. The importance of drinking parties in the development of men's public personalities (as economic, social and political agents) and as sources of social and emotional support cannot be overemphasised. They are supposed to be lavish but frequent affairs, during which men who engage in cycles of reciprocity come together to reaffirm their relationships over the best drinks and food their money can buy. However, such gatherings too are about building trust, and constitute spaces in which men discuss whatever personal problems are troubling them. Inasmuch as drinking parties provide a form of social support, they may be understood as a central means by which men share the burden of their troubles.

Typically composed of the host and just three or four others, the aim of drinking parties is not necessarily to make new acquaintances but to strengthen and deepen ties with existing ones. The rule in Madampe is that men who drink together collaborate: the drinking circle defines the scope of a man's economic and by extension social and emotional world. Thus, men who are teetotal complain that their sobriety leads to forms of social exclusion and a barrier to their passage into other men's social worlds. One medical doctor who drank a little beer on special occasions complained: 'People don't trust me!' His comment reflected a wider sentiment that men who do not drink together cannot properly get to know one another, and therefore cannot be relied upon for help when troubles might arise.

Reflecting their exclusivity, drinking parties are normally held at men's *ge:*. I have also attended parties for particularly important friends – and those with whom men would probably not discuss personal problems – in the bars of local tourist hotels. However, by inviting men into the *ge:*, the host is making an explicit declaration of kinship, regardless of whether such a relationship exists or not. However, even if the men are unrelated, they will begin to refer to each other as '*maçaŋ*', the informal and friendly term for *massina*. This is more than just a symbolic label: *maçaŋ* assumes an essential relationship of amity that is supposed to exist between proper *massina* (see Chapter 4).

Home-based drinking parties usually take place in the evening, after younger children have gone to bed. However, men prefer to hold parties when the rest of the family is away, otherwise they become subdued affairs. All parties, regardless of whether the wife is at home, begin calmly. Men in Madampe tend to be shy when sober, and highly conscious of the need to maintain an image of good character. Despite their exclusivity, men behave no differently when arriving at drinking parties.

Nevertheless, after a few glasses, men and their tongues start to loosen up and for a while the conversation is freely flowing and witty. It is during this time that men may share problems they are experiencing, for example, with work or business, and wives or children. The other men listen and give advice, perhaps sharing similar experiences and providing solutions. During one party Ruwan told about how his teenage sons had discovered masturbation and his wife was concerned about what to do; Upali suggested he explain to his wife that masturbation is an ordinary part of growing up. At another party Jeewan shared some gossip concerning his wife's fidelity and sought advice on how to respond. In so doing, Jeewan signalled a level of trust with his drinking friends – one of whom was even his wife's brother – whose advice Jeewan found to be satisfying and helped him to manage his concerns. At a subsequent party, Shelton told about how he was struggling to find Rs.40,000 (£2,000) to pay for the roof on the house he was building. As a signal of their friendship, Jeewan agreed to lend Shelton the money, with no interest.

When the family is present, at around midnight the host's wife will begin to ask the men to behave quietly so as not to disturb the children. It is normally at this time that conversation is dying due to the effects of advanced inebriation, and singing takes its place.

Singing is viewed as an essential part of any drinking party, as men say it extends their drinking capacity by at least one more bottle. The content of songs tends to be funny, often smutty, and usually about lost or unrequited love. One or two men lead the songs, with others beating out a rhythm on their legs, the arms of their chairs or on tables. As the momentum increases and men find their musical souls, so does the volume. It is not unusual for drummers to send glasses and plates flying as they become unconscious of the force they are using. Now husband and wife begin a spiralling discourse in which the wife asks the husband to quieten his guests, to which he pretends to cower and look afraid, and his guests respond with a nudge and a chuckle. Eventually the wife pretends to lose her temper and demands that they take their rice and curry (and thus cease drinking), and in response the husband affects anger that he must ask his guests to leave. By this time, however, the guests have usually drunk and sung all they can, and thankfully take their rice and curry before departing on wobbly legs, bicycles or motorcycles. These kinds of spousal disputes are regarded as being part of drinking parties and are not treated very seriously, and certainly not risking suicide.

In Madampe, alcohol and drinking parties provide everyday opportunities for the pursuit of fearlessness through movements of various kinds. Physically, drinking entails leaving the *ge:* and creating spaces of male sociality in bars, on roadsides or at the beach; alternatively, it occupies the *ge:*, a normatively female domain, if only for a few hours. Bodily, too, drinking allows for freedom of movement: dancing in the street, urinating in the night air, creating music out of tabletops, chairs and the family dinner set. Socially, then, drinking marks out wealth and status, and facilitates men's entry into and maintenance of circles of patronage and emotional support. At the same time, however, drinking can either stake or affirm *pura:ŋə* and *estate* status in one's own and others' eyes, or explicitly seek to transcend them. On the other hand, the financial and health burdens of drinking create many more problems for men and their families, not to mention, as we will see, high levels of domestic violence and suicide. The paradoxical nature of alcohol – its status as a 'barrier' to suicide as well as a 'risk' – is found too in a less everyday form of movement against which masculinities in Madampe are judged: overseas migration.

Men and migration

'These days migration is like a fashion: everybody thinks they can go abroad to work and solve all their problems', said one middle-aged male ex-migrant, who had worked in the Maldives and Europe for several years. Many people in Madampe thought that international labour migration was a means by which economic uncertainty could be avoided, and was a marker against which one's own status and the status of others could be judged. Across the Division, men and women from poor backgrounds returned from abroad with the money to purchase land, build a large house, equip them with all-new consumer goods, and invest in a range of business ventures. By migrating for a couple of years, so the story went, *ge:* could leap in socioeconomic standing. Unmarried men in Madampe migrated for the purpose of raising economic capital to buy land, build a house, start a business, and eventually marry. Married men, meanwhile, migrated in order to provide for their *ge:*. For most men I knew, migration was assumed to offer a quick route to economic success and pride, as well as a chance to see something of the world and have an adventure.

Although the kinds of labour available were typically in the construction and service sectors, the nature of the work did not affect the class status associated with it. Working-class migrants came to hold middle-class status when they returned home, and middle-class men who were employed in decidedly working-class positions overseas nevertheless retained their original status back home. For this reason, the number of legal routes for migration was far lower than the number of men wishing to migrate. Thus, of the five men in Madampe I knew who had migrated abroad to work, only one had done so legally.

Similar to men's stories of migratory successes recorded by Osella and Osella (2006), masculinities in Madampe are often tied to men's successful pursuit of careers in a globalised economy. One evening I had drinks with two male friends aged in their mid-thirties and early forties, Shelton and Lalith. Shelton had previously worked abroad and had returned to Alutwatta to establish himself as a migration broker, the first link in a chain of agents from the village to the Gulf. Lalith ran an upmarket bar and guesthouse at Marawila catering to local middle-class families and the odd tourist who had strayed off the beaten track to the south coast. Both men were married, had young children and were financially successful. The two often drank at Lalith's bar and when they met would spend their evenings reminiscing about how they had made their money and how successful they had become. Both proudly told about how a life of hard work, an earlier testing period of migration, on-going entrepreneurial acumen and an ability to 'play the system' had paid off. By this, they had been able to provide for their *ge:* and *pavula* and so proved themselves 'honest' husbands, fathers and *massina*. Shelton and Lalith thought of themselves as the embodiment of the 'successful man', standing out among their peers as economically savvy who, despite lowly beginnings (Shelton was an orphan and had left school at the age of sixteen), rose in stature within their communities.

In Madampe, young men consider overseas labour migration as a principal economic strategy and barrier to suicide. Men who have migrated and returned with wealth and tales of glittering cityscapes in Singapore, Dubai or London are treated with a huge amount of respect. One weekend I was invited to meet Chinthaka, forty-six, who had travelled back to Madampe from London, where he had been living for the past two years. The owner of the local bar, Ruwan, took Chinthaka, three other friends and I to a new guesthouse recently opened on the outskirts of Chilaw, where we drank whisky, ate crab and swam in the luxury pool. Later in the evening, we returned to Ruwan's bar where we opened an expensive bottle of brandy from his personal stash and Chinthaka regaled a growing group of new friends with tales of life in the UK. Throughout the day, Chinthaka was treated like a 'chief guest', an honour only reserved for men of special economic and political prestige and who, through their social position, represent a model of masculinity in Madampe.

If men like Shelton, Lalith and Chinthaka are held aloft as examples of the promise of migration, others come to exemplify its failure through the inherent difficulties men face in trying to actually move abroad. The subject was a popular one in the bar where I drank, and I knew several men who tried to migrate to the Middle East, Europe or Australia during my stay. A few of my friends had calculated the succession of countries through which one had to pass in order to gain a visa for the next with a minimum of difficulty, and also, importantly, without having to put oneself at the mercy of traffickers.[3] They were also rather coy about revealing their plans to me, but I learned enough to know that it involved passing through some combination of India, Russia, Africa and the Baltics, finally to fetch up in Germany, then France, and eventually the UK.

In early 2006, one of these men, Chandrasiri, aged thirty-four, attempted the journey himself. Chandrasiri, a resident of a *pura:ṇə* village, had a professional technical job and had recently married. As is often the case, Chandrasiri decided that in order to build a proper home for his family he needed to travel abroad to earn money. Chandrasiri disappeared from Madampe without much fuss two months after his wedding. For a week, his friends in the bar heard nothing. Then one day Chandrasiri telephoned to say that he was in southern India, and was making his way north. Chandrasiri next called his friends one month later to say that he had made it to the Czech Republic. Another month passed, and I heard rumours that he was in North Africa. Finally, four months after he had left Sri Lanka, Chandrasiri returned to Madampe, tail firmly between his legs, apparently having failed in his attempts to get into France and subsequently being deported from Spain. Having spent more than Rs.500,000 (around £2,500) on the venture, Chandrasiri put any ideas about migrating behind him, and by luck returned to his old job. Nevertheless, Chandrasiri's failure was the subject of much ribbing and he avoided his old drinking friends for the rest of my time in Madampe.

As with alcohol and drinking parties, migration provides a paradoxical measure of masculinity. On the one hand, migratory movements away from *ge:* can demonstrate men's economic and social savvy and 'strong mind', setting them up in the eyes of peers as fearless men worthy of respect. Yet the promise of migration is tempered by its realities. When I spoke to Chinthaka privately about his experiences in the UK, a more complex story emerged. Chinthaka was in the UK illegally and although he had the paperwork to move freely between London and Colombo, was always terrified he would be caught and expelled. Moreover, Chinthaka worked as a low-level help in an Indian restaurant and shared a house with eight other men in a poor neighbourhood of southeast London: very different from the glitz and glamour conveyed to his friends. Like many other men, Chinthaka also feared that his migration would lead to the breakup of his marriage as his wife had stayed behind in Madampe. It is to this issue that I now turn.

When the party's over: suicide and the cessation of movement

In providing forms of economic, social and emotional support, men's attempts at movement in the fearless pursuit of fun necessarily run counter to local imaginings of good family lives. Across villages, courts and clinics, different theories of male suicidality that were being generated held up both alcohol and migration as the primary causes of self-harm and self-inflicted death, either in men themselves or else in wives and children who fell victim to their effects. At the core of each was a concern with the ways in which men and their families dealt with alcohol and drinking, which in turn were understood through their relationship with movement: of women and men or their children being 'left behind' by migrant husbands and wives or parents; of drunken men returning home and entering the female space of *ge:* in a highly intoxicated state; of wives being left alone by husbands who spend too much time away from the *ge:* and opening up space for infidelity. In villages and clinics especially, this last problem, of marital discord and extra-marital affairs, proved to be a particularly popular idiom through which to understand the paradox of movement and its relationship with suicide.

Kalu Yaka: the 'Black Demon'

In Madampe, most people fear that marriage will be the first casualty of migration. Bandara, an Udagama resident and teacher at a primary school in an *estate*, was particularly interested in the effects of migration on *ge:*. Many of Bandara's students came from families in which a parent, often the mother, had migrated. Bandara explicitly linked such backgrounds to poor performance and delinquency at school; when family members attempted or committed suicide, Bandara argued a clear link between the cause and the migrant. We often had long discussions about how the separation of wife and mother from husband and children was 'bad', but the most interesting account arrived in my email in-box one day several months after my return from Sri Lanka. The email began by describing for me what made a family (the bold typeface is his) which, for Bandara, was best understood as a 'machine':

> Father, mother and their children make a family. It's like a machine. [For it to] work ... properly, all the parts must work [together] and proper maintenance is very much needed. We must oil it, grease it and service it at the right time for good performance.
>
> A family also needs good maintenance. What is needed ... is love, sex, compassion, sacrifice, money and so on. If one of them is missing then the trouble begins.
>
> According to my point of view, **having good sex is a great bond to unite husband and wife**. (Of course you can have good sex in many ways but what I mentioned above is different from that.)
>
> **Sleeping with his own wife not only gives perfect sex but it gives him love, care, kindness, selflessness, etc.**
>
> Most Sri Lankan men and women just after getting married go abroad searching for green pastures [in] their **prime age** (between **twenty-eight and thirty-five years**).
>
> When husband or wife is away during this time I think I need not say the outcome. Of course they earn money but eventually ruin the whole family.
>
> Now I think you can imagine the massive destruction caused to families in Sri Lanka by **the migration of Sri Lankan men and women**.

In this description, Bandara was applying the *pura:nə* ideal of respectable households to the situation he saw in an *estate*.

One of the 'worst' effects of labour migration that people often spoke about concerned husbands' and especially wives' fidelity. Although sometimes seen as the victims of unscrupulous employment agents who were said to trade jobs for sex, women were more often accused of starting affairs on their own volition. Husbands of migrant women often heard gossip that while abroad the wife would form a 'connection' with another man; if it was the husband who migrated, he was told his wife had an affair with a local man. Both men and women I knew in Udagama and Alutwatta discussed the risk of wives' infidelity in terms of women's sexual being, which was said to be always in danger of flaring up in the absence of male authority and guidance. As one young man in Udagama put it: 'They [women] cannot control their urges and if allowed will have affairs with other men. It's in their nature to do this.' The misogynistic assumption prevalent in Madampe – and one expressed by 'respectable' middle-class women as much as men – that women who lose male authority become sexually promiscuous may be understood as forming one of the most important consequences of movement in Madampe.

Rumour, gossip and innuendo questioning the fidelity of migrant wives or wives of migrant husbands circulated widely across Madampe. Informants in both Udagama and Alutwatta told stories about Krishantha, who lived at a third village, and who was widely assumed to be suffering from family problems due to his migration and his wife's subsequent infidelities. Krishantha had migrated to Germany on a tourist visa (sponsored by his brother who lived there) in 2002, where he stayed for two years. Krishantha explained that during his stay he became very lonely, and began drinking as a way of dealing with the social isolation he experienced. However, while Krishantha told me that other men would visit prostitutes as a way of dealing with this, he would 'make do with a bottle of whisky and late night pornography'. In the two years that Krishantha was away, he claimed never once to have thought about cheating on his wife.

However, in time Krishantha came to hear stories that his own wife, Chulani, had begun an affair with a married man at her place of work. Although Krishantha told me that he was sceptical about this and said the stories were *boru* (lies), he nevertheless returned to Sri Lanka. Once home, Krishantha received a number of telephone calls from a man whose voice he did not recognise. The calls were infrequent but continued for a number of years. The caller claimed to have information about the affair, but this could not be confirmed. The 'other man' as well as the caller remained nothing more than ephemeral figures. Nevertheless, Krishantha said he could not help but become suspicious of Chulani and started to keep watch over her movements.

The outcry over international labour migration holds a particular appeal for ordinary Sri Lankans. Yet it may also be understood as just the latest in a long line of outcries to movements of people – both internal and external – that have defined Sri Lankan society for the past two centuries (Spencer 2003). In this sense international labour migration may be regarded as providing the most recent problem in a long-running debate held mostly by and for the interests of the Sri Lankan middle classes concerning the social and cultural consequences of development, modernisation and urbanisation (another is the 'open economy' policy of '1977': see Chapter 3). Therefore, it is perhaps not surprising that even though 'migration' has become a dominant explanatory paradigm for all kinds of social problems including suicide, it is far from the only context within which people assume that marriages and families might be at risk of breakdown due to infidelities.

Somewhat ironically, Bandara himself became embroiled in gossip concerning the state of his own marriage, from which neither partner had migrated. Towards the end of my fieldwork, stories began to circulate around Udagama that Bandara's wife Padmini, a teacher in a school in Madampe New Town, was having an affair with the headmaster of the school in Udagama. When I asked Udagama men why they thought Padmini was being unfaithful they pointed to the fact that Padmini taught science in a high-status secondary school while Bandara himself taught in a mere primary school. Popular opinion assumed that Padmini would be uncontrollable and as a result would fall victim to her own sexual urges. In this way, Padmini was assumed to be as susceptible to infidelity as any migrant wife or woman left in Sri Lanka by a migrant husband. The only difference in Bandara's case was that the 'other man' had a face and a name, and was far from ephemeral; to add insult to injury, he was a school principal and so Bandara's superior. Other male friends heard similar stories about their own wives, but in those cases the 'other man' remained ephemeral as they had in Krishantha's case.

That families entirely unconnected with migration should also become subject to the same kinds of stories as migrant families illustrates the broader base upon which critics of migration develop their claims. It is not migration per se that is assumed to be the cause of infidelity and family breakdown, but the conditions of modernisation and globalisation that facilitate movements of many kinds, including of wives away from the home in pursuit of careers and thus into contact with unknown dangers, including those created by their own sexualities. The indistinct yet assumed ever-present threat of wives' infidelity and the faceless and nameless nature of those tempting their betrayals or spreading malicious gossip link men's fears of movement with the world of malign supernatural forces. In Sri Lanka, gossip and rumour form mechanisms of social control as well as an idiom for making sense of misfortunes in people's lives. Seneviratne (1999) highlights how these processes stretch from the intimate everyday socialities of people's lives to questions of national and nationalist concern. Speaking of outcries over the establishment of Mahayana Buddhist preschools in Sri Lanka,[4] Seneviratne suggests that paranoia concerning the malevolent actions of ephemeral others 'is an example of Sinhala paranoia about the vulnerability of their culture' (ibid.: 267). He continues:

> Instances of this paranoia are extensive and varied. Its agents are, for example, the CIA, America in general, India, the Tamils, the Muslims, the

Christians, the World Bank. ... This is a national-level expression of the local and domestic paranoia expressed in the suspicion of magical and other harm that can emanate any moment from kinsmen, neighbors, fellow workers, and even friends.

(Ibid.: 226fn)

For Krishantha, there was little question that human agents were behind the stories he was hearing and that the conditions giving rise to them were also considered the work of human agents. Yet he had little idea as to who in his social world it could be: all his friends and acquaintances were as well-off, if not better-off, than he. Krishantha had certainly made money while abroad and now owned a few acres of coconut land, but he was not wealthy to the extent that he considered any of his friends jealous of him and thus the source of negative influences in his life, either this-worldly or other-worldly. In any case, Krishantha was a self-proclaimed 'rationalist' and a 'non-practising Roman Catholic', as he put it, and had no time for 'silly stories' of malevolent spirits. Even so, Krishantha came to make sense of the gossip he was hearing through a framework clearly borrowed from local belief systems of ritual, sorcery and magic.

Men's suspicions and fears of wives' infidelities may be understood as another form of paranoia through which they make sense of the perceived threats of migration to Sinhala culture, family and their own masculinities. This paranoia takes the form of fears about nameless and faceless men existing always on the borders of their world and waiting to snatch away women whose sexuality was permitted to flourish through uncontrolled movements.

In both form and function, these men resemble the demon Kalu Kumara (Black Prince) and his incarnation Kalu Yaka: (Black Demon). Kalu Yaka: is feared because he seeks women tirelessly, lusting after them and killing their children (Kapferer 2000: 10). Kapferer (ibid.) describes the various myths that explain the coming into being of Kalu Kumara and Kalu Yaka: as expressing 'a Buddhist morality, the ultimate annihilating destructiveness of obsessive Desire and Lust ... [and] as the construction of male fantasies concerning the all-consuming capacity of the female sexual appetite'. Thus, while Kalu Kumara is usually explicitly absent from men's suspicions and paranoia concerning wives' fidelity, the moral themes of the demon and his myth are nevertheless present. 'Going somewhere' is akin to people's criticisms of 1977 and migration and the aspirational 'running after material things' (*salli passe duvənəva*) lamented by Udagama resident Don Appuhami in Chapter 3. Desire and lust in this context are not merely sexual but also material; the pursuit of material, selfish gain is what exposes men and their wives to the dangers of ephemeral Casanovas and Don Juans (cf. Kapferer 2000: 10–11).

The fear of Kalu Yaka: and abusive men surfaced in the many tales of child sexual abuse that circulated around Madampe and were especially associated with migrant households. By the end of my fieldwork I could often predict exactly where a conversation about migration would be going. Most informants held in their minds a three-step scheme: (1) wife migrates; (2) husband becomes alcoholic; (3) daughter is raped by her father or other male relative due to lack of maternal care. A training manual issued by the Sri Lanka Bureau of Foreign Employment (BFE), *Health and Reproductive Health for Women Migrant Workers* (2001), repeated the assumption:

> [Mothers] leave behind young children, sometimes infants as young as 2 to 3 months. The children they leave behind are psychologically affected without the love of their mother. Especially the girl child is very badly affected when there is no woman guardian to protect her or provide advice and care at times of need. Very often the children of these women are abused sexually by relatives.

A similar view was put forward in *Ravaged Innocence: A Study of Incest in Central Sri Lanka* (Silva *et al.* 2002), a report published by the Centre for Women's Research, a Sri Lankan NGO. Assessing prosecutions of incestuous rape in one province, Silva and colleagues (ibid.: 16) concluded that the absence of the mother, especially in the context of migration, was a special factor in causing the sexual abuse of young girls. My own survey of thirty-eight incestuous rape cases that passed through the Chilaw clinic on the way to court found that mothers were listed as absent in 37 per cent of cases. Although in 21 per cent of cases mothers were reported as living at home at the time of abuse (and in several cases of being complicit), in 42 per cent the records lacked any information to judge. In any event, child sexual abuse, and especially of young girls by older male relatives, is now said to be at 'epidemic' proportions in the country, with 'three to five' children raped every day (*Time*, 13 August 2013).

Pathological jealousy: the clinicians' verdict

Popular theories of the social consequences of drinking and labour migration also worked their way into Chilaw clinicians' diagnoses of patients they saw, where they were treated in medical terms. Within self-harm patients' case histories, migration was identified as a primary causal factor in 11 per cent of males and 9 per cent of females. Compared with this, the level of migration from the Puttalam District was just 5 per cent (Department of Census and Statistics 2003).

On this basis, clinicians coined two phrases for the social and psychological problems they saw in patients somehow involved in migration: 'Middle East syndrome' and 'Italian syndrome'. Those diagnoses were never recorded in patients' files, being replaced instead by a formal diagnosis like depression, adjustment reaction, or some other problem. However, they did provide a convenient label for clinicians when describing the effects of female and male labour migration respectively, as the diagnoses acknowledged the assumption that female migrants typically travel to the Gulf, while male migrants travel to Italy. Middle East syndrome and Italian syndrome meant slightly different things according to patients' actual experiences of migration. Among migrants' dependants, Middle East syndrome referred to the consequences of absent wives and mothers, while Italian syndrome referred to the consequences of absent husbands and fathers. As one clinician told me:

> Middle East syndrome is what children suffer from when their mother goes abroad to work: mental problems, social problems, and educational problems, including learning disabilities. They also suffer from a lack of energy and lack of interest. Middle East Syndrome is caused by the breaking of the mother–child bond and subsequent loss of mother's love. Meanwhile, father becomes a drunkard, and sometimes sexually abuses his children ... Italian syndrome is what children suffer from when their father goes abroad to work. Although he sends money, the children miss his love. They become addicted to alcohol and drugs, visit prostitutes, and miss school. They don't learn how to spend the money he provides because he is not there to guide them.

In relation to clinicians' diagnoses of returned migrants they saw, either syndrome could refer to the consequences of long-term separation from families, abuse suffered at the hands of employers, difficulties experienced when reuniting with spouses, children and other kin, and the effects of alcoholism. Within this, suspicions and accusations of infidelity were again paramount, either on the part of spouses left behind or due to accusations that the migrant had engaged in extra-marital affairs when abroad.

As with Krishantha's case, however, the material causes of Middle East and Italian syndromes in the context of infidelities were at times hard for clinicians to pin down. Clinicians found that men's claims of wives' infidelities were rarely made based on sound evidence but usually unsubstantiated gossip. This led clinicians to tag men who expressed such sentiments as suffering from 'pathological jealousy': a psychotic disorder also known as 'morbid jealousy' often found in alcoholic men who fantasise that their wives or partners are being unfaithful, and leads them to committing violent acts. Thus, while pathological jealousy may be a diagnosis attached to an act of self-harm committed by a man or woman where one party had migrated, it was also often attached to cases where a male self-harmer or the husband of a female self-harmer was deemed 'alcoholic'.

When interviewing patients who could be associated with migration or alcoholism in one way or another, clinicians made much of talk of infidelity when it arose and often probed for it when it did not. Thus patients' files routinely noted 'evidence of pathological jealousy' or 'no evidence of pathological jealousy', and this was subsequently understood as the cause of self-harm and set directions for intervention. Thus, for example, a female self-harm patient's file might contain the following note:

> Husband alcoholic and accuses her of being unfaithful
> Experiences domestic violence
> Occasional suicidal thoughts
> No active suicidal plans
> Pathological jealousy present in husband.

Likewise, where infidelity had been 'proven', or at least the rumours seemed 'more certain' than in other cases, or indeed where no rumours of infidelity had been voiced at all, clinicians would reject the diagnosis of pathological jealousy:

> Patient took poison while under the influence of alcohol
> Followed an argument with his wife
> No pathological jealousy present.

Thus, both women and men were deemed to be at risk of self-harm in the context of rumour. In the cases of self-harm I reviewed at the Chilaw clinic very few men swallowed poison after hearing rumours of infidelity, and that was when wives were abroad. When wives were at home, men more often resorted to direct forms of violence and abuse, in response to which wives themselves swallowed poison. The following three cases provide illustrations of the relationship among village rumour, diagnoses of pathological jealousy, and men's and women's suicidalities. In the original recorded in clinicians' shorthand, for the purposes of readability I have restructured them into narrative case histories. While showing the links clinicians draw between the social processes of village rumour and mental processes of pathological jealousy and its suicidal effects, they also show the grounds on which clinicians admit or omit the diagnosis of pathological jealousy at all, and in so doing seemingly struggle with the psychiatric logic on which it is based.

Case 16: Maurice

> Maurice, aged thirty-five, is married with two children. He was admitted to Chilaw hospital after swallowing eighty tablets of paracetamol. Two years previously his wife had migrated abroad, and around one year previously he began to hear stories that she was having an affair. Six months after that Maurice started to hear that she was involved in a second affair. Although Maurice is suspicious that someone in their village is trying to create problems in his family by spreading these rumours, he developed a depressive episode, pathological jealousy, and swallowed paracetamol with an intent to die.

In this case, the clinician recorded a chain of events leading from migration through rumour to self-harm. It shows how entirely unsubstantiated gossip, which Morris himself suspected had been started for malevolent reasons, led to what the clinician called 'depression' and 'pathological jealousy', and a resulting suicide attempt. On the surface, the chain appears to be self-evident, but in fact it involves a series of assumptions that while in this case they are obscured from view, in the following two cases they pose problems for clinicians' thinking.

Case 17: Nishantha

Nishantha, aged thirty, had been a solider in the army for the past eight years, the past two of which he has been absent without leave. Nishantha has been married once before, prior to his joining the army, but he ended the relationship because he suspected his wife of having an affair. However, the couple had children together and because of this Nishantha maintains a friendship with his wife. Nishantha married again soon after joining the army, but has come to suspect his new wife of also having affairs. Nishantha's new wife is also unhappy that he continues to see his first wife and also became suspicious of another woman in the village. These suspicions have led to numerous arguments between the couple, during one of which Nishantha swallowed weedicide in front of her.

This case shows how clinicians dealt with rumours of infidelity as they were expressed by women and men. While both husband and wife made unsubstantiated claims of infidelity based on rumour, the clinician decided that Nishantha was suffering from pathological jealousy but his wife was not. Ostensibly, this was because Nishantha drank arrack but the wife did not; the psychological diagnosis of pathological jealousy is, of course, only generally found in alcoholics, and in Madampe women are assumed not to drink. Yet by failing to account for the wife's unfounded suspicions in medical terms – that is, by admitting the validity of village gossip in her case but not in the husband's – the clinician undermines his own diagnosis of Nishantha.

Case 18: Priyanthi

Priyanthi, aged twenty-seven, swallowed pesticide after arguing with her husband. He began hearing rumours about her infidelities with several men. Priyanthi denies the rumours and her husband is unable to prove his allegations. However, he violently abused her over this issue, prevents her from leaving the house, and also prevents her from speaking with family members. Over the past eighteen months Priyanthi has self-harmed three times, twice by swallowing *kane:ru* seeds and most recently by swallowing pesticides. Priyanthi's marital problems are caused by the husband's pathological jealousy brought on by his excessive drinking. However, the husband's family also accuses Priyanthi of having affairs.

This case illustrates how diagnoses of pathological jealousy in men can form the basis of a diagnosis of suicide in women. What is also interesting about the case, however, is the fact that Priyanthi's in-laws were also accusing her of infidelity, even though they apparently were not alcoholic and showed no signs of (presumably mass) pathological jealousy. As with the previous case, the clinician's search for a medically sensible explanation was undermined by the very facts presented, which suggested that rumours and jealousies of infidelities were generated by a far wider set of individuals than alcoholic men alone.

Collapsing the paradox: reconsidering alcohol, migration and suicide

Veena Das (2007: 108) argues that rumour has 'the potential to make us experience events, not simply by pointing to them as something external, but rather by producing them in the very act of telling'. Rumours that gnaw at men's fearless pursuit of fun ironically generate fears which challenge that pursuit. At the village level, the high rate of suicide in middle-aged men, and in particular men and households involved in the migration economy, stands as paradox to the usual stories that manhood and masculinity manifest by men's involvement in the global economy, and of the suffering suicides of respectable middle-class men. Indeed, they may be understood as acts of sabotage by those 'left behind', the nameless and faceless men who, excluded from the supposed wealth and glamour of international lives, find themselves increasingly on the wrong side of widening gaps between rich and poor in contemporary Sri Lanka. In many ways the suicides of men who have been frozen in space and time resemble those of lovelorn male youth recoiling from a rejection.

At the level of the clinic, however, men's tales of rumour and rejection make little medical sense except as a form of psychosis, while women's tales of rumour find no substantiation at all. In psychiatric terms suicide should not proceed from imaginary infidelities; however, the additive of alcoholism is enough to push clinicians into a diagnosis that makes sense to them. Here we find a professionalised critique of migration that fulfils many of the same functions as the vernacular fear of Kalu Yaka, the Black Demon. At both levels it is the existential fear of movement and cessation of movement that shapes the contexts and conditions of men's suicides. These are especially concerns for the broad middle class – Udagama teachers, Chilaw mental health clinicians – who generate theories of suicide about the lower status men they encounter in daily life. Contexts of movement that link family breakdown with the exposure of women and men to various kinds of negative sexual and social influence and violence are regarded as the root of suicidal practice. The folk belief in Kalu Kumara and the clinical diagnosis of pathological jealousy capture in single frames the genesis and consequences of those experiences and anxieties.

Viewed from such perspectives, the paradox that I have explored begins to break down. We are once again dealing with ethos and evidence. The alcohol that fuels fearlessness leads to its own terrors, creating a space for violence at once fantasy and forceful. But the courage to face those fears is also to be found in masculine spaces, of which the drinking party is the exemplar. What the material suggests is a far more complex relationship between alcohol and suicide and migration and suicide than has hitherto been discussed in Sri Lanka. There is no simple causal link between alcohol and suicide, and migration and suicide, or even alcohol and migration, as alcohol and migration provide crucial – and *valid* – forms of movement. There is of course more than a semblance of puritanism in the equation between alcohol and suicide, and a semblance of chauvinism in laying blame on migration, which is usually to lay blame on women.

What is required is a more dynamic view of social practice and representation generated in this space, which grants the complex overlay of *jolly time*, movement, fearlessness, thwarted lives, challenged identities, formless threats, domestic violence and self-inflicted deaths. Moving beyond ideas of perpetrators and victims and causes and consequences, we must instead consider how and why the cessation of movement is figured as a risk or a cure, and the relational politics of doing so.

Insights for prevention

Summary of the argument

- Masculinities are constructed in many ways, but in Madampe having the means as reasons for *'going somewhere'* – and of having *'somewhere to go'* – are vital. Drinking parties and migration represent two of these.
- Drinking and migration may not suit everyone but in and of themselves they do not cause suicide or violence and in some cases may provide barriers to suicide and violence.
- Problems mount up when men's ability to 'move', both literally and figuratively, are *challenged* – often this is experienced in terms of a *perceived threat to women's sexuality and the mythical 'Black Demon'*.
- Forms of violence stemming from masculinities that have nowhere to go may either be directed *'inwardly' through forms of suicidal practice* or *'outwardly' through forms of relational violence*, which cause their own suicidal practices in victims.

Practical applications

- Intervention programmes promoting abstinence from alcohol are *unlikely to be effective* not only because drinking forms an important construction of masculinity but drinking parties can offer men an *important and legitimate form of social and emotional support*.
- Greater attention needs to be paid to the creation of a *responsible drinking culture* and education and awareness for men concerning *gender and relational violence*.
- At the same time more support should be provided to women and children who are the *victims* of drinking violence. This requires not only the development of short-term solutions including state support but fostering a long-term change in attitudes towards relational violence.
- Ultimately it must be men themselves who lead this change, and at all levels of society.

Notes

1 By 'taking men's point of view' I want to stress, however, that I am not validating the reasons that men give for engaging in suicidal practices, which are often expressions of gender inequality and may involve the exclusion or oppression of women. If men's suicides are to be understood and tackled effectively, then their reasons for doing so must

be taken seriously in and through their own terms; it is not enough to simply view them as misogynistic expressions but as contributing to the factors leading men to report suicide rates four times those of women, in Madampe and across Sri Lanka.
2. Further associations were made between 'hot' and 'cold' drinks, including the notion that hot drinks (i.e. spirits) are suitable for men, while cold drinks (i.e. beer and wine) are suitable for women. They also have medicinal properties: hot drinks are good when you have a cold, but beer is chilling so should be avoided.
3. My middle-class friends in Madampe could neither afford to travel abroad legally (unless they were fortunate enough to have a sponsor in the destination country or secure employment via some means) nor willing to be trafficked, smuggled or travel on false documents. Having heard countless horror stories of Sri Lankans who had ended up in slavery or worse, their comfortable lives at home precluded the possibility of 'risking it all' to leave the country using high-risk means.
4. Sri Lankan Buddhists are Theravada Buddhists. In recent years, evangelical Christian orphanages and preschools have begun attracting the same kinds of fears.

8 The search for compassion

We had to tell them they were depressed!

Chilaw mental health clinician

In Madampe, suicidal practices are often specifically public events that draw attention to the social and moral challenges and conflicts in people's lives. If the popular imaginary of suicidality in Euro-American contexts is of the lonely individual slipping quietly away in the privacy of their own home, in Sri Lanka it is of the frustrated or angry person brandishing a bottle of pesticide or a packet of Panadol tablets in their hand, 'up close and personal' in the presence of those whom they blame for their troubles and misfortunes. The exception to this – and ones that do not figure so centrally in popular imaginary – is of the suffering person who retreats to some isolated spot, or who quietly strings up a rope in the house when the family is asleep, and kills him- or herself without an audience. Yet, even in those cases, the body will usually be discovered and a crowd quickly form, giving the deceased the public showing he or she may or may not have wished for. In the same way, when survivors of self-harm are admitted for emergency treatment, crowds of relatives, friends and neighbours often congregate outside the hospital ward, eager to hear how the person is doing, swap theories about what may have happened, and figure out who might be to blame and whether retaliation is called for.

The cases described throughout this book have shown how suicidal practices seek to preserve or challenge the social order. This chapter explores the practices and representations attendant to suicide prevention and treatment work carried out in Madampe. Far from existing as a benign activity, I show how suicide interventions may be understood as forming a crucial role in how suicidal practices may achieve social conservatism or transformation. How suicidal people and their families and friends engage with – and seek to encourage suicidal people to engage with – intervention services springs from how they consider the relational and emotional causes of suicidal practice and how they envision the 'good family life'. If the suicidal act is often one of conscious performance committed with the intent of drawing attention and sympathy to the self, then preventive intervention may be understood as an imposition of silence: an attempt to damp down the suicidal person's claims and present matters in a very different way. Intervention may be understood as an effort to frame and reframe past and future to fit the concerns of those who are the *object* of suicidal practices as much as similar concerns are the aim of suicidal people themselves. By seeking to temper or remove suicidal responses from people's repertoires of action, suicide intervention may be understood as practices of power and control that perpetuate the causes of suicide *here* as much as they promote the welfare of the suicidal – and perhaps more so.

This chapter explores these themes through a consideration of village-, court- and clinic-generated intervention strategies existing in Madampe. When I asked informants what kinds of help were available to them, most mentioned three possibilities. First, seeking emotional support and help with problem solving, either in partnership with some trusted relative or friend, a monk, priest, pastor, teacher, or otherwise alone; second, seeking the help of a health or social work professional like the Child Probation Officer, Family Counsellor or the Grama Niladhare; third, but very rarely, visiting mental health clinicians at Chilaw. These responses thus echoed those gathered by Jeanne Marecek (1998: 78) in her survey of preferred intervention strategies in Sri Lanka, which suggested that emotion-focused responses, problem-focused responses and expert healing systems were turned to in approximately equal measure.

Alongside voluntary intervention services are those into which self-harmers may be funnelled involuntarily, usually as a result of family intervention, a child welfare court order, a medical request for restraint, or because a self-harm patient is unconscious and decisions are taken by relatives or doctors. Sariola and Simpson (2013) have studied the processes through which self-poisoning patients in the North Central Province of Sri Lanka are co-opted into clinical trials of poisoning antidotes. Sariola and Simpson argue that through this process suicidal people move from the status of 'abject', having engaged in a stigmatised act that 'places them at the very limits of physical and social life', to a status of 'object', the focus of scientific clinical trial, to a status of 'subject', bestowed by their participation in experimental research that grants them protection through international ethical mandates. In Madampe it is far from the case that villages, courts and clinics routinely ascribe suicidal people to an abject status, and this has ramifications for how interventions play out in individual cases as they become 'objects' of court or clinic intervention and 'subjects' of legal and mandated codes of conduct for the management and treatment of self-harming individuals.

So far in this book I have described a world that is riven by relational violence. It is a bleak view and one that offers little hope for its victims. In this chapter, my aim is to balance that view through a consideration of how people in Madampe attempt to resolve crises in their lives. Following my informants, my intention is to search for compassion. The underlying concept discussed in this chapter is *metta*, the Buddhist value of 'loving kindness' and 'compassion'. The chapter first considers how *metta* is imagined in relation to suicide and its causes, including how *metta* can become a form of violence in its own right. Yet the principal objective of the chapter is to demonstrate the pacific opportunities of *metta* and its potential role in the prevention of suicide. Thus the chapter describes the social effects of suicide interventions as they are deployed in Madampe, evaluates them in relation to a theoretical 'search for compassion' and seeks to develop a model of compassion that offers alternative ways of thinking about self-harm and suicide prevention.

Village-generated interventions: sympathy or silence?

In Madampe, *metta*, loving kindness or compassion, is widely considered the cure for the causes of suicide *here*, especially family problems. *Metta* is routinely reflected upon by ordinary Buddhists observing the *dasa sil* (ten precepts)[1] on *poya* (full moon) days (Obeyesekere 1985: 140); *metta* is also something that people seek to reflect upon in their daily lives with the intention of reducing suffering and the risk of frustration and anger. Ravi's death, which introduced this book, was explained by people in terms of his mother's loss of *metta*, which allowed her to 'abandon' her son, and Ravi's subsequent loss of his 'mother's love' (*ammage a:dare*) which exposed him to dangerous influences that eventually cost him his life. We can follow this concern with the loss of *metta* and absence of love through the relational violence of suicidal practice, the mounting feelings of suffering, frustration and anger that come with them, and the love problems of youth and disruptive movements of men. In each instance, suicidal practices may be explained in relationship with compassion and love in two ways: the first as the product of *metta*'s loss, and the second as the consequence of the suicidal person's search for *metta*. Thus, people in Madampe suggest, suicide interventions should focus on providing *metta* for whom it is in deficit.

When Udagama villagers complained that Ravi's mother 'did not have love in her heart', they were seeking to lay blame upon her alone. Yet, in so doing, they were also giving credence to a wider discourse in Madampe that expresses concerns about the absence of *metta* in daily life more generally. This absence is something that many people feel keenly, and to some extent take a share of the blame for. 'We should have love in our hearts' (*hite: mana:pəyak tiyennə o:ne*) is a common answer to a range of problems, and especially seeks to counterbalance the processes of blaming and shaming that otherwise regulate social and moral life. Indeed, this dichotomous representation, of a community on the one hand riven by *necessary* conflict that is generative of the relational, political and societal, but which on the other hand is held together by an *equally necessary* ethic of *metta* for oneself, one's relatives, friends and neighbours, and 'humanity' at large, offers an explanation for both the high levels of suicidal practice and commitments to generosity, charity and hospitality found in Sri Lanka.[2] If the manifestation of the 'deficit' of *metta* is suicide, then its remedy and surplus becomes the loving gift – an act of *metta*. When one or the other is in abundance, problems may ensue; when they are in balance, social and moral harmony may prevail.

Thus, suicidal practices may be understood as a search for *metta* and not simply the consequence of lost *metta*. So far, I have represented suicidal people as, if not revengeful people, then at least as people seeking redress. Yet, in so doing, I have developed an argument that is itself in deficit of *metta*: I have not adequately shown how those caught within processes of blaming and shaming may also be understood as calling for *metta*. Here again we find that suicide is not understood simply as the ends of a means but the means to an end other than death. By engaging in suicidal practices, people are hoping to receive from others what they feel to be lacking: an expression of love, compassion, and a general concern for their welfare. A central component of the suicidal act becomes a questioning of the absence of, and thus a call for, *metta*, and this is what many people in Madampe say should be at the heart of any relevant suicide prevention programme. Yet it is never the case that all people at all times are thought to deserve *metta* or can equally claim *metta*, and it is in the decisions around how to respond to suicidal practices – that is, with sympathy or not – that the crises highlighted by suicidal acts may be silenced. This also means that 'too much' *metta* may be seen as encouraging, not reducing, suicide risk.

As always, the decision to respond with sympathy or silence reflects gender, generational and class concerns. At the most general level, the suffering suicides of *pura:ṇə* men and the middle class are considered more worthy of sympathy than the anger suicides of *estate* women and the working class, the silencing of which is sought. Once, two young male informants argued over whether a suicide could ever be justified, and if not how suicidal people should instead seek to respond to their problems. Roshan, aged twenty-one, and Kumara, aged twenty-six, and I had spent the best part of the day at the Kuliyapitiya Coroners' Court translating files. After work, we retired to a teashop to discuss our findings. Roshan and Kumara were particularly struck by the fact that many suicides appeared to manifest in the context of everyday conflicts of blaming and shaming. Roshan explained: 'I cannot believe these things! I cannot believe our people live like this!'

Our conversation moved on to the issue of whether any of the cases we read could be justified and if so deserved sympathy and our compassion. Neither men raised any of the obvious Buddhist objections to suicide, for example, the principle of non-violence, of *kamma*, or that suicide is a manifestation of desire for and attachment to material things. Instead, Roshan argued that people committed suicide because their problems became too much to bear. If people committed suicide, Roshan said, it was because they had no other choice available to them: they 'are suffering from frustrations' that cannot be remedied by any means except their own death. For Roshan the epitome of a suffering suicide that deserved sympathy was of a man struggling with work and financial problems. Roshan suggested:

> Suicide is the only solution for some people because their problems are too big for them. By committing suicide, they are hoping to solve their problems. When this is the case, we should not blame him. This is why I don't think suicide is always a problem.

Roshan was providing justification for the idea that suicidal behaviour could be used as a means by which irresolvable problems could be addressed. He expressed sympathy for the suicidal and, by inference, condemned those individuals who could be blamed for causing the problems leading to suicide. In that case, then, further attention should be paid to the crisis and, far from being silenced, the suicidal person should be given proper opportunity to speak. However, Kumara countered that suicide was wrong because problem solving is 'the purpose of life itself'. For this reason, Kumara added, problem solving was always possible regardless of the nature or extent of the problem faced, because problem solving is part of what makes us, human beings, what we are:

> I know many people [who have killed themselves]: it is worrying. It is bad because taking a life is not the solution, facing the problem is the solution. Some people can't face their problems because they have no backbone. Their mental situation is not ready to face reality. Problem solving is life, no? But they don't try to solve their problems.

For Kumara, the argument that suicide is a last-resort strategy was not convincing. Instead, Kumara argued that suicide was a strategy chosen by people who lacked the 'education' (a phrase also implying a more general social and moral maturity) to solve their own problems, think of alternatives, or who relied too heavily on others:

> They always try to escape the problem. But that is not life. We can always find a solution. Many people think that it's not possible ... and they always try to depend on others. Then their problems get bigger. If they have a loan, they think that they can't pay it back and so he thinks he will give up his life. Sometimes people think 'I do not have a good girl' and they give up their life. But everyone has someone.

Thus, while for Roshan suicide was justified and alternatives were not forthcoming because they cannot rely on others to support them, for Kumara suicide was not justified because people did seek to rely on others instead of their own mettle. The best reaction in that case would be not to respond with sympathy but instead with *incomprehension*: to disavow the apparent causes, refuse loving kindness, and impose silence lest the suicidal person be tempted to self-harm again. While Kumara was prepared to include suffering men in his example of suicides who did not deserve sympathy, both he and Roshan agreed that women's and youths' anger suicides deserved only silence.

Roshan's and Kumara's arguments were echoed across Udagama and Alutwatta, and Madampe more widely. According to Soma, a fifty-six-year-old Buddhist widow living in Udagama, suicide was also evidence of poor problem-solving skills and a general lack of education, and therefore should not be responded to with sympathy but with silence. Soma explained:

> [T]hey are unable to solve their problems. They are weak; suicide is the only solution for them. They are weak in the mind. Every problem has a solution; they should have tried to find it. You shouldn't take poison because of a love problem. They should think about it.

Soma further argued that suicidal behaviour often led to problems for families. She pointed out that even if a person committed suicide with no ill intent towards another, village gossip would nevertheless ensure that some third party was blamed for it, and usually a family member:

> It is bad for the family when someone kills themself. Society [the village community] will say bad things about the family. If you kill yourself because of an economic problem villagers will start rumours that something else was the problem. They won't speak about the real reason.

Soma's concern links suicidal practice again with the problem of *boru* – the telling of lies and 'obvious pretence' – that acts as a moral levelling device (see Chapter 3). Just as the intended outcome of the suicidal act itself can never truly be known, the appropriateness of an intervention can only be similarly vague. And to respond inappropriately – in fact to respond at all – is to become caught up in the suicide process and the claims and counter-claims that surface concerning who is to blame and what must be done.

The question of whether to respond with sympathy or with silence was raised by people in most suicide cases I investigated and formed an important part of the overall repertoire of suicidal acts. The decision was of concern for the families of suicidal people, who are usually assumed to have caused the act, as well as agents of the state tasked with their treatment and management. Given that in the vast majority of cases suicidal acts are known only through *post hoc* rationalisations, and given that this fact is as true for suicidal people as it is for their interlocutors and witnesses, the timeframe within which sympathy can be expressed and crisis maintained or silence imposed has significant effects on how people come to know about suicides occurring around them. Due to the suicidal person's survival, the management of self-harm cases was particularly fraught: he or she may lobby for sympathy at the same time as others' attempts at silencing them. Two examples illustrate the contexts and conditions within and under which sympathy and silence played out. In so doing I show how suicidal individuals, their families and other interested parties use a variety of mechanisms to build sympathy or impose silence, and how in one case I became an unwitting part of that process.[3]

Case 19: Champika

During my fieldwork at the Chilaw Mental Health Clinic, one case I investigated was that of Champika, aged forty-one, and Piyadasa, aged forty-two, who both lived in the same village in the Chilaw area. Champika and Piyadasa had been involved in an affair for a few months before being discovered, following which Piyadasa's wife and children left home and Piyadasa committed suicide. Following Piyadasa's funeral, his relatives found Champika and blamed and assaulted her, after which she swallowed a dozen or so paracetamol tablets. In retaliation, Champika's own relatives blamed Piyadasa's relatives, and a fight ensued.

In this case, claims for sympathy and attempts at imposing silence played out across multiple scenarios. These included through the use of violence that shows how sympathy for a suicide can generate different kinds of responses. First, Piyadasa's relatives expressed sympathy and anger over his death through violence committed against Champika, while Champika's relatives also expressed sympathy and anger over her self-harm in the same way. Thus, sympathy for a kinsman or kinswoman demanded retaliation against the other group, and this was considered a means through which *metta* could be restored and equilibrium maintained.

Case 20: Ravi

The second case involves Ravi, whose death, as I have shown, generated a huge amount of sympathy but also an attempt to impose silence. Ravi's friends, other Udagama villagers and people across Madampe at large discussed the case at length. Even more than a year afterwards, people were still telling me about Ravi's death with no seeming connection with Udagama at all. However, from the moment I stepped off the bus in Madampe and returned home that first evening I had heard about the death, I was treated to a concerted effort on the part of local government officials, who then knew nothing of my research interests in suicide, to downplay the incident and define it as an accident. That night my host family received a telephone call from the local Grama Niladhare informing them that a boy from Udagama had drowned and that I should steer clear of the village because it was a 'dangerous' place. The next morning the Grama Niladhare paid a visit to my lodging place to repeat the information and warning. Subsequently I spoke to the Madampe Child Probation Officer, Bandara, a resident of Udagama and friend since 2001. The conversation was strained, and while I have no doubt that it was a difficult subject for him, what he told me seemed to be a conscious attempt to divert the issue. Because Bandara's response was so striking, I wrote it down verbatim at the time:

> Ravi did have a love problem a while ago but not any more. He wasn't that affected by it. Some people are saying it was a suicide, some even that his friends pushed him. People say things. The correct thing to say is that it was an accident ... yes, that is the correct thing to say.

There are a number equally valid reasons why the Grama Niladhare took such an interest in my knowledge of the case and why Bandara thought describing Ravi's death as an accident would be 'the correct thing to say'. Some of these reasons include the wish to limit gossip for the good of the family left behind, a desire to control information about the suicide and thus risk of 'copycat' cases, and a concern for the country's reputation when a foreign researcher was working in the area. These explanations notwithstanding, another interpretation is that as agents of the state, the Grama Niladhare and Child Probation Officer felt a responsibility to silence a crisis generated from Ravi's family life and by Ravi's death: a crisis that exposed, as witnessed by Udagama villagers' attempts at making sense of the case by laying blame, the absence of *metta* and its implications for 'normal' social life.

The concern to silence the suicidal has also been documented by Jeanne Marecek and Chandanie Senadheera (2012: 76–77). Marecek and Senadheera recorded the narratives of teenage women who self-harmed in southern Sri Lanka, and of their parents. In twenty-two pairs of interviews with the women who self-harmed and a primary caregiver (usually an older adult female), the expressions 'foolish thing' and 'foolish act' were used over forty times (ibid.: 76). Marecek and Senadheera suggest that the reference to foolishness fulfils a social function, on the one hand used by the self-harming women to distance themselves from agentic intent and thus blame for their actions, and on the other hand providing those who might be implicated in the case with a 'get-out' clause. This distancing operates as a diversionary tactic, drawing attention away from the relational violence of suicide, and placing in its stead an explanation of 'momentary foolishness'. Marecek and Senadheera (ibid.: 77) suggest that in so doing the silencing of the suicidal '[seals] off family strife from further probing ... [enabling] family members to co-exist; it may thus serve as a collective need'.

Marecek and Senadheera's highlighting of the importance of silence in the management of the conflicts that produce suicidal practice is related to Alex Argenti-Pillen's (2002) study of violence in southern Sri Lanka. Argenti-Pillen described how language was used by women living side by side with neighbours who had previously engaged in the JVP uprisings of the late 1980s and early 1990s, during which they engaged in killings, abductions and torture (see also Hughes 2013). In that context, silence and other forms of 'linguistic containment' were used to draw attention away from unresolved conflicts, crimes and problems, and to maintain a level of social accord. Thus, the search for silence in conditions of extreme 'noise' enables the co-existence of people who would otherwise perhaps quickly collapse into further violence. 'Not talking about it' becomes as much a strategy for self-survival as it does one of social harmony. At the same time, however, there is never any doubt that silence is illusory. When people in Madampe spoke of both suicide and those suspected of orchestrating violence during the JVP years, it was often in hushed tones, but the perpetrators were always known.

Yet the removal of intent from a suicidal act and the imposition of silence also functions to deflect the karmic implications of violence. As I described in Chapter 3, if suicidal acts are consciously targeted to damage others then it is the suicidal person him- or herself who accrues *pav* (demerit). In this sense, the imposition of silence may also be understood as a concern to protect the *pin* (merit) of the suicidal person, which is an act in itself that may be understood as one of *metta*. Thus, even as silence extends the possibilities of violence and perpetuates the structures of inequality that generate violence, the exhibition of *metta* pursues a caring path and one that is concerned with the well-being of the suicidal person. To designate *metta* as simply being a false belief or consciousness in the service of power here would not remain faithful to the ethnographic project. The search for compassion even in the midst of such suffering is a real one, and it offers hope. As I will describe more fully below, if our anthropological understanding of Sri Lanka's suicide epidemic is to be found in the ontological subjectivities of practice, so too will the possible solutions it calls for. First, however, I discuss how attempts to silence the suicidal have also been a key strategy deployed by the agents of courts and clinics in Sri Lanka, and in so doing highlight the inadequacy of existing approaches in the search for compassion.

Court-generated interventions: dealing with frustration

Up until 1997, in Sri Lanka an attempt to commit suicide was a criminal offence and could be dealt with through legal prosecution. While legal proceedings often accompanied suicidal acts, they usually depended on medical officers reporting them to the police, and in Madampe at any rate this happened only vary rarely (interview with Head of Health Services Puttalam, 8 February 2006). In the vast majority of self-harm cases, patients returned home to their family lives with no formal legal interference. Today, an attempt to commit suicide is decriminalised but abetment to suicide – that is, encouragement of another person to attempt suicide either through maltreatment or through assisted suicide – remains illegal. The Sri Lankan police sometimes threaten to charge people who through their actions cause someone to attempt or commit suicide with abetment to suicide as a way of reducing conflicts leading to suicide and thus the suicide rate (*News 1st*, Thursday, 19 September 2013). Through this action, then, the Sri Lankan police may be understood as instigating a formal policy of encouraging people to take heed of their actions and the spread of *metta* throughout society.

Abatement to suicide is an old charge in Sri Lanka, and may be traced back through several centuries. In 1660 Robert Knox, an employee of the British East India Company, was captured and held by the Kandyan king for twenty years. Knox kept detailed and fascinating descriptions of everyday life that he observed and, upon his escape, published. Knox (1981: 267) reported that under Kandyan law, a suicide by those considered to be of 'sound mind' was seen to be the fault of other people, who were accused of having failed in their duty of care for that person – of 'not letting one another alone' (Chapter 4). In some cases it seems that entire villages were fined for neglect, although more commonly specific individuals were held to account:

> They have an odd usage among them to recover their debts.... They will sometimes go to the house of their debtor with the leaves of the Neiingala a

certain plant, which is rank Poyson, and threaten him, that they will eat that Poyson and destroy themselves, unless he will pay him what he owes. The debtor is very much afraid of this, and rather than the other should Poyson himself, will sometimes sell a Child to pay the debt: Not that the one is tender of the life of the other, but out of care for himself. For if the party dyes of the Poyson, the other for whose sake the man Poysoned himself must pay a ransom for his life. By this means also they will sometimes threaten to revenge themselves of those with whom they have any contest, and do it too. And upon the same intent they will also jump down some steep place or hang or make away with themselves; that so they might bring Adversary to great damage.

Amerasinghe (1999: 306), quoting Davy in *The Legal Heritage of Sri Lanka*, suggests that suspected suicides were referred to the Coroners' Court for ruling. It was upon his judgement that culpability for a suicide was established:

In the case of a suicide occurring in a village, the suicide having been of sound mind, or subject to only temporary fits of insanity, the *sāke-ballaṇḍa* (coroner court) inflicted a fine on the inhabitants of fifty *ridīes* (about twenty-nine shillings).... If the suicide were a confirmed idiot or lunatic, no fine was inflicted. In the first instance, the inhabitants were punished for want of attention to an individual who required it, and whose life might have been preserved had such attention been paid; whilst in the latter, they were excused because they were not supposed to have time to spare to watch individuals who required incessant vigilance.

Later in his book Knox (ibid.: 283) also tells us, however, that the Kandyans possessed 'excellent skill' in the healing of poisons such as Neiingala, suggesting that once the debt or other duty had been agreed to be paid, a remedy for the poison was administered, saving the life of the person. If so, then such 'protest suicides' may rarely have been fatal, and were instead practised with the express intent of scaring another into action.

During the nineteenth and early twentieth century the suicide rate itself was relatively low. Despite this, the character of Knox's 'protest' suicides appealed to the interest of the British, who reported instances of debt collection using suicide threats, and suicidal behaviour received a level of attention that it might not otherwise have. In 1821, the London *Morning Post* carried a story concerning 'The Treatment of Debtors in Ceylon', which included such a reference:

Frequently the creditor will go to the person indebted to him, and say he will poison himself, unless he pays him directly. Instances have occurred of such threats being put into execution, and the debtor, who is considered the cause of his creditor's death, also forfeits his life.

A week later a retired 'Member of the Ceylon Establishment' wrote to the *Post* to dismiss the story and the reports of suicidal 'barbarisms' contained within it, perhaps due to efforts being conducted in Ceylon to stamp out such practices at the time. However, in 1833, Sir John D'Oyly (1929: 37, 80), an administrator of the colony, wrote that among the Ceylonese suicide was 'easily provoked ... [by] ... slander, non-payment of debt, damage to crops, and thwarted love affairs'. Similarly, in 1902 H.R. Freemen (*Administration Report* 1902: S3, G24), administrator of the Chilaw District, commented:

> Attempt to commit suicide – a rather prevalent offence – should be punishable with rigorous as well as simple imprisonment. Would-be suicides generally want pulling together by the tonic of hard work.

Despite these proposed sanctions the suicide rate continued to climb. In 1955, the *Times of Ceylon* ran a story on the increasing number of suicides by ascetic acid, a chemical used in the rubber industry. The *Times* reported that J.N.C. Tiruchelvam, Batticaloa City Coroner, had said at his verdict on a suicide case that:

> [T]he ease with which ascetic acid was obtainable in Ceylon had led to a number of persons, especially among the younger generation, committing suicide by swallowing it. Of late, the number has assumed alarming proportions.

Like their British forebears, Ceylonese members of the legal establishment also viewed the suicidal practices of their subordinate countrymen and women with a great deal of disdain. Newspaper reports at the time captured this attitude, which tended to be dismissive of suicide and treat the subject lightly. To take just one example from 1955 published in the English-language *Times of Ceylon*:

> *Set himself afire after family row*: A man poured kerosene on his head and set himself on fire because of a quarrel with his wife over their child. This was related to the Additional Colombo Magistrate, Mr V.S. Gunawardena, when Nagoor Cassim of Vincent Street was charged with attempting to commit suicide. When Cassim pleaded guilty to the charge, the Magistrate told him that differences between man and wife were not unusual. They tended to relieve the monotony of everyday life. Cassim was bound over in Rs100 for one year. His wife stood surety.
> (*Times of Ceylon*, 3 January 1955)

The flippant tone of these reports has also been characteristic of most suicide journalism in the country over the decades since, to the point where the news media have been accused of feeding the epidemic. The Sri Lankan think-tank, the Centre for Policy Alternatives and UK charity PressWise Trust studied Sinhala-language newspaper stories published in Sri Lanka between March and May 2003. The research showed how the newspaper stories they reviewed tended to include intimate details of each case and to portray suicide in a 'glorified' or 'heroic' way (Centre for Policy Alternatives and PressWise Trust

2003: 3), two elements said to encourage 'copycat' cases and spark suicide contagion. Often stories were found to adopt a male-centred perspective: women were portrayed as the cause of the problem, with men acting to solve the problem through acts of violence, including suicide. The *Handbook* concludes that suicide journalism in Sri Lanka should be concerned to report suicide stories in a way that excludes the sensational and highlights the pathological. Drawing from popular psychological and medical theories, they argue that suicide is the consequence of long periods of mounting depression and is practised for psychological, not social, reasons.

This small selection of official court and media reporting from the past century illustrates the ways in which theories of frustration generated by the court arena have influenced legal interventions in suicide. While suicide is today decriminalised, legal officers and coroners in Madampe continue to feel duty-bound to attempt to prevent suicide through measures aimed at addressing social causes of suicide, including frustration and the contexts that produce frustration. The response of the Grama Niladhare and Child Probation Officer to Ravi's suicide is one indication of this. Another is the ways in which police officers and coroners sometimes act to rein in a suicide case, either by purposively misclassifying a suicide as an accident or through intimidation of witnesses and survivors. In Chapter 2, I described how in some cases it proved difficult to establish a cause of death, and this was especially so with drownings, which were easily classifiable as accidental. During an interview with a local officer, I discussed Ravi's case and learned that the Madampe police had eagerly classified the case as accidental. Ravi's father and uncle were both friends of one of the officers and there was little enthusiasm for causing the family further shame, blame and guilt by adding to the already strong rumours circulating around the village that Ravi had died because of family problems. This was, then, a case of court-generated intervention seeking explicitly to silence a suicide death, not out of sympathy for the suicide but his family.

Court-generated theories of suicidal practice build on the proximate causes of family problems to develop accounts based on theories of frustration. When it comes to intervention, police officers and coroners are interested to limit this interpretation in order to avoid validating common-sense understandings of suicidal practice and to damp down crises into silence, while expounding the virtue of treating one another with loving kindness, for example, by threatening to charge people with abetment to suicide. People in Madampe, who view the police force as highly corrupt and randomly violent, treat the fact that police officers do attempt to promote loving kindness as being deeply ironic. Since decriminalisation, however, their ability to do this has diminished somewhat, and their role has been usurped by health professionals and mental health clinicians.

Clinic-generated interventions: the transformation of suffering

When court interventions dominated the scene, health interventions beyond first aid work remained limited. Commenting on this, the Director of Health Services for the Puttalam District, Dr Rathnayake, whose office is located in Madampe, described the various ways in which medical doctors sought to influence self-harm patients not to attempt suicide again. These ranged from giving stern lectures on the futility of suicide, through informal bedside counselling sessions, to more formal attempts at creating longer lasting support for suicidal people. However, Dr Rathnayake explained, medical intervention was difficult because doctors were obliged to report suicide attempts to the police:

> When I was practising I had to report suicides to the police. But like many of my colleagues I tried not to do so. We thought what would be the point of causing more problems for the fellow? Instead I wanted to treat them in my own way. So I asked them to bring a plant from their home and plant it in the hospital grounds. That way whenever they came back they would see the plant growing.

Dr Rathnayake's solution was to encourage suicidal people to reflect on how their actions can and do have meaning, in this case by giving life to something where once they almost met their own death. Those who attempted suicide more than once would also see the plant and think the same thing. However, Dr Rathnayake suggested that during his five-year posting in the emergency ward he encountered less than a dozen such cases, and intimated that his intervention had been effective. But when people did commit repeat attempts, Dr Rathnayake reported them to the police. If a prior patient died from suicide, he would have been liable, he said.

In the new era of decriminalisation, the 2004 tsunami pushed clinic-generated interventions to the forefront of suicide prevention work in Madampe. When the Chilaw clinic expanded and began mental health education and awareness-raising programmes, village- and court-generated theories of suicide and theories of suicide intervention began to slowly transform. Commenting on the success of the outreach programme, Chilaw clinician Dr Herath boasted:

> Before we went into the villages the people suffered from their problems, but didn't know what caused them. They didn't come to us for help. We had to go and tell them they were depressed. Now they come to our clinic!

Chilaw clinicians consider their work to be at the cutting edge of the Global Mental Health movement that is currently crossing Sri Lanka. Advocates of Global Mental Health (GMH) argue that poor mental health infrastructure, insufficient spending, and an erroneous belief that psychiatric illnesses are culture-bound syndromes indigenous only to Euro-American cultures have left the vast majority of the world's population without adequate mental health care – leading to significant social, health and economic problems. Part of the solution is said to lie in education and awareness with the aim of improving take-up of and retention in mental health services (Prince et al. 2007).

The idea that ordinary people in Sri Lanka do not know how to identify mental health problems and do not even know when they might be suffering from some kind of psychological illness is widespread in Sri Lanka's medical community. This has led one health NGO to comment that in Sri Lanka 'a large number of people do not know that they have mental health problems' (Basic-Needs 2010: 8). Similarly, psychiatrists D'Souza and Singh (2005: 68) argued that '[d]ue to the ... very limited psychological mindedness [of Sri Lankan culture] ... psychiatric morbidity usually remains unrecognised and not treated'. At Chilaw, the problem of 'uneducated villagers' failing to recognise their own psychological problems and the efficacy of psychiatric interventions was a subject of constant discussion and concern among staff. Self-harm patients were viewed as problematic not only because the typical self-harm case they reviewed did not fit neatly with psychiatric models, but also because self-harm patients did not act like (clinicians thought) they should. This led to very common problems in terms of treatment recommendations.

A chief concern was of how self-harm patients failed to follow prescribed courses of anti-depressants. Clinicians told me that either the patient would not take them in the correct quantities or consistently at the right times of day, or if they did they would stop taking them as soon as they felt better, thus risking relapse. As Dr Herath put it:

> We tell them to follow the whole course, even if they feel well again. But they are not educated. They don't listen to us. And then they have to come back to the clinic again because their depression returns.

Another problem facing clinicians was said to be patients' unwillingness to return to the clinic for follow-up appointments. The vast majority of referrals only visited the clinic once, and did not become repeat patients even if this was strongly recommended by the clinician. This problem was said to be especially the case for self-harm patients. The reason for this was again seen to be a lack of education, as well as patients' disbelief in or suspicion of psychiatric medicine.

Sometimes, however, patients' complaints were considered too serious for pharmaceutical intervention alone, or else of a kind where some form of counselling was more appropriate. Both the doctors and the consultant psychiatrist – and also the clinic's male nurse during busy periods – engaged in counselling of varying degrees. The doctors and the male nurse considered counselling to be part of their consultation time, and so the ten minutes spent with a patient might include obtaining a history as well as advising them on how to deal with their problems. The consultant Dr Meddagama spent longer than the doctors on this, but engaged in the same kind of approach. Medical staff who engaged in counselling had read Aaron Beck (e.g. 1979), the chief exponent of cognitive behavioural therapy (CBT). For them, the main lesson to be taken from Beck was that the holding of false beliefs about self and the world caused psychological problems such as depression. The aim of counselling was to make patients recognise this fact, and thus, I was told, to 'correct their thinking'. In this way counselling appealed to clinicians' paternalistic views of uneducated villagers and their perceived inability to deal with problems offered an opportunity to 'correct thinking' more generally, including in terms of how to be a 'good patient'.

Clinicians' narratives were littered with references to these challenges they perceived to be halting their own abilities of being 'good doctors'. The consultant psychiatrist complained that self-harm was very difficult for such patients to deal with 'because they lack education'. A lack of education was both a cause of self-harm (it led to a failure to work out solutions to problems) as well as a failure to respond to treatment. Thus, the focus of clinic-generated interventions was as much concerned with drilling patients into becoming 'good patients' as it was with helping them with psychosocial problems. Indeed, the first had to precede the second. By creating 'patients' out of self-harmers, Chilaw clinicians were also pacifying, atomising and individualising their suffering, frustration or anger, and stripping them of their social crises to make them silent. While this is the aim of many people at village level as well as police officers and coroners, in the arena of the clinic the process envelops self-harmers within the GMH movement which – accompanied by the globalisation of psychiatry behind it – reforms suicidal people in the image of their Euro-American counterparts. Self-harmers are not merely silenced by this process, but relocated to the modern waiting room of idealised mental health facilities built on very different ontological grounds.

In the new psychiatric era, suicide is being transformed into something different from what it once was. If in the village arena people seek to achieve balance between sympathy and silence and in the court arena police officers and coroners seek to regulate conflicts leading to and emanating from self-harm, in the clinical arena the social is being muted in favour of a mental health prescription that models suicide as the result of personalised suffering. The battles that raged between sociologists and psychiatrists across Europe in the nineteenth century about where to locate the causes of suicide (see Chapter 1) are being replayed in Sri Lanka today. Since the time of my original fieldwork, this battle has only intensified. As the self-harm epidemic continues to grow, renewed national attention in the form of a growing field of mental health professionals and international attention in the form of World Health Organisation and World Bank initiatives is placing suicide back on the government agenda. In early 2013, a policy director in the Ministry of Health explained to me how national programming had stalled on this very issue. According to my informant, the ministries of health and social services were at loggerheads over which organisation should lead national suicide interventions. They are arguing about *where* to locate the causes of suicide: in macro-level social forces or internal emotional states.

At stake is more than just the flow of money and policy influence. By redefining suicide as a mental health issue, the claims of suicidal people themselves are being silenced. In the eyes of Chilaw clinicians, this is the most sympathetic thing to do – for them it is the best expression of loving kindness – as it removes 'dysfunctional' concepts of self-harm that legitimise the act as a meaningful social practice.

But as with village and court attempts at doing the same, it leaves unanswered the question of how suicidal people might be able to express themselves or exert influence when other options are unavailable. An uncomfortable but significant truth is that suicidal practices offer the powerless and abused in society an especially potent form of social action. Interrupting this process, and seeking to transform the representation of suicide and its causes, risks re-creating the very conditions giving rise to suicide in the first place, including perpetuating gender, generation and class inequalities, and relational violence. During my research in the Chilaw clinic a forty-six-year-old woman presented following self-harm. This was the third time she had self-harmed; the first time she had swallowed poison, the second time she had tried to hang herself, and the third time she had swallowed poison again. The first suicide attempt had left her partially blind. Each suicide attempt had been preceded by harassment and abuse committed by her husband. Each time she presented at the clinic she was diagnosed with depression and recommended for anger management counselling, and placed on a course of anti-depressants. The domestic environment remained off limits to intervention.

It was not possible, during my research in the clinic, to question patients very closely about their views on the care they received. However, in Udagama and Alutwatta I was able to question informants freely about what they thought of the Chilaw clinic and mental health services more broadly. Interestingly, I did not encounter a great deal of 'mental health illiteracy' or indeed stigma and shame attached to the issue. Certainly, the views expressed about mental illness were not 'enlightened' but neither were they simply discriminatory. The majority of my informants seemed willing to accept that some people might need such services and if so that was because they had a certain kind of 'mental problem' that could be dealt with at the Chilaw clinic. What I encountered more of, however, was the sense that mental health clinicians simply were not going to be useful in the vast majority of cases of 'mental problems' and self-harm, especially in the context of frustration and anger. Loving kindness and visits to temples, churches and shrines were considered as having much greater potential.

Once, I was able to observe at close quarters the reasoning involved when deciding between professional mental health and other forms of intervention. On the day of the Sinhala New Year in 2006, Jamis, a twenty-four-year-old informant in Udagama, began to feel feverish, complain of a headache, and at one point started speaking in tongues: symptoms 'traditionally' associated with demonic interference if not possession. Worried, and clearly subscribing to the more 'modern' view, some of his friends suggested that he visit the Chilaw clinic. However, Jamis' sister's husband, his superior by age and social standing, vetoed this. Instead, he suggested that Jamis should see the local Buddhist priest, who would be able to advise on how to remedy the problems in his life that were manifesting these symptoms.

When I asked why Jamis should not see the doctor, he told me: 'Because all they do is give you drugs. But that's not a solution. Addressing the problem is the solution.' The temple was seen as a place where Jamis could achieve a more 'calm and quiet' or 'contented' (*sǝhane*) state of mind over the long term. This was not something that psychopharmaceuticals could promise. Although not suggesting that Jamis was possessed or required any kind of supernatural intervention, his *massina* – a lower-rung civil servant – did clearly think that mental health intervention would be unhelpful. For the *massina*, Jamis' problems were a manifestation of relational problems combined with occupational problems. These were understood as involving difficulties finding employment in a context where Jamis had few patronage networks from which to draw, combined with an unimpressive curriculum vitae on which to trade. Given the nature of these problems, Jamis' *massina* suggested a solution that focused on relational issues should be sought, and subsequently set about tapping his own networks to find Jamis a job.

However, the promise of psychiatry not only confounds the social aetiology of relational problems that most people assume to be significant. By focusing on the inner, individualised experience of suicide, opportunities for silence and the disavowal of agency are also presented. In this sense, the medicalisation of suicide would appear to complement rather than contradict existing approaches to the management and prevention of suicide in Madampe, and indeed endow it with a 'scientific' method. In her study of depression in Japan, Junko Kitanaka (2011) describes the shifting focus of anthropological and critical social scientific studies of the medicalisation of psychological experience. Kitanaka shows how an early interest in medicalisation as a 'top-down' process of domination over the mentally ill later turned into an interest in medicalisation as a form of 'self-discipline' in which the mentally ill appropriated medical models for their own ends. Kitanaka's own concern is to show how there is no biomedical monopoly on depression but instead the field is better viewed as a bundle of concepts claimed by different actors in different ways.

In Madampe, we also find 'top-down' and 'self-disciplinary' approaches at work, generating a field of bundled concepts where the work of psychiatry is unfolding in different ways. What is especially interesting here are the attempts at sympathy or silence that have evolved across these arenas over the years, with various actors – ordinary villages, government administrators, global mental health professionals – trying generation after generation to fit Sri Lankan suicidal practices into forms shaped by other moulds. Dynamics of power and control are not simply between an external force (be it colonialism, the state or globalisation) on the one hand, and a subjugated, abject population on the other. In Madampe, the balancing of sympathy – respect for the suicidal, respect for their families – with silence – denying the suicidal their claims, denying families their defence – is simply another means by which the relational conflicts of suicidal practice continue. When compassion is withheld and silence is imposed, intervention can be a form of suicide by other means.

Finding compassion

At the wider level is the question of what all these attempts at intervention add up to, or at least are supposed to add up to. On the one hand frustration and anger suicides are seeking social transformation, while their 'cure' through loving kindness, legal dispute, mental health counselling or psychopharmaceutical prescription is seeking a repression of this revolt. The antithesis of the social and emotional states fuelling the process, frustration and anger, is the state of calm and quiet contentedness. In Madampe, *sǝhane* is considered a cure for suicidal practice through the intervention of religious prescriptions, and is a vision of society desired by members of the *pura:ṇǝ* class, for example, men like Don Appuhamy whom we met in Chapter 3. 'If only people would simply stop running after material things,' goes the argument, 'the suicide problem would be solved.' Madampe people consider 'something unsettling' to be at work in contemporary society, producing the conditions that create the contradictions and conflicts of gender, generational and class inequalities. They are, in rhetorical forms, 'modernisation', 'globalisation' and 'change'. Suicidal practices expose these conflicts, and become part of them. The purpose of intervention is to paper over them, and to perpetuate the status quo.

Yet for thoughtful people in Madampe, the causes of suicide and the failures of intervention cannot be forever ignored, and at some point real solutions will have to be addressed. The challenge rests in finding the counterpoint to the ontological grounds of suicidal practice in the village arena, and to learn the lessons of failures in the courts and clinics. A local problem requires a local solution. The concept of *metta* provides that solution, existing as a sentiment poised to address the deficit of compassion in relational lives and so in principle standing as a meaningful practice through which suicide might be addressed. However, where might we find real compassion – compassion that does not re-create the conditions of its own deficit? This is not to call for more or truer Buddhist practice in everyday life, even though the conceptual root of *metta* is of course Buddhism. Such a call would ignore the distinctions between religious texts and religious contexts that anthropology has described so well, and could be misconstrued as an argument for a more 'pure' Buddhism to replace a supposedly 'corrupt' Buddhism of modern society.

Rather, my interest is to explore how the popular sentiments of *metta* might offer a local resource for driving change. By way of their popularity in Sri Lankan society, the sentiments of *metta* or compassion extend beyond just the Buddhist community to encompass the island's ethnic and religious diversity. Compassion is required not only in the deficits that are created at relational level but also at the institutional level, in terms of how suicidal people are treated. Compassion can offer a new approach to silence that pacifies the causes of conflict while ensuring that other voices continue to be heard. However, compassion is also a work in progress and one that extends beyond the scope of this chapter. Yet we understand little of the ethnographic context and practice of compassion that does not re-create the need for itself. The challenge lies in the unravelling of response and oppression to ensure that the forms of violence that generate and are generated by suicide are addressed in ways that offer scope for moving beyond the terms they themselves set down and demand. The aim of this chapter has simply been to map out the terrain of compassion in suicide interventions and to mark out some lessons we may carry forward into the future. The work of compassion has only just begun.

Insights for prevention

Summary of the argument

- Suicide prevention is always a *social and political practice*: to prevent suicide is to deny a choice, to deny a means of communication, and ultimately to impose *silence*, re-creating the conditions that cause suicide.
- In Madampe the Buddhist concept of *metta* (loving kindness/compassion), popularly expressed through the saying 'we should have love in our hearts' for the suicidal, *regulates the politics of prevention*.
- Village-, court- and clinic-generated interventions engage with the principles of *metta* in different ways, with village interventions *allowing a space for sympathy*, and court and clinic interventions largely *imposing silence*.
- Although the search for *metta* does risk re-creating the causes of suicide, as a local resource it also offers the most relevant framework for ontologically grounded suicide prevention work.

Practical applications

- *Local problems require local solutions* – the ontologically subjective nature of suicidal practice requires an ontologically subjective method of suicide prevention.
- Care must be taken to ensure that prevention activities *do not re-create the conditions* of their own need. Suicide prevention is a social and political act that will *deny agency*, which may be a cause of suicide itself.
- Working closely with suicidal people using ethnographic research methods can help suicidologists to better understand the *power dynamics* involved in suicide prevention.
- Detailed study of relational and emotional contexts of suicidal practice can provide frameworks for understanding how local resources can be effectively mobilised for suicide prevention.

Notes

1 These include: (1) Refrain from killing living things; (2) Refrain from stealing; (3) Refrain from unchastity (sensuality, sexuality, lust); (4) Refrain from lying; (5) Refrain from taking intoxicants; (6) Refrain from taking food at inappropriate times (after noon); (7) Refrain from singing, dancing, playing music or attending entertainment programmes (performances); (8) Refrain from wearing perfume, cosmetics and garlands (decorative accessories); (9) Refrain from sitting on high chairs and sleeping on luxurious, soft beds; (10) Refrain from accepting money.
2 The extent of Sri Lankan generosity, charity and hospitality has long been noted, with Robert Knox (1981) commenting that he knew of no other people in the world that were so well disposed. More recently, Sri Lanka has topped global league tables in terms of levels of charitable giving in the country (Charities Aid Foundation 2012). See Osella *et al.* (in press) for an overview of charitable practices in Sri Lanka.
3 The 'observer effect' – the impact that researchers have on their subjects because they are conscious of being watched – is of obvious relevance here. However, what seems

clear is that my presence provided just one more mechanism through which sympathy could be sought or silence imposed, albeit one that had the 'prestige' of difference attached to it. Whether or not my willingness to listen to people's stories about their own or others' problems and self-harm had any real impact on the ways in which sympathy or silence played out however, I cannot say.

9 The suicide process

How can suicidal practices generate social life? The overwhelming approach to suicide as an academic subject and a social and health problem is to treat it as an effect of a cause: of macro-level social changes or micro-level psychological states. However, suicide is undoubtedly the cause of its own effects: most obviously for the suicidal individual and for his or her family and friends but also for society as a whole. It could be argued that suicide is simply too infrequent to have any real socially productive effects on a substantial scale. Gender, generational and class formations may very well generate suicidal practices and epidemiologies, but how could those practices and epidemiologies ever generate gender, generational and class formations? Sri Lanka, with its 'epidemic' of suicide and 'endemic' of self-harm, may well be an unusual case – but when are cases ever not unusual?

The theoretical approach adopted in this book illustrates how an ontological subjectivity of suicide gives rise to an epistemological objectivity, how particularism gives rise to normativism, and how practice gives rise to representation. Theories of suicide generated across villages, courts and clinics have wider effects on popular understandings of suicidality, the contexts and conditions that cause them, and ultimately of the nature of those contexts and conditions. By this view, suicidal practices may be thought of as forming a chain in longer running social processes and of being a social relationship in their own right. Suicidal dispositions are acquired through agentive learning processes that are both structured and structuring.

This concluding chapter develops a processual model of suicide that shows how practices give rise to representation and embeds them in chains of action and consequence. The model is developed from my analysis of the Sri Lankan situation but has global significance. The processual model I am proposing encompasses three timeframes: long-term timeframes at societal level, medium-term timeframes at the life-course level, and short-term timeframes at the event level. Thus the temporal also encompasses the socio-spatial: societal timeframes incorporate the processes through which suicide causal theories come into being across Sri Lanka at large, through village, court and clinic institutions as well as through central government; lifespan timeframes encompass the learning processes in families, peer groups and communities through which individuals come to develop their own understandings and repertoires of suicidal practice and to lay down cognitive frameworks of suicidal practice; event timeframes are the manifestation of societal and lifespan timeframes in quotidian spaces. Obviously, this is a looping process: event level shapes the life-course level shapes the societal level.

In Madampe, the suicide process at societal level encompasses the subjective ontologies of villages, courts and clinics, and their relationships to the Sri Lankan state. Under British colonial rule, suicide was understood as an expression of anger, in the post-colonial era as an expression of frustration, and increasingly today as an expression of depression. Each diagnosis is more than a way of making sense of individual cases of suicide but also defines a particular historical moment. For the British this was the inherent criminality of the native population; for Ceylonese governments the struggles of a newly independent nation emerging in the world system between East and West; for neoliberalist ('post-1977') Sri Lankan governments the globalisation of psychiatry and the spread of Global Mental Health movements across the island following the tsunami. Each provides a vehicle for the operations of power over colonised, liberated and commercialised populations and their ailments. These include: the rise of a bourgeois notion of the 'good family life'; the spread of proposal marriage as the normative type; and increased opportunities for and restrictions on expressions of masculinity through movement. These may all be seen as part of the long play of this process, lived through class and status concerns that in Madampe tie into *pura:ṇə* and *estate* identities.

The suicide process at the level of the lifespan condenses this down into chunks of lived time and space. Children's and youths' concerns with the moral actions of self, friends and family manifest regulating forms of suicide play and suicide practice. Adults' and elders' concerns with the demands and expectations of household members and extended kin provide another generative for suicidalities. The developmental implications of this have only just begun to be explored in this book. However, it appears that life-historical forms, as at societal level, build upon one another. Children and youth imitate and innovate suicidal practices, and these are just as likely to shape their 'suicidal personalities' in adulthood and old age as do the practices of adults and elders shape those of children who learn from them. The cognitive foundations of suicidal practice are laid down from childhood through processes of cultural transmission that exist at societal, lifespan and event levels, and regulate individual lives in terms of gender, generational and status concerns.

This is especially clear in the emotional languages that people use and the emotional model of suicide that lies behind them. If historically suicide in Sri Lanka has been a matter of anger, frustration and depression, then within individual lives, and between genders, generations and social classes, it has been a matter of suffering, frustration and anger. The correspondence between court- and clinic-generated languages of the emotions of suicide and those generated in the village is of course more than coincidence and reflects the extent to which each affects the other. I have explored this in more detail elsewhere (Widger

2012b), but the implication I wish to point out is how the structured and structuring processes of suicide form people in different ways. The suffering suicides of men and the *pura:ṇə* class seek to preserve the social order as much as the frustration and anger suicides of women, youth and the *estate* class seek to challenge it. The terms themselves owe as much to the stigmatising effects of their colonial, post-colonial and mental health appropriations as they do their relationships to local concepts of coolness and heat, and their gender, generational and status components.

The suicide process at the event level further condenses societal and lifespan timeframes into hours, minutes and seconds. This is the level of the 'impulsive' suicidal act in its many forms, from the suffering suicides of the *pura:ṇə* class through the frustration and anger suicides of the *estate* class. Here, the relationships between gender, generation and social class played out over long- and medium-term timeframes are lived in a matter of moments, often passing by too quickly to be explicit but integral to the performance of the act and the reception of the performance. It is also at the event level that the ramifications of societal and lifespan levels are felt most keenly, and at which such emotional and social consequences take effect that they have ramifications for the lifespan and societal levels.

As the suicide process unfolds and passes first from the village arena and into court and clinic arenas, the representations of suicidal practices generated also change. This includes how suicide *here* may be defined at all – as a 'real' attempt at death or 'lies and make-believe' – and how this decision is come to, across arenas. Then there is the question of causality, which proximately is often understood in terms of family problems and their accompanying emotional consequences, which may in turn be defined through recourse to 'indigenous', 'Western' and 'hybrid' classifications and diagnoses. Finally, there is the problem of consequences, including how suicidal practices ought to be responded to, which is to say with sympathy or silence, and what this means for the claims of the suicidal person. Answers to these questions are posed and challenged and, perhaps, eventually agreed upon, at all stages of the suicide process and by the myriad actors involved across villages, courts and clinics. Through the telling and retelling of the story of any particular suicide event, which is inevitably set against the backdrop of lifespan and societal timeframes, the timeframe of the event is itself established.

To make sense of this process I introduce a theory of the 'suicide drama' based on Victor Turner's (1957) classic theory of the social drama. Turner's model is useful because it suggests a processual map of social conflicts that illustrates the relationships between individual experiences and their collective effects. Turner described social dramas as sudden disputes occurring between groups or individuals and which passed through four distinct stages.

The first stage, *breach*, is characterised by the failure of 'norm-governed relations' between individuals or groups. The second stage, *crisis*, is characterised by mounting tensions and troubles between the two sides that, if unchecked, can eventually encompass 'the widest set of relevant social relations to which the conflicting parties belong'. Within this stage, the fundamental structural bases of society, normally invisible in the course of stable everyday relations, are exposed. The third stage, *redressive action*, involves the intervention of high-status members of the group who implement a set of informal or formal mechanisms responsive to the problem in hand. This leads to the fourth stage, *reintegration* or *recognition*. Reintegration is characterised by the reunification of the disputing parties and the continuation of pre-breach social norms, and the second by an adjusted set of social norms encompassing the demands of the breach.

With elaboration, Turner's model provides a framework for understanding suicide. Like social dramas, suicide events in Madampe followed a processual form. This included a first-stage breach of social norms (family problems), a second stage of mounting crisis (blaming and shaming), a third stage of redress (in this case not an intervention but a suicidal reaction), and a fourth stage of recognition or reintegration (sympathy or silence). Depicted in this way the suicide process is cleanly linear. Yet, because the process traverses three socio-spatial arenas and three timeframes, this apparent linearity is upset. Practices associated with each stage generate the representations of those practices that both preceded them and follow from them. The breach of social norms is rarely formally acknowledged until the fourth stage when processes of recognition or reintegration have finished. Until then, they occupy a space of *possibilities* only. Nevertheless, the second and third stages commence, and equally these remain *possibilities* until the fourth stage is reached. It is only when the whole process has played out that any single suicide case may be defined as such.

What does this mean for the suicide process? First, it depicts how practices give rise to representations. Second, it depicts how social practices are contingent upon timespans for their significance. Third, it depicts how 'storytelling' – the ways in which generated narratives of suicidality are used to make sense of things past through their causal simplification and time straightening – turns the whole suicide process around to give the illusion of representation giving rise to practice, and of there being a neat series of steps from a 'culture of suicide' to a 'practice of suicide'. Fourth, it depicts the importance of memory in this process, of the ways in which memories are stored, recollected and recalled through narrative form (Bloch 2012: 189–191). When suicide events are described, it is through a process of *post hoc* recollecting and recalling in which the suicidal individual is cast as the lead player, and through which he or she responds to social or emotional stimuli. The narrative form is obviously linear and exclusivist: it is impossible, through language, to explain the sequence of events in any other way, or to include every possible detail. Much 'goes without saying' (Bloch 1998, 2012), especially at lifespan and societal levels.

Thus, the operations of power, in gender, generational and class terms, shape the processes through which event, lifespan and societal timeframes are first stored in memory, and later recollected and recalled. What is *possible* and what is *impossible* differ for groups of people (men and women, old and young, pura:ṇə class and *estate* class), and how the *possibilities* of the suicide process are eventually defined in sympathy or silence reflects those operations. The narrative forms of suicidality generated by villages, courts and clinics are idealised versions only. At the analytical level, they give insights into evidence as well as ethos, an objective view of the world as well as a subjective rendering of the world. Of course, this is true for all kinds of social action and not just for suicide, but with suicide the implications are crucial because so much of what is done for or to suicidal people in terms of treatment and management depends on a reading of the narrative form. It must be recognised that suicide prevention becomes part of the process through which the possibilities of suicidality are structured into definitive kinds, and that these kinds may ultimately perpetuate the same inequalities, abuses and conflicts that give rise to suicidal practice in the first place.

The concertina of suicidal practice from event level through lifespan level to societal level and back through lifespan level to event level – processes continually occurring across the seconds, days, months and years of practice – means that the suicide process is never complete. Time, and the representations, practices, counter-representations and counter-practices it generates, progresses, circles back upon itself, and sets off in new trajectories at every stage. The 'truth' of any one suicide, the causes, consequences, and intentionality involved, unfolds through dialogues and monologues proposed, established, held, countered, disputed and resolved, over multiple levels of time, action and narrative. By traversing time and space through the minutiae of life, long-term ethnographic fieldwork can offer a unique perspective on this suicide process, providing a distinctly human account of self-harm and self-inflicted death while also offering the opportunity to situate suicide as an anthropological problem. This ultimately is a problem of human life and death, of how we desire to start each day of our lives, and see it through to an end of our own choosing.

The aim of this book has been to develop an anthropological analysis of suicide in Sri Lanka, a country where rates of suicide and self-harm have been among the highest in the world. Adopting an approach elaborated from practice theories of social life, I have swung back and forth between viewing suicide as a constructed and constructing phenomenon. Using ethnographically gathered data, I have sought to show how suicidal practices in one small place and time can only be understood through a careful appreciation of the arenas of social action that generate them. This process of generation takes a multi-layered and circular form which turns diverse practices into formalised representations akin to something like a 'culture' of suicide. Yet to see this culture of suicide as anything other than a stereotypical rendering distal to the originating practice is to risk misunderstanding what is really at stake: the struggles of people seeking to live life in a way that is meaningful to them. An anthropological approach to suicide is an approach that seeks to give life back to suicidal people by helping to make visible what is turned invisible through the operations of power across social arenas. Anthropology offers a distinctive humanistic ethical approach to suicide that seeks to balance the suicidal person's right to die with a concern for their potential to live. As a proposal for an anthropological charter of suicide studies, this book has only set the most basic framework. Nevertheless, an anthropological perspective is deeply valuable and, for relevant and meaningful interventions ever to be made, anthropology must form a central plank of endeavours to reduce practices of self-harm and self-inflicted death, and the conditions of inequality that produce them.

Glossary

a:dambərə   Excessive or unjustified pride
a:dərə praʃnə   Love problems
ahiŋsəkə   Non-violence, innocence
akka   Elder sister
asəhane   Frustration, discontent, restlessness
ayya   Elder brother
baɲinəva   Blame, scold
bayə   Fear
be:badda, be:badukəmə   Alcoholic, alcoholism
boru   Lies, make-believe
dukə   Suffering, sorrow, one of the Four Precepts of Buddhism
e:kə ehe   That is there
estate   Modern housing colony
ge: Household, family
goyigamə   Cultivator caste, highest caste
hoňdə lamay   Good [well-behaved] boy/child
hoňda pavul ji:vite   Good family life
ikmaŋ tarəha   Sudden anger
kaɖe   Small shop, convenience store
kane:ru   Yellow oleander
kane:ru æṭa   Yellow oleander seeds
kasippu   Illicit liquor
læjja   Shame, shy
lingikə asəhanəyə   Sexual frustration
maḷə gedərə   Funeral house
malli   Younger brother
ma:ma: Mother's brother
ma:nəsikə asəhane   Mental frustration
massina   Male cross-cousin, wife's brother, sister's husband
metta   Loving kindness, compassion
næ:na   Female cross-cousin, husband's sister, brother's wife
niyəngəla   Glory lily
parampara:və   Ancestor, generation

pav Sin/demerit
pavul praʃnə Family problems
pavul tatve Family status
pura:ṇə Old, ancient, traditional
pura:ṇə gam Old, ancient, traditional village said to pre-date the LDO
puta Son
rada: Washer caste, low caste
səhane Calm and quiet, content/peaceful [state of mind, society]
salli passe duvənəva Running after material things
sanskrutiyə Culture/tradition
siya divi nasa: gæni:mə To take one's own life [suicide]
tarəha Anger
taruŋəkamə Youthfulness
vaha bonə ekə Poison drinking

Bibliography

Books and articles

Abeyasinghe, R. and Gunnell, D., 2008, 'Psychological Autopsy Study of Suicide in Three Rural and Semi-rural Districts of Sri Lanka', *Social Psychiatry and Psychiatric Epidemiology*, 43(4), 280–285.

Achenbach, T.M. and Rescorla, L., 2001, *ASEBA School-age Forms and Profiles*, Burlington: Aseba.

Alvarez, A., 2002 [1971], *The Savage God: A Study of Suicide*, London: Bloomsbury.

Amerasinghe, A.R.B., 1999, *The Legal Heritage of Sri Lanka*, Colombo: The Royal Asiatic Society of Sri Lanka.

Anderson, J.R. and Chamove, A.S., 1985, 'Early Social Experience and the Development of Self-aggression in Monkeys', *Biology of Behaviour*, 10(2), 147–157.

Argenti-Pillen, A., 2003, *Masking Terror: How Women Contain Violence in Southern Sri Lanka*, Philadelphia: University of Pennsylvania Press.

——, 2007, 'Obvious Pretence: For Fun or For Real? Cross-cousin and International Relationships in Sri Lanka', *Journal of the Royal Anthropological Institute*, 13(2), 313–329.

Astuti, R., Parry, J. and Stafford, C. (eds), 2007, *Questions of Anthropology*, London: Berg.

Atkinson, J.M., 1978, *Discovering Suicide: Studies in the Social Organization of Sudden Death*, London: Macmillan.

Bandarage, A., 1983, *Colonialism in Sri Lanka: The Political Economy of the Kandyan Highlands, 1833–1886*, Berlin: Mouton.

Bandura, A., 2001, 'Social-cognitive Theory: An Agentic Perspective', *Annual Review of Psychology*, 52, 1–26.

BasicNeeds, 2010, *A creative approach to Mental Health and Development at work in Sri Lanka: Challenges, good practices, and lessons learnt*, www.basicneeds.org/download/PUB-A_creative_approach_to_Mental_Health_and_Development_at_work_in_Sri_Lanka.pdf (accessed 16 October 2012).

Beautrais, A.L., 2006, 'Suicide in Asia', *Crisis*, 27(2), 55–57.

Beck, A.T., 1979, *Cognitive Therapy and the Emotional Disorders*, London: Penguin.

Beck, B., 1969, 'Colour and Heat in a South Indian Ritual', *Man*, 4(4), 553–572.

Becker, C.B., 1990, 'Buddhist Views of Suicide and Euthanasia', *Philosophy East and West*, 40(4): 543–556.

Bemme, D. and D'souza, N., 2012, *Global Health and its Discontents*, Somatosphere website, http://somatosphere.net/2012/07/global-mental-health-and-its-discontents.html (accessed 5 April 2014).

Bibliography

Bloch, M., 1973, 'The Long Term and the Short Term: the Economic and Political Significance of the Morality of Kinship', in J. Goody (ed.), *The Character of Kinship*, Cambridge: Cambridge University Press, pp. 75–87.

——, 1998, *How We Think They Think: Anthropological Approaches to Cognition, Memory, and Literacy*, Oxford: Westview Press.

——, 2005, *Essays on Cultural Transmission*, London: Berg.

——, 2012, *Anthropology and the Cognitive Challenge*, Cambridge: Cambridge University Press.

Bohannan, P., 1960, 'Theories of Homicide and Suicide', in P. Bohannan (ed.), *African Homicide and Suicide*, Princeton, NJ: Princeton University Press, pp. 3–29.

Boldt, M., 1988, 'The Meaning of Suicide: Implications for Research', *Crisis: The Journal of Crisis Intervention and Suicide Prevention*, 9(2): 93–108.

Bourdieu, P., 1977, *Outline of a Theory of Practice*, Cambridge: Cambridge University Press.

——, 1984, *Distinction: A Social Critique of the Judgement of Taste*, London: Routledge.

——, 1990, *The Logic of Practice*, Stanford, CA: Stanford University Press.

Brown, M.F., 1986, 'Power, Gender, and the Social Meaning of Aguaruna Suicide', *Man* (n.s.), 21(2), 311–328.

Brown, R.M., Dahlen, E., Mills, C., Rick, J. and Biblarz, A., 1999, 'Evaluation of an Evolutionary Model of Self-preservation and Self-destruction', *Suicide and Life-threatening Behavior*, 29(1), 58–71.

Caldwell, D.B., 1999, *Marriage in Sri Lanka: A Century of Change*, New Delhi: Hindustan Publishing Corporation.

Camus, A., 1955, *The Myth of Sisyphus, and Other Essays*, London: Random House.

Centre for Policy Alternatives and The PressWise Trust, 2003, *Suicide Sensitive Journalism Handbook*, www.cpalanka.org/research_papers/suicide_report.pdf (accessed 1 June 2009).

Charities Aid Foundation, 2012, *World Giving Index 2012*, www.cafonline.org/PDF/WorldGivingIndex2012WEB.pdf (accessed 6 April 2014).

Chua, J.L., 2011, 'Making Time for the Children: Self-temporalization and the Cultivation of the Antisuicidal Subject in South India', *Cultural Anthropology*, 26(1), 112–137.

——, 2012, 'Tales of Decline: Reading Social Pathology into Individual Suicide in South India', *Culture, Medicine, and Psychiatry*, 36(2), 204–224.

——, 2014, *In Pursuit of the Good Life: Aspiration and Suicide in Globalizing South India*, Oakland, CA: University of California Press.

Collins, P.Y., Patel, V., Joestl, S.S., March, D., Insel, T.R., Daar, A.S., Bordin, I.A. *et al.*, 2011, 'Grand Challenges in Global Mental Health', *Nature*, 475(7354): 27–30.

Colucci, E. and Lester, D. (eds), 2012, *Suicide and Culture: Understanding the Context*, Cambridge, MA: Hogrefe Publishing.

Cooper, J., Kapur, N., Webb, R., Lawlor, M., Guthrie, E., Mackway-Jones, K. and Appleby, L., 2005, 'Suicide After Deliberate Self-harm: A 4-year Cohort Study', *American Journal of Psychiatry*, 162(2), 297–303.

Counts, D.A., 1980, 'Fighting Back Is Not the Way: Suicide and the Women of Kaliai', *American Ethnologist*, 7(2), 332–351.

Cross, H.A. and Harlow, H.F., 1965, 'Prolonged and Progressive Effects of Partial Isolation on the Behaviour of Macaque Monkeys', *Journal of Experimental Research in Personality*, 1(1), 39–49.

Daniel, E.V., 1984, *Fluid Signs: Being a Person the Tamil Way*, Berkeley, CA: University of California Press.

Das, V., 2007, *Life and Words: Violence and the Descent into the Ordinary*, Berkeley: University of California Press.
de Munck, V.C. 1996, 'Love and Marriage in a Sri Lankan Muslim Community: Toward a Reevaluation of Dravidian Marriage Practices', *American Ethnologist*, 23(4), 698–716.
de Silva, D., 2003, 'Suicide Prevention Strategies in Sri Lanka: The Role of Sociocultural factors and Health Services', *Ceylon Medical Journal*, 48(3), 68–70.
de Silva, K.M., 2005, *A History of Sri Lanka*, Colombo: Vijitha Yapa Publications.
de Silva, P., 1989, 'The Logic of Attempted Suicide and its Linkage with Human Emotions', in *Suicide in Sri Lanka*, Kandy: Institute of Fundamental Studies.
de Silva, V.A., Senanayake, S.M., Dias, P. and Hanwella, R., 2012, 'From Pesticides to Medicinal Drugs: Time Series Analyses of Methods of Self-harm in Sri Lanka', *Bulletin of the World Health Organization*, 90(1), 40–46.
Dissanayake, S.A.W. and De Silva, W.P., 1974, 'Suicide and Attempted Suicide in Sri Lanka', *The Ceylon Journal of Medical Science*, 23(1/2), 10–27.
Donner, H., 2008, *Domestic Goddesses: Maternity, Globalization and Middle-class Identity in Contemporary India*, London: Ashgate Publishing.
D'Oyly, J., 1929, *A Sketch of the Kandyan Kingdom*, Colombo: Cottle.
D'Souza, R. and Singh B., 2005, 'The Mental Health Challenge in Sri Lanka from Working Within the Disaster Area', *World Psychiatry*, 4(2), 68.
Durkheim, E., 1951, *Suicide: A Study in Sociology*, trans. J.A. Spaulding and G. Simpson, London: Routledge & Keagan Paul.
Eddleston, M., Sheriff, M.R. and Hawton, K., 1998, 'Deliberate Self Harm in Sri Lanka: An Overlooked Tragedy in the Developing World', *BMJ: British Medical Journal*, 317(7151), 133–135.
Eddleston, M., Ariaratnam, C.A., Meyer, W.P., Perera, G., Kularatne, A.M., Attapattu, S. and Warrell, D.A., 1999, 'Epidemic of Self-poisoning with Seeds of the Yellow Oleander Tree (Thevetia Peruviana) in Northern Sri Lanka', *Tropical Medicine and International Health*, 4(4), 266–273.
Eddleston, M., Gunnell, D., Karunaratne, A., De Silva, D., Sheriff, M.R. and Buckley, N.A., 2005, 'Epidemiology of Intentional Self-poisoning in Rural Sri Lanka', *The British Journal of Psychiatry*, 187(6), 583–584.
Eriksen, T.H., 2001, *Small Places, Large Issues: An Introduction to Social and Cultural Anthropology*, London: Pluto Press.
Fincham, B., Langer, S., Scourfield, J. and Shiner, M., 2011, *Understanding Suicide: A Sociological Autopsy*, London: Palgrave Macmillan.
Fortes, M., 1969, *Kinship and the Social Order: The Legacy of Lewis Henry Morgan*, London: Routledge & Keagan Paul.
——, 1978, 'An Anthropologist's Apprenticeship', *Annual Review of Anthropology*, 7, 1–30.
——, 1983, *Rules and the Emergence of Society, Occasional Paper no. 39*, London: Royal Anthropological Institute.
Fuller, C.J. and Narasimhan, H., 2008, 'Companionate Marriage in India: The Changing Marriage System in a Middle-class Brahman Subcaste', *Journal of the Royal Anthropological Institute*, 14(4), 736–754.
Gamburd, M.R., 2000, *The Kitchen Spoon's Handle: Transnationalism and Sri Lanka's Migrant Housemaids*, London: Cornell University Press.
——, 2008a, 'Milk Teeth and Jet Planes: Kin Relations in Families of Sri Lanka's Transnational Domestic Servants', *City and Society*, 20(1), 5–31.

——, 2008b, *Breaking the Ashes: The Culture of Illicit Liquor in Sri Lanka*, New York: Cornell University Press.

——, 2013, *The Golden Wave: Culture and Politics after Sri Lanka's Tsunami Disaster*, Bloomington: Indiana University Press.

Geertz, C., 1983, 'From the Natives' Point of View', in C. Geertz, *Local Knowledge*, New York: Basic Books, pp. 55–70.

Gellner, E., 1983, *Muslim Society*, Cambridge: Cambridge University Press.

Giddens, A. 1965, 'The Suicide Problem in French Sociology', *British Journal of Sociology*, 16(1), 3–18.

Goffman, E., 1961, *Asylums: Essays on the Social Situation of Mental Patients and Other Inmates*, Garden City, NY: Anchor Books.

Goldman, L.R., 1998, *Child's Play: Myth, Mimesis, and Make-believe*, New York: Berg.

Gombrich, R.E.F. and Obeyesekere, G., 1988, *Buddhism Transformed: Religious Change in Sri Lanka*, Chicago, IL: University of Chicago Press.

Gunnell, D., Fernando, R., Hewagama, M., Priyangika, W.D.D., Konradsen, F. and Eddleston, M., 2007, 'The Impact of Pesticide Regulations on Suicide in Sri Lanka', *International Journal of Epidemiology*, 36(6), 1235–1242.

Hacking, I., 1995, 'The Looping Effects of Human Kinds', in D. Sperber, D. Premack and A.J. Premack (eds), *Causal Cognition: A Multidisciplinary Approach*, Oxford: Oxford University Press, pp. 351–383.

Harvey, P. and Gow, P., 1994, 'Introduction', in P. Harvey and P. Gow (eds), *Sex and Violence: Issues Representation and Experience*, London: Routledge, pp. 1–17.

Hewamanne, S., 2003, 'Performing "Dis-respectability": New Tastes, Cultural Practices, and Identity Performances by Sri Lanka's Free Trade Zone Garment-factory Workers', *Cultural Dynamics*, 15(1), 71–101.

——, 2008, *Stitching Identities in a Free Trade Zone: Gender and Politics in Sri Lanka*, Philadelphia: University of Pennsylvania Press.

Hezel, F.X., 1984, 'Cultural Patterns in Trukese Suicide', *Ethnology*, 23(3), 193–206.

Hughes, D., 2013, *Violence, Torture and Memory in Sri Lanka: Life After Terror*, London: Routledge.

IRIN News, 2009, 'SRI LANKA: Suicide Rate Drops, but More People Using Poison', www.irinnews.org/report/83435/sri-lanka-suicide-rate-drops-but-more-people-using-poison (accessed 5 April 2014).

Jadhav, S., 1996, 'The Cultural Origins of Western Depression', *International Journal of Social Psychiatry*, 42(4), 269–286.

Jadhav, S., Weiss, M.G. and Littlewood, R., 2001, 'Cultural Experience of Depression among White Britons in London', *Anthropology and Medicine*, 8(1), 47–69.

Jayasinghe, N.R. and Foster, J.H., 2011, 'Deliberate Self-harm/Poisoning, Suicide Trends: The Link to Increased Alcohol Consumption in Sri Lanka', *Archives of Suicide Research*, 15(3), 223–237.

Jeganathan, P., 2000, 'A Space for Violence: Anthropology, Politics and the Location of a Sinhala Practice of Masculinity', in P. Chatterjee and P. Jeganathan (eds), *Community, Gender and Violence*, New York: Columbia University Press.

Joiner, T., 2005, *Why People Die By Suicide*, London: Harvard University Press.

Jones, I.H. and Daniels, B.A., 1996, 'An Ethological Approach to Self-injury', *The British Journal of Psychiatry*, 169(3), 263–267.

Kapferer, B., 2000, 'Sexuality and the Art of Seduction in Sinhalese Exorcism', *Ethnos*, 65(1), 5–32

Kearney, R.N. and Miller, B.D., 1985, 'The Spiral of Suicide and Social Change in Sri Lanka', *Journal of Asian Studies*, 45(1), 81–101.
——, 1987, *Internal Migration in Sri Lanka and its Social Consequences*, Boulder, CO: Westview Press.
——, 1988, 'Suicide and Internal Migration in Sri Lanka', *Journal of Asian and African Studies*, 23(3/4), 287–304.
Keown, D., 1996, 'Buddhism and Suicide: The Case of Channa', *Journal of Buddhist Ethics*, 3, 8–31.
Kitanaka, J., 2011, *Depression in Japan: Psychiatric Cures for a Society in Distress*, Princeton, NJ: Princeton University Press.
Knox, R., 1981 [1681], *An Historical Relation of Ceylon*, Colombo: Tisara Prakasakayo.
Konradsen, F., Hoek, W.V.D. and Peiris, P., 2006, 'Reaching for the Bottle of Pesticide – A Cry for Help: Self-inflicted Poisonings in Sri Lanka', *Social Science and Medicine*, 62(7), 1710–1719.
Kusumaratne, S., 2005, *Indigenous Medicine in Sri Lanka: A Sociological Analysis*, Nugegoda: Sarasavi Publishers.
Lave, J. and Wenger, E., 1991, *Situated Learning: Legitimate Peripheral Participation*, Cambridge: Cambridge University Press.
Laye-Gindhu, A. and Schonert-Reichl, K.A., 2005, 'Nonsuicidal Self-harm among Community Adolescents: Understanding the "Whats" and "Whys" of Self-harm', *Journal of Youth and Adolescence*, 34(5), 447–457.
Leach, E.R., 1961, *Pul Eliya, A Village in Ceylon: A Study of Land Tenure and Kinship*, Cambridge: Cambridge University Press.
Lester, D. and Goldney, R.D., 1997, 'An Ethological Perspective on Suicidal Behaviour', *New Ideas in Psychology*, 15(1), 97–103.
Lynch, C., 1999, 'The "Good Girls" of Sri Lankan Modernity: Moral Orders of Nationalism and Capitalism', *Identities: Global Studies in Culture and Power*, 6(1), 55–89.
——, 2002, 'The Politics of White Women's Underwear in Sri Lanka's Open Economy', *Social Politics: International Studies in Gender, State and Society*, 9(1), 87–125.
——, 2007, *Juki Girls, Good Girls. Gender and Cultural Politics in Sri Lanka's Global Garment Industry*, London: Cornell University Press.
Lynch, O.M. (ed.), 1990, *Divine Passions: The Social Construction of Emotion in India*, Berkeley: University of California Press.
MacAndrew, C. and Edgerton, R.B., 1969, *Drunken Comportment: A Social Explanation*, Oxford: Aldine.
Mahāthera, N., 1988, *The Buddha and His Teachings*, Buddhist Missionary Society.
Malinowski, B., 1949 [1926], *Crime and Custom in Savage Society*, London: Routledge & Kegan Paul.
Marasinghe, R.B., Edirippulige, S., Kavanagh, D., Smith, A. and Jiffry, M.T., 2012, 'Effect of Mobile Phone-based Psychotherapy in Suicide Prevention: A Randomized Controlled Trial in Sri Lanka', *Journal of Telemedicine and Telecare*, 18(3), 151–155.
Marecek, J., 1998, 'Culture, Gender, and Suicidal Behavior in Sri Lanka', *Suicide and Life-threatening Behavior*, 28(1), 69–81.
——, 2006, 'Young Women's Suicide in Sri Lanka: Cultural, Ecological, and Psychological Factors', *Asian Journal of Counselling*, 13(1), 63–92.
Marecek, J. and Senadheera, C., 2012, '"I Drank It to Put an End to Me": Narrating Girls' Suicide and Self-harm in Sri Lanka', *Contributions to Indian Sociology*, 46(1/2), 53–82.
Marshall, M., Ames, G.M. and Bennett, L.A., 2001, 'Anthropological Perspectives on

Alcohol and Drugs at the Turn of the New Millennium', *Social Science and Medicine*, 53(2), 153–164.
Martin, J., 2004, 'Self-regulated Learning, Social Cognitive Theory, and Agency', *Educational Psychologist*, 39(2), 135–145.
McGilvray, D.B., 1998, *Symbolic Heat: Gender, Health and Worship among the Tamils of South India and Sri Lanka*, Ahmedabad: Mapin Publishing.
McGilvray, D.B. and Gamburd, M.R., (eds), 2013, *Tsunami Recovery in Sri Lanka: Ethnic and Regional Dimensions*, London: Routledge.
Menninger, K.A., 1938, *Man against Himself*, New York: Harcourt, Brace & Co.
Minois, G., 1999, *History of Suicide: Voluntary Death in Western Culture*, trans. L.G. Cochrane, Baltimore, MD, and London: Johns Hopkins University Press.
Mody, P., 2008, *The Intimate State: Love-marriage and the Law in Delhi*, London: Routledge.
Muggah, R., 2008, *Relocation Failures in Sri Lanka: A Short History of Internal Displacement and Resettlement*, London: Macmillan.
Nichter, M., 1987, 'Cultural Dimensions of Hot, Cold and Sema in Sinhalese Health Culture', *Social Science and Medicine*, 25(4), 377–387.
Nissan, E. and Stirrat, R.L., 1990, 'The Generation of Communal Identities', in J. Spencer (ed.), *Sri Lanka: History and the Roots of Conflict*, London: Routledge, pp. 19–44.
Nye, R.A., 1984, *Crime, Madness, and Politics in Modern France: The Medical Concept of National Decline*, Princeton, NJ: Princeton University Press.
Obeyesekere, G., 1981, *Medusa's Hair: An Essay on Personal Symbols and Religious Experience*, London: University of Chicago Press.
——, 1984, *The Cult of the Goddess Pattini*, Chicago, IL: The University of Chicago Press.
——, 1985, 'Depression, Buddhism, and the Work of Culture in Sri Lanka', in A. Kleinman and B. Good (eds), *Culture and Depression: Studies in the Anthropology and Cross-cultural Psychiatry of Affect and Disorder*, Berkeley: University of California Press, pp. 134–152.
——, 1990, *The Work of Culture: Symbolic Transformation in Psychoanalysis and Anthropology*, London: University of Chicago Press.
Ondaatje, C., 2005, *Woolf in Ceylon: An Imperial Journey in the Shadow of Leonard Woolf, 1904–1911*, London: HarperCollins.
Osella, C. and Osella, F., 1998, 'Friendship and Flirting: Micro-politics in Kerala, South India', *Journal of the Royal Anthropological Institute*, 4(2), 189–206.
——, 2006, *Men and Masculinities in South India*, London: Anthem Press.
Osella, F. and Osella, C., 1996, 'Articulation of Physical and Social Bodies in Kerala', *Contributions to Indian Sociology*, 30(1), 37–68.
——, 2000, 'Migration, Money and Masculinity in Kerala', *Journal of the Royal Anthropological Institute*, 6(1), 117–133.
Osella, F., Stirrat, R.L. and Widger, T., in press, 'Philanthropy, Charity, and Development in Colombo', in B. Morvaridi (ed.), *New Philanthropy and Social Justice*, Bristol: University of Bristol, Policy Press.
Parry, J.P., 2001, 'Ankalu's Errant Wife: Sex, Marriage and Industry in Contemporary Chhattisgarh', *Modern Asian Studies*, 35(4), 783–820.
Patel, V. and Bloch, S., 2009, 'The Ethical Imperative to Scale Up Health Care Services for People with Severe Mental Disorders in Low and Middle Income Countries', *Postgraduate Medical Journal*, 85(1008), 509–513.
Peebles, P., 1995, *Social Change in Nineteenth Century Ceylon*, New Delhi: Navrang.

Petryna, A., Lakoff A. and Kleinman, A. (eds), 2006, *Global Pharmaceuticals: Ethics, Markets, Practices*, Durham, NC: Duke University Press.
Pfeffer, C.R., Klerman, G.L., Hurt, S.W., Kakuma, T., Peskin, J.R. and Siefker, C.A., 1993, 'Suicidal Children Grow Up: Rates and Psychosocial Risk Factors for Suicide Attempts during Follow-up', *Journal of the American Academy of Child and Adolescent Psychiatry*, 32(1), 106–113.
Popper, K.R., 1962, *Conjectures and Refutations*, New York: Basic Books.
Pradhan, G., 2001, 'Economic Cost of Sri Lanka's Ethnic Conflict', *Journal of Contemporary Asia*, 31(3), 375–384.
Prince, M., Patel, V., Saxena, S., Maj, M., Maselko, J., Phillips, M.R. and Rahman, A., 2007, 'No Health without Mental Health', *The Lancet*, 370(9590), 859–877.
Ranasinghe, H. and Jayawardene, C.H.S., 1966, 'Suicide in the Southern Province', *Ceylon Journal of Medical Science*, 15(1), 31–40.
Rogers, J.D., 1987, *Crime, Justice and Society in Colonial Sri Lanka*, London: Curzon Room.
Rose, N., 1999, *Inventing Our Selves: Psychology, Power, and Personhood*, Cambridge: Cambridge University Press.
Sahlins, M.D., 1965, 'On the Sociology of Primitive Exchange', in M. Banton (ed.), *The Relevance of Models for Social Anthropology*, London: Routledge, pp. 139–186.
——, 2011a, 'What Kinship Is (Part One)', *Journal of the Royal Anthropological Institute*, 17(1), 2–19.
——, 'What Kinship Is (Part Two)', *Journal of the Royal Anthropological Institute*, 17(2), 227–242.
——, 2013, *What Kinship Is – And Is Not*, Chicago, IL: University of Chicago Press.
Said, M., 2014, 'Suicide and Shame in Southern Sri Lanka: Networks of Dependency', *South Asia Research*, 34(1), 19–30.
Samarasinghe, D., 2006, 'Sri Lanka: Alcohol Now and Then', *Addiction*, 101(5), 626–628.
Samaraweera, S., Siribaddana, S.H., Sumathipala, A. and Bhugra, D., 2010, 'RCT of Cognitive Behaviour Therapy in Active Suicidal Ideation – A Feasibility Study in Sri Lanka', *European Journal of Psychiatry*, 21(3), 175–178.
Samaraweera, S., Sumathipala, A., Siribaddana, S., Sivayogan, S. and Bhugra, D., 2008, 'Completed Suicide among Sinhalese in Sri Lanka: A Psychological Autopsy Study', *Suicide and Life-threatening Behavior*, 38(2), 221–228.
Sariola, S. and Simpson, B., 2013, 'Precarious Ethics: Toxicology Research among Self-poisoning Hospital Admissions in Sri Lanka', *BioSocieties*, 8(1), 41–57.
Scheff, T.J., 1966, *Being Mentally Ill: A Sociological Theory*, Chicago, IL: Aldine.
Searle, J.R., 1995, *The Construction of Social Reality*, New York: The Free Press.
Seneviratne, H.L., 1999, *The Work of Kings*, Chicago, IL: University of Chicago Press.
Shneidman, E.S., 1998, *The Suicidal Mind*, Oxford: Oxford University Press.
Shneidman, E.S. and Farberow, N.L., 1961, *The Cry for Help*, New York: MacGraw-Hill.
Silva, K.T., 2000, 'Suicide as a Form of Protest and its Implications for Public Health: The Case of Sri Lanka', *Violence and Health. Proceedings of a WHO Global Symposium*, World Health Organization, Kobe, Japan, pp. 62–78, http://apps.who.int/iris/handle/10665/66480?mode=full (accessed 5 April 2014).
——, 2006, 'Body as Ultimate Weapon: Cultural Roots of Suicidal Violence in Sri Lanka', *African Safety Promotion*, 4(4), 48–58.
——, 2009, '"Tsunami Third Wave" and the Politics of Disaster Management in Sri Lanka', *Norsk Geografisk Tidsskrift-Norwegian Journal of Geography*, 63(1), 61–72.

Silva, K.T. and Pushpakumara, W.D.N.R., 1996, 'Love, Hate and the Upsurge in Youth Suicide in Sri Lanka: Trends in a Mahaweli New Settlement', *Sri Lanka Journal of Social Sciences*, 19, 1–2.

Silva, K.T., Athukorala, V. and Herath, D., 2002, *Ravaged Innocence: A Study of Incest in Central Sri Lanka*, Colombo: Centre for Women's Research.

Singh, A.T. and Uberoi, P., 1994, 'Learning to "Adjust": Conjugal Relations in Indian Popular Fiction', *Indian Journal of Gender Studies*, 1(1), 93–120.

Skegg, K., 2005, 'Self-harm', *The Lancet*, 366(9495), 1471–1483.

Spandler, H., 2001, *Who's Hurting Who? Young People, Self-harm and Suicide*, Gloucester: Handsell Publishing.

Spencer, J., 1990a, 'Collective Violence and Everyday Practice in Sri Lanka', *Modern Asian Studies*, 24(3), 603–623.

——, 1990b, *A Sinhala Village in a Time of Trouble: Politics and Change in Rural Sri Lanka*, New Delhi: Oxford University Press.

——, 1992, 'Representations of the Rural: A View from Sabaragamuva', in J. Brow and J. Weeramunda (eds), *Agrarian Change in Sri Lanka*, London: Sage, pp. 357–387.

——, 1997, 'Post-colonialism and the Political Imagination', *Journal of the Royal Anthropological Institute*, 3(1), 1–19.

——, 2003, 'A Nation "Living in Different Places": Notes on the Impossible Work of Purification in Post-colonial Sri Lanka', *Contributions to Indian Sociology*, 37(1/2), 1–23.

Staples, J. and Widger, T., 2012, 'Situating Suicide as an Anthropological Problem: Ethnographic Approaches to Understanding Self-harm and Self-inflicted Death', *Culture, Medicine and Psychiatry*, 36(2), 183–203.

Steinmetz, S.R., 1894, 'Suicide among Primitive Peoples', *American Anthropologist*, 7(1), 53–60.

Stirrat, R.L., 1975, 'Compadrazgo in Catholic Sri Lanka', *Man* (n.s.), 10(4), 589–606.

——, 1982, 'Caste Conundrums: Views of Caste in a Sinhalese Catholic Fishing Village', in D.B. McGilvray (ed.), *Caste Ideology and Interaction*, Cambridge: Cambridge University Press, pp. 8–33.

——, 1987, 'A View from Britain', *Contributions to Indian Sociology* (n.s.), 21(1), 67–75.

——, 1992, *Power and Religiosity in a Post-colonial Setting: Sinhala Catholics in Contemporary Sri Lanka*, Cambridge: Cambridge University Press.

Straus, J.H. and Straus, M.A., 1953, 'Suicide, Homicide, and Social Structure in Ceylon', *The American Journal of Sociology*, 58(5), 461–469.

Tambiah, S.J., 1965, 'Kinship Fact and Fiction in Relation to the Kandyan Sinhalese', *The Journal of the Royal Anthropological Institute of Great Britain and Ireland*, 9(5/2), 131–173.

Taylor, S., 1982, *Durkheim and the Study of Suicide*, London: Macmillan.

Thalagala, N., 2009, 'Suicide Trends in Sri Lanka 1880–2006: Social, Demographic and Geographical Variations', *Journal of the College of Community Physicians of Sri Lanka*, 14(1), 24–32.

Thiranagama, S., 2011, *In My Mother's House: Civil War in Sri Lanka*, Philadelphia: University of Pennsylvania Press.

Toren, C., 1994, 'Transforming Love: Representing Fijian Hierarchy', in P. Harvey and P. Gow (eds), *Sex and Violence: Issues, Representation and Experience*, London: Routledge, pp. 18–39.

Trawick, M., 1990, 'The Ideology of Love in a Tamil Family', in O.M. Lynch (ed.),

Divine Passions: The Social Construction of Emotion in India, Berkeley: University of California Press, pp. 37–63.
——, 1992, 'Death and Nurturance in Indian Systems of Healing', in C. Leslie (ed.), *Paths to Asian Medical Knowledge*, London: University of California Press, pp. 129–159.
Turner, B.S., 1996, *The Body and Society*, London: Sage.
Turner, V.W., 1957, *Schism and Continuity in an African Society: A Study of Ndembu Village Life*, Manchester: Manchester University Press.
Widger, T., 2009, *Self-harm and self-inflicted Death amongst Sinhalese Buddhists in Sri Lanka: An Ethnographic Study*, Doctoral thesis, London School of Economics.
——, 2012a, 'Suicide and the Morality of Kinship in Sri Lanka', *Contributions to Indian Sociology*, 46(1/2), 83–116.
——, 2012b, 'Suffering, Frustration, and Anger: Class, Gender and History in Sri Lankan Suicide Stories', *Culture, Medicine, and Psychiatry*, 36(2), 225–244.
——, 2013, 'Reading Sri Lanka's Suicide Rate', *Modern Asian Studies*, 1–35.
——, n.d., 'Learning Suicide and the Limits of Agency: Children's "Suicide Play" in Sri Lanka', unpublished manuscript.
Williams, J.M.G., 2001, *Suicide and Attempted Suicide: Understanding the Cry of Pain*, London: Penguin Books.
Wiltshire, M.G., 1983, 'The "Suicide" Problem in the Pāli Canon', *Journal of the International Association of Buddhist Studies*, 6(2), 124–140.
Wolf, M., 1975, 'Women and Suicide in China', in M. Wolf and R. Witke (eds), *Women in Chinese Society*, Palo Alto, CA: Stanford University Press, pp. 111–141.
Wood, A.L., 1961, 'Crime and Aggression in Changing Ceylon: A Sociological Analysis of Homicide, Suicide, and Economic Crime', *Transactions of the American Philosophical Society* (n.s.), 51(8).
Wood, K., Lambert, H. and Jewkes, R., 2008, '"Injuries are Beyond Love": Physical Violence in Young South Africans' Sexual Relationships', *Medical Anthropology*, 27(1), 43–69.
Woolf, L., 1981 [1913], *The Village in the Jungle*, London: Hogarth Press.
——, 1997 [1962], *Diaries in Ceylon, 1908–1911*, Dehiwala, SL: Tisara.
World Health Organization, 2012, *Public Health Action for the Prevention of Suicide: A Framework*, http://apps.who.int/iris/bitstream/10665/75166/1/9789241503570_eng.pdf?ua=1 (accessed 17 April 2013).
Yalman, N., 1967, *Under the Bo Tree: Studies in Caste, Kinship, and Marriage in the Interior of Ceylon*, Berkeley: University of California Press.
Yip, P.S.F. (ed.), 2008, *Suicide in Asia: Causes and Prevention*, Hong Kong: Hong Kong University Press.
Zola, I.K., 1972, 'Medicine as an Institution of Social Control', *The Sociological Review*, 20(4), 487–504.

Government of Sri Lanka ministries and departments

Department of Census and Statistics, 2001, *Census of Population and Housing – 2001, Population and Housing Data*, Puttalam District, Colombo.
Department of Census and Statistics, n.d., *Population by Sex and District, Census Years*, Colombo.
Mental Health Directorate, 2005, *The Mental Health Policy of Sri Lanka, 2005–2015*, Colombo: Ministry of Healthcare and Nutrition.

National Youth Service Council, 1999, *Sri Lanka Youth Vision*, June, Colombo: Ministry of Youth Affairs.
——, 1999, *Sri Lanka Youth Vision*, July, Colombo: Ministry of Youth Affairs.
Report of the Presidential Committee on Prevention of Suicide, 1997, *National Policy and Action Plan on Prevention of Suicide*, Colombo: Presidential Secretariat, 3 December.
Sri Lanka Bureau of Foreign Employment, 2001, *Health and Reproductive Health for Women Migrant Workers*, Colombo: Ministry of Labour.

Sri Lanka National Archives (SLNA)

Administration Report, 1877, 1895, 1902, 1917, 1954.
Sessional Paper III, 1967, *Youth in Ceylon Part 1: Analysis of Youth Needs in Ceylon*, Colombo: Government Press.
Times of Ceylon, 3 January 1955.

Index

Page numbers in *italics* denote tables, those in **bold** denote figures.

abetment to suicide 161–2, 164
Abeyasinghe, R. 7
accidental death/self-harm 17, 80–2
affinal relationships 84–91
age 15, 16, 27, 28, **29**, 30, 112, 113
agency 12, 14, 15, 16
agricultural land use 25, *26*
alcohol/alcoholism 7, 19–20, 32, 41, 53, 141, 147, 150; and pathological jealousy 103, 147; *see also* drinking culture
altruism 5, 92
altruistic suicide 6
Alutwatta 23, 32–5, 36, 53; occupational classes *34*; religious communities 35
Aluwihare, Sir R. 39
Alvarez, A. 6
ambiguities of suicidal language and practice 62–6
Amerasinghe, A.R.B. 8, 162
Anderson, J.R. 9
anger 96, 97, 113, 114, 131, 155, 174
anger suicide 97, 98, 103, 109–12, 114, 121, 170; female 109–11, 156, 175; male 113; pathology of 111–12
anomic suicide 6
anomy 5
anthropology of suicide 8–13
anti-depressants 166
arenas of suicidal practice 13–14, 18
Argenti-Pillen, A. 65, 69, 73, 160
arranged marriage 7, 19, 117, 118
assisted suicide 161
Astuti, R. 9
Atkinson, J.M. 38
attempted suicide 3, 4

Bandarage, A. 31

Bandura, A. 14, 15
Bastian, A. 95
Beck, A.T. 166
Beck, B. 97
Becker, C.B. 58
Bemme, D. 113
blame/blaming 19, 70, 71–3, 81, 91, 126–7, 156, 176
Bloch, M. 8–9, 11, 14, 92, 176
Bloch, S. 12
Bohannan, P. 9
Boldt, M. 11
Bourdieu, P. 14, 15
Brown, R.M. 9, 11
Buddhism 12–13, 52, 58–60, 71, 96, 98, 99, 170, 174
Buddhist community 25, 27, 30, 35, 58, 63, 134
Burgher population *25*, 27
burning 28

Caldwell, D.B. 117, 119
Camus, A. 15
caste structure 7, 32, 33, 35, 54, 55, 90
Catholics *see* Roman Catholic community
causing self-harm/suicide 60, 161
Centre for Policy Alternatives 163
Centre for Women's Research 146
Chamove, A.S. 9
character self-harm 124
Chilaw Mental Health Clinic (CMHC) 45–6
children 174; and maternal migration 142, 146, 147; sexual abuse of 145–6; suicide play 65, 80–2, 84
Christian communities *see* Evangelical Christian community; Protestant Christian community; Roman Catholic community

Chua, J.L. 56
civil war 7, 8, 69
class 3, 15, 24, 32, 33, 112, 113, 156, 173, 175; inequality 96, 170; and power 96, 176; *see also* labouring class; middle class; working class
clinic-generated interventions 164–9
clinic-generated theories of suicide 23, 43–7, *48*, 49
coconut economy 25, 26, 31, 35, 36
coercion, suicides of 19, 125–8
Collins, P.Y. 12
Colombo 27
colonial period 31, 38, 54–5, 174
Colucci, E. 11
communities of practice 14
compassion (*metta*) in suicide interventions 20, 154–70
consumerism 54, 59
cool behaviour 97, 112, 113, 175
Cooper, J. 17
counselling 45, 166–7
Counts, D.A. 11
court-generated interventions 161–4
court-generated theories of suicide 23, 37–43, *48*, 49
criminality 5, 161
Cross, H.A. 9
'cry for help' theory 6
culpability for suicide 162
cultural theory approach to suicide 11
culture 13; Sinhala, vulnerability of 144–5; of suicide 177

Daniel, E.V. 32, 97
Daniels, B.A. 9
Das, V. 150
de Munck, V.C. 117, 118
de Silva, D. 7
de Silva, K.M. 31
de Silva, P. 96
de Silva, V.A. 4, 28
de Silva, W.P. 7
death drive (Thanatos) 6
death wish 6
deception 65; *see also* lies and make-believe
decriminalisation 161, 164
depression 6–7, 12–13, 95, 104, 113, 166, 174
development, Sri Lankan experiences of 3, 54, 144
dialogue suicides 7–8
disposition for suicide 15

Dissanayake, S.A.W. 7
distant-knowledge 67
Donner, H. 117
D'Oyly, J. 8, 38–9, 163
drinking culture 19, 20, 132, 133, 134–9; *see also* alcohol/alcoholism
drinking parties 137–9, 150
drowning 28, 41, 42, 164
D'Souza, R. 113, 166
Durkheim, E. 5–6, 9, 17, 60–1, 67, 108

economic reforms (1977) 54, 55–6, 144
economic/financial problems 41, 56, 62, 105
economy 25, 26–7
Eddleston, M. 4, 27, 28
Edgerton, R.B. 134
education 57; and aspiration 40; and employment 7, 56; lack of 157, 166, 167
educational frustrations 58
egoism 5
egositic suicide 5–6
emotion-focused responses 154
emotional flows 19, 95–8; *see also* anger; frustration; suffering
employment 104–5, 108; by sector *26*; and education 7, 56
epistemological objectivity 9, 10–11, 173
Eriksen, M. 8
Eros (life drive) 6
estate settlements 31–2, 33
ethnic communities 25, *33*, 58
ethnic distribution of suicide 27
ethnography 8, 9
ethnopsychiatric model of suicide 112–14
ethos model of suicidality 23, 47, 62, 113, 150
Evangelical Christian community 25, 30, 35
evidence model of suicidality 23, 47, 62, 113, 150
experience-distant concepts 66–7
experience-near concepts 66

family life 91–2; breakdown of 32, 35, 54, 92; and migration 142–4, 150; and modernisation/globalisation 144
'good' 3, 18–19, 35–7, 80, 82, 91, 117, 118, 128, 153, 174
family problems 2–3, 38, 41, 42, 63, 64, 70, 83–4, 175, 176
Farberow, N.L. 6
farming communities 52–3, 63
fatalism 5

fatalistic suicide 6
fear/fearlessness 132, 137, 139, 150
femininity 71
financial/economic problems 41, 56, 62, 105
Fincham, B. 47
Fortes, M. 92
Foster, J.H. 7
Freeman, H.R. 39, 163
Freud, S. 6
friends, disputes with 76, 77
friendship 82–3, 91
frustration 42, 96, 97, 113, 114, 131, 155, 164, 174; youth 39–41, 52, 54, 56–8
frustration suicide 97, 98, 103, 104–9, 112, 114, 121, 170–1, 175
frustration-aggression hypothesis 39, 96
Fuller, C.J. 117, 118, 119

Galmuruwa Peripheral Health Unit (GPHU) 28, 44–5
Gamburd, M.R. 35, 44, 132
Geertz, C. 66
Gellner, E. 61
gender 3, 15, 19, 27, 70, 112, 113, 156, 173, 174, 175; inequality 96, 170; and power 176; roles 35, 36; and suicide play 82
generation 3, 96, 156, 170, 173, 174, 175
Giddens, A. 4
Global Mental Health (GMH) movement 12, 13, 113, 165, 167, 174
globalisation 3, 8, 16, 35, 71, 144, 170
Goffman, E. 12
Goldman, L.R. 14, 81
Goldney, R.D 9
Gombrich, R.E.F. 54, 55, 99, 117
'good' and 'bad' moral conduct 71
good family life 3, 18–19, 35–7, 80, 82, 91, 117, 118, 128, 153, 174
Gow, P. 70
Gunnell, D. 4, 7, 28

habitus 14, 15, 16
Hacking, I. 4, 5
hanging 28, 30, *31*, 41, 64
Harlow, H.F. 9
Harvey, P. 70
health interventions *see* mental health services
heat/hot behaviour 97–8, 112, 113, 175
Hewamanne, S. 36, 69, 71
Hezel, F.X. 11
Hindu community 27, 30

historical sources 8
homicide 38, 39, 69
honour 71
honour suicide 104
Hughes, D. 40, 69, 160
human rights 20
hypergamy 90

independence, national 174
individualisation 56
inequality 7, 96, 170
infidelity 149, 150; female 20, 143, 144, 147–8
intentionality 9, 17, 59–60, 63–4
intervention strategies *see* suicide interventions
Italian syndrome 146, 147

Jadhav, S. 12
Jaffna 27
Jayasinghe, N.R. 7
Jayawardene, C.H.S. 7
jealousy 83; pathological or morbid 103, 146–9, 150
Jeganathan, P. 132
Joiner, T. 6–7
Jones, I.H. 9
journalism, suicide 163–4
jumping 28

Kalu Kumara (Black Prince) 103, 145
Kalu Yaka (Black Demon) 20, 145, 150
Kandyan village 36, 37
Kapferer, B. 145
karmic consequences of suicide 59–60
kasippu 136
Kearney, R.N. 4, 7, 27, 40, 53
Kegalle 27
Keown, D. 58
kinship 7, 19, 32, 54, 70–1, 79, 80, 84–91, 91–2
Kitanaka, J. 11, 169
Knox, R. 8, 161–2
Kohut, H. 66
Konradsen, F. 69
Kusumaratne, S. 96

labour: domestic division of 35, 105; migration *see* migration
labouring class 104, 112; drinking practices 136
land colonisation 31, 53
Land Development Ordinance (LDO) 31
language of suicide, ambiguities of 62–6

Lave, J. 14
Laye-Gindhu, A. 17
Leach, E.R. 36–7, 90
learning 14–15: agentive processes of 14, 15; situated 14, 15
legal codes 8
Lester, D. 11
lies and make-believe (*boru*) 18, 65, 71, 73, 80, 103, 158, 175
life drive (Eros) 6
loitering and drinking 122, 124
love, romantic 19, 105, 117, 121–2
love marriage 7, 19, 54, 55, 64, 117–20, 122
love problems 2, 3, 16, 41, 56, 64, 105, 116–30
loving kindness *see* compassion
Lynch, C. 36, 69, 71
Lynch, O.M. 117

MacAndrew, C. 134
Madampe Division 23, 24, 25–7; agricultural land use 25, *26*; economy 25, 26–7, 36; ethnic communities 25; family life 35–7; female labour participation 35–6; land colonisation 31; and mental health policy 44; religious communities 25; suicide patterns 28–30, *31*
Madampe Police Station (MPS) 28, 41, 42, 43
Mahāthera, N. 59
Mahaweli Development Authority 27
Mahaweli Irrigation Development Programme 53
Malinowski, B. 9–11, 13
Marasinghe, R.B. 7
Marecek, J. 7–8, 27, 43, 59 69, 70, 95, 111, 154, 160
market capitalism 54
marriage 36–7, 91, 116; arranged 7, 19, 117, 118; breakdown of (migration and 142–4; modernisation/globalisation and 144); companionate 117, 119, 120, 129; equality in 128; love 7, 19, 54, 55, 64, 117–20, 122; personalisation of 128; proposal 118, 122, 174; and status 90
Marshall, M. 134
Martin, J. 14, 15
masculinity 19, 20, 131–2, 150, 174; and female labour migration 19, 132; ideals of 71; migration as measure of 141; and violence 70

massina relationship 90, 138
Matara 27
material success 56
materialism 54, 55, 59, 145, 156, 170
McGilvray, D.B. 44, 97
media reporting 163–4
medical anthropology 11–13
medical intervention *see* mental health services
medicinal drugs: as suicide method 4, 28; as treatment method 166
memory 176
men 27, 28, 92, 131–52; anger suicide 113; character self-harm 124; drinking culture 19, 20, 132, 133, 134–9; frustration suicide 104, 105–9; and migration 132, 133, 139–41, 146, 150; movement and 'pursuit of fun' 19, 20, 133–41, 174; relational flows of suicide/self-harm 74, **75**, 76, 77–9; romantic suicide 121, 122–3, 124–5, 129; suffering suicide 99–102, 150, 156, 175; unmarried 74, **75**, 78, 79, 139; violent acts 70, 81, 102, 132; *see also* masculinity
Menninger, K.A. 6
mental health policy 43–4, 167
mental health programmes 12
mental health services 43–7, 164–9; assessment of suicide causation 46
mental illness 6, 12, 113
methods of suicide/self-harm 4, 28, 30, *31*, 41, 42
metta see compassion
middle class 19, 31, 33, *48*, 111, *112*, 117, 144, 150, 156; drinking culture 135–9; migration 139–40; religious practice 99
Middle East syndrome 146–7
migration 7, 19, 20, 26, 31, 35, 36, 80, 86, 133; female 19, 33, 35, 132, 142, 143, 145–6, 146–7; internal 7; and marital/family breakdown 142–4, 150; men and 132, 133, 139–41, 146, 150; middle-class 139–40; overseas 19, 20, 26, 27, 35, 36, 57, 80, 90, 134, 139–41, 142–4; as threat to Sinhala culture 145; working-class 139
Miller, B.D. 4, 7, 27, 40, 53
Minois, G. 4
modernisation 7, 8, 16, 35, 54, 71, 131, 144, 170
Mody, P. 117, 121
monologue suicides 7, 8
moral conduct 71, 81, 82, 83

Morseli, G. 9
mothers, absence of, through migration 142, 146, 147
movement: cessation of 141–9, 151; men's freedom of 20, 132–4, 174; *see also* migration
Muggah, R. 53
Muslim community 25, 27, 30, 58, 60, 61–2
mutuality of being 92

Narasimhan, H. 117, 118, 119
narratives of suicidality 176–7
National Youth Service Council (NYSC) 40–1
near-knowledge 67
newspaper stories 163–4
Nichter, M. 97
Nissan, E. 40
Nye, R.A. 12

Obeyesekere, G. 7, 12–13, 54, 55, 69, 72, 97, 98, 99, 104, 117
occupational life 104–5
Ondaatje, C. 69
ontological subjectivity 9, 10, 13, 173
open economy policy (1977) 54, 55–6, 144
Osella, C. and Osella, F. 97, 117, 121, 131, 140

pansil 110–11
paranoia, about threat to Sinhala 144–5
parents, disputes with 76, 77, 78
Parry, J.P. 117
Patel, V. 12, 113
patriarchy 85, 92, 99, 112, 120; dead-end of 100, 132
patterns of suicide 27–30, *31*
Peebles, P. 55
pesticides 4, 8, 28, 43
Petryna, A. 12
Pfeffer, C.R. 80
poison drinking 63, 64, 65, 66, 79, 123
poisoning 28, 30, *31*, 41, 42, 43, 162
police: classifications of causes of suicide 42–3; investigations 41–2
policy interventions 43–4, 167
Polonnaruwa 27
Popper, K.R. 49
power 96, 113, 176; of women 99
practice theory of suicide 11, 13–16, 18
practices of concern 62
Pradham, G. 4
PressWise Trust 163

prevention efforts *see* suicide interventions
pride 72
Prince, M. 12, 165
problem-focused responses 154
problem-solving 156, 157–8
processual model of suicide *see* suicide process
protest 7–8
protest suicides 162
Protestant Christian community 25, 30
psychache 6
psychiatric anthropology 11–13
psychiatry 4, 5, 6, 12, 13, 67, 95, 167, 169, 174
psychological states 6–7, 8, 95, 96, 173
psychology 6
psychopathology 19, 95
Pushpakumara, W.D.N.R. 4, 7, 27, 40, 53, 117
Puttalam District 31

Ranasinghe, H. 7
relational flows 69–94; of male and female suicides 74; of married self-harmers 77–80; of unmarried self-harmers 74, *75*, 76
relational violence 7, 8, 19, 69–71, 91, 116
religion 3, 32, 58–62, 108, 168–9, 170; and release from suffering 98; of suicides 24, 25, 27, **29**, 30; *see also* Buddhism
religious communities *25*, 35; *see also* Buddhist community; Evangelical Christian community; Hindu community; Muslim community; Protestant Christian community; Roman Catholic community
representations of suicide 7–8, 11, 13–14, 18, 173, 176; clinic 23, 43–7, *48*, 49; court 23, 43–7, *48*, 49; village 23, 35–7, 49
Rogers, J.D. 38, 69
Roman Catholic community 25, 30, 35, 58, 60–1, 98, 134
romantic suicide 116, 118, 121–9
Rose, N. 12
rumour 144, 150; and pathological jealousy 148–9

Sahlins, M.D. 92
Said, M. 69
Samarasinghe, D. 134
Samaraweera, S. 7, 95
Sariola, S. 154
Scheff, T.J. 12

Schonert-Reichl, K.A. 17
Searle, J.R. 9
self-cutting 122, 123, 129
self-harm 17–18; character 124; epidemic 3–4; female 28, **29**, 30, 74, 76, 77–9; Madampe Division 28, **29**, 30, *31*; male 28, 74, **75**, 76, 77–9; methods of 4, 28, 30, *31*; as protest or complaint 7–8; relational flows of 74, **75**, **76**, 77–80; and religion 25, **29**, 30; social 124
Senadheera, C. 7–8, 59, 69, 70, 111, 160
Seneviratne, H.L. 144
sexual abuse 76, 145–6
sexual frustration 105, 124
shame/shaming 19, 64, 69, 70, 71–3, 81, 126–7, 156, 176; avoidance of 65; fear of 132
Shneidman, E.S. 6
sibling disputes 76, 77, 78
silence, as response to suicidal practices 20, 153–4, 156, 157–8, 159, 160–1, 164, 167, 169, 175, 176, 177
Silva, K.T. 4, 7, 40, 53, 117
Simpson, B. 154
Singh, A.T. 118
Sinhala population 25, 27
situated learning 14, 15
Skegg, K. 17
social change 5–6, 7, 8, 170, 173
social class *see* class
social drama, theory of 175–6
social suicide/self-harm 122, 124
social support, loss/lack of 5–6, 99, 100
socialisation 14, 15
sociality, denial of 92
Spandler, H. 123
Spencer, J. 40, 54, 60, 69, 72, 79, 85, 143
Sri Lanka Federation of Youth Clubs (SLFYC) 41
Sri Lankan Mental Health Directorate 44
Staples, J. 4
status 71, 85, 113, 174, 175; conflicts 69, 86; inequality 79; and marriage 90
Steinmetz, S.R. 9
Stirrat, R.L. 40, 69, 90, 98
Straus, J.H. and Straus, M.A. 7, 27, 39, 54, 69, 117
suffering 96, 97, 98, 113, 114, 131, 155, 174
suffering suicide 97, 98–105, 109, 112, 113, 114, 150, 156, 175
suicide: as criminal act 5, 161; culture of 177; definition of 16–18; disposition for 15; as epistemically objective phenomenon 9, 10–11, 173; methods 4, 28, 30, *31*, 41, 42; as ontologically subjective phenomenon 9, 10, 173; origin of term 4–5
suicide drama 175
suicide interventions 20, 43–4, 153–72; clinic-generated 164–9; compassion in 20, 154–70; court-generated 161–4; as imposition of silence 20, 153–4, 156, 157–8, 159, 160–1, 164, 167, 169; village-generated 155–61
suicide notes 41
suicide play 65, 80–2, 84
suicide process 173–8; at event level 173, 174, 175, 176, 177; at lifespan level 173–4, 175, 176, 177; at societal level 173, 174, 175, 176, 177; possibilities of 176–7
suicide rates 5; global 3, 4; Sri Lanka **5**

Tambiah, S.J. 90
Tamil community 25, 27, 58
Taylor, S. 7
Thalagala, N. 27
Thanatos (death drive) 6
Thaniwelle Devalaya shrine 121
Thaniya Vallabha 121
there and here, distinction between 51–2, 63
Thiranagama, S. 32
threat of suicide 64–5, 162–3
Times of Ceylon 163
Tiruchelvam, J.N.C. 163
Toren, C. 70
train suicides 28, 41, 42
Trawick, M. 121
tricks, suicide performances as 65, 66
Trobriand Islands 9–10
tsunami (December 2004) 43–4, 165, 174
Turner, B.S. 12
Turner, V.W. 175

Uberoi, P. 118
Udagama 23, 32–5, 36; occupational classes *34*; religious communities 35
United National Party (UNP) 54
urban/rural divide 27
urbanisation 7, 54, 144

Vavuniya 27
villages 7, 31–7, *48*; 'ancient' 31, 32, 33; estate 31–2, 33; and suicide interventions 155–61; and suicide representations 23, 35–7, 49

violence 7, 8, 161; against women 70, 81, 102; male 70, 81, 102, 132; relational 7, 8, 19, 69–71, 91, 116

Wenger, E. 14
Widger, T. 4, 8, 13, 24, 38, 40, 49, 52, 55, 65, 69, 70, 71, 81, 92, 96, 100, 113, 120, 174
Williams, J.M.G. 6
Wiltshire, M.G. 58
Wolf, M. 70, **29**, 30, 92, 164; anger suicide 109–11, 156, 175; and infidelity 20, 143, 144, 147–8; labour participation 35–6; marriage preferences 120, 128, 129; migration 19, 33, 35, 132, 142, 143, 145–6, 146–7; power in domestic economy 99; relational flows of suicide/self-harm 74, **75**, 76, 77–9; romantic suicide 116, 118, 121, 123–4, 125–8, 129; suffering suicide 102–4; unmarried 73, 76, 79; violence against 70, 81, 102; *see also* femininity; mothers
Wood, A.L. 7, 8, 27, 39, 54, 117
Wood, K. 70
Woolf, L. 69
working class 33, 104, 112, 156; drinking practices 136; migration 139
World Bank 167
World Health Organization 3, 167

Yalman, N. 36, 90
Yip, P.S.F.
youth: frustration 39–41, 52, 54, 56–8; insurgency 69; love problems 116–30; relational flows of suicide practice 82–4
Youth in Ceylon report (1967) 39–40
youth clubs 41
youthfulness 57–8

Zola, I.K. 12